A YEAR IN WHITE

A YEAR IN WHITE

Cultural Newcomers to Lukumi and Santería in the United States

C. LYNN CARR

RUTGERS UNIVERSITY PRESS

New Brunswick, New Jersey, and London

Library of Congress Cataloging-in-Publication Data

Carr, C. Lynn.
    A year in white : cultural newcomers to lukumi and santería in the United States /
C. Lynn Carr.
        pages cm
    Includes bibliographical references and index.
    ISBN 978–0-8135–7120–1 (hardcover : alk. paper)—ISBN 978–0-8135–7119–5 (pbk. :
alk. paper)—ISBN 9780813571218 (e-book (web pdf))—ISBN 978-0-8135-7266-6
(e-book (epub))
    1. Santeria—United States. 2. Priests—Training of—United States.
3. Priesthood—Santeria. I. Title.

    BL2532.S3C38 2016
        299.6'7461—dc23
        2015012451

A British Cataloging-in-Publication record for this book is available from the British
Library.

Copyright © 2015 by C. Lynn Carr

Visit our website: http://rutgerspress.rutgers.edu

Manufactured in the United States of America

In honor of the memory of Karen McCarthy Brown

CONTENTS

ACKNOWLEDGMENTS

Moyuba Olorun, Moyuba Olofin, Moyuba Olodumare
Moyuba Baba, Moyuba Yeye
Moyuba ara, Moyuba ilé
Araonu iba'ye baye tonu
Theresita Ariosa Ochun Funke (iba'ye)
Belen Apoto Gonzales Ochun Alaibo (iba'ye)
Luisa "La China Sylvestre" Ochun Miwa (iba'ye)
Jose Urquiola "Jose Pata Palo" Echu Bi (iba'ye)
Aurora La Mar Obá T'ola (iba'ye)
Antonia Terry Shango oro Agayu Shango L'aye (iba'ye)
Juana Nuñez Banguala (iba'ye)
Rita Miranda Ewin L'ade (iba'ye)
Felicita (Fela) Mendez Shango Gumi (iba'ye)
Luis Rivera Oke Ewe (iba'ye)
Wifredo Cruz Ode Ilu (iba'ye)
Roberto Clemente Aña Bi Osun (iba'ye)
Iba'ye baye tonu gbogbo egun araonu orí Iyatobi Ode Lenu
Iba'ye baye tonu gbogbo egun araonu orí Baba Ala Esu
Iba'ye baye tonu gbogbo egun araonu orí Okandekun
Iba'ye baye tonu gbogbo egun araonu orí Ogun Gbemi
Iba'ye baye tonu gbogbo egun araonu orí emi nani Chango Dina ...

In every undertaking in the Lukumi religious traditions, we begin by honoring those who have come before us. In this manner I acknowledge the many who assisted in the creation of this book by first reciting praise and gratitude in a shortened form of a traditional prayer. I pay homage to God, my biological parents, the earth and my house, priests in my lineage who are no longer living, and the ancestors and spiritual guides of my godmother, *ayubona*, *oriaté*, and myself. I thank also Elegua, Ogun, Ochosi, Obatalá, Oya, Oshun, Agayu, the Ibeji, Olokun, Yemaya, and Chango. And I thank my first Lukumi godfather, Clay Keck Afolabi (Shloma Rosenberg), *iba'ye*.

As for the living, I thank my godmother, who took me under her wing when I was in need; offered consistently sane, smart, and witty advice; and taught me patiently. I appreciate her years of encouragement while I was writing this book, for looking over parts of my manuscript, and for honoring me with the gift of the beautiful cover art that includes Orisha from whom mine were born. Similarly, I wish to thank Gloria Chaidez Okandekun, my adoptive *ayubona*, for taking me in, for generously teaching me, and for always treating me like family. I have been blessed with near and extended godkin and those I have met and communed with along the Ocha road—Afefe Alada, Eshu Okan Lade, Oya Leti, Oshun Alade Koide, Omi L'ade, Omi Ala, Odofemi, Ala Bero, Ade Kola, Omi Laye, Omi Tokunbi, Omi Lana, Omi Saide, Omi Tola, Obadi Meji, Omi Dina, Odula Aja-gun, and all the others too numerous to list here. These people have offered me emotional support, reassurance, guidance, inclusion, laughs, and inspiration.

I thank also my biological family and close friends for being there for me. A mounted Obatalá once said of me, "You love books but you need people." To the extent that book writing requires a modicum of sanity, I do need people. I thank Mom, Ari, Melanie, Laura, T. J., Amara, Peter, Beth, Joey, Tom, Chris, Marah, and Selwa for companionship and for bearing with me even when it wasn't easy.

This book is an undertaking I began a decade ago, and there are many in the academic world I must acknowledge for assistance in its writing. I thank Seton Hall University for a University Research Council Research Grant in 2006 and the Foundation for the Scientific Study of Sexuality for a Grants-in-aid Research Grant in 2007 that paid for most of the interview transcription I needed. I also thank Seton Hall University for a one-semester sabbatical in 2008, during which I was able to draft several chapters, and for a small grant to pay for professional indexing services. I received professional assistance to redraw many of the figures used in this book from Christopher Petruzzi at Seton Hall's Teaching, Learning and Technology Center.

The book was improved by the generous priests, scholars, professionals, and the occasional friend who assisted me. Obás Ernesto Pichardo and Miguel "Willie" Ramos both consulted with me at different points in the creation of the book. I am grateful to have a gem of a colleague, Peter Savastano; I thank him for comments on many chapter drafts and for years of scholarly counsel and friend-ship. Another wonderful colleague, Leslie Bunnage, provided encouragement after reading pieces of my book in a writing group. I am beholden to an anony-mous peer reviewer whose tough yet encouraging critique caused me to rethink several aspects of the text; s/he turned my attention especially to the importance of terminology. I am indebted to Salvador Vidal-Ortiz, who read the entire man-uscript a second time after his anonymous peer review of the manuscript helped me create an improved draft. I thank Christopher McGinn for helping me shape the book title. I also thank my editors at Rutgers University Press, Peter Mickulas and Carrie Hudak. The book was also improved by the many comments of copy editor, Kate Babbitt. Although many have assisted in the creation of this book, its faults are, of course, all my own.

Finally, without the many *olorishas, iyawos, aleyos,* and *oluwos* who inter-viewed with me, passed on announcements about the project, and answered my survey, this book could not have been written. Although some knew me, to others I was a stranger they entrusted with detailed and intimate stories. In the context of a tradition with a history of secrecy, persecution, and stigma, these offerings to me (and through me to you) at times required courage and trust. Many gave so generously of their time, words, advice, and stories that on several occasions I have been overwhelmed with gratitude. It is to the many research participants of this book that I owe the greatest debt.

. . . Kinkamashe Sarah Jones Ode Lenu
Kinkamashe Nina Baba Ala Eshu
Kinkamashe Gloria Chaidez Okandekun
Kinkamashe Maria Concordia Ogun Gbemi
Kinkamashe Rosa Parilla Eshu Alaiwo
Kinkamashe gbobo olorisha of my ilé
Kinkamashe gbobo oyaremi
Kinkamashe orí emi nani Chango Dina
Kinkamashe gbogbo abure, ashire, Oluwo, Iyalosha, Babalosha.

I ask that no misfortune befall my godmother, my *ayubona,* my *oriaté,* the *olori-shas* of my house, my family, and myself. For all who come to these pages, I wish *omi tutu, ona tutu, ashé tutu*—refreshing water, a cool path, and divine grace.

A YEAR IN WHITE

INTRODUCTION

I wrote very little in the days immediately following my initiation into the service of the Orisha in the Lukumi religion, although I have fragments of memory from that time. I remember clearly the brightness and confusion of the market on the first day I was freed from the seven-day ceremonial seclusion—mostly spent in an area five feet by nine feet designated as the *trono*—plus the additional pre-initiation days I had spent in my godmother's care undergoing preparatory rites. I recall the mixing and shifting feelings of exhilaration, anxiety, optimism, and disorientation on that weirdly dazzling May morning in the state of Washington. Newly bald, covered head to toe in white layers—a long white skirt; *chokotos* (ankle-length pants); a roomy, long-sleeved blouse; and multiple head coverings—I was extremely self-conscious about my appearance. I worried about the ubiquitous shiny surfaces on car and shop windows. My godsister told me not to be concerned, to just forgo focusing on the reflections I was obligated to avoid during my first few months of the year in white. I recollect also the tentative, awkward way I moved about the public space, as if I really was taking the first steps of a new life in my previously unworn clothes and shoes. And I remember at the airport the next day, on my journey home across the country, feeling both unsettled and excited by the great numbers of people around me, enthusiastic about the sense of fresh potential, empowered to have passed through security so seamlessly despite my bizarre dress, musing about whether it was a coincidence or if I enjoyed mystical protection during the *yaworaje*, the year in white that follows the *kariocha* initiation in the Lukumi tradition.

Once I recovered somewhat from the initial shock of the year in white I began to write regularly in my journal. I recorded people's reactions to me and my responses to them. I tried to make sense of the many instructions and messages I had received during my initiation. I noted the internal changes I sensed and the external changes I found difficult, wonderful, frustrating, liberating, and transformational.

A month into my year in white, I made the trip back to the West Coast for another godsister's *ocha* ceremony. As the most recent initiate of my godmother, I was required to accompany my godsister on the *trono* (throne) during part of the seven-day ritual, just as one of my godsiblings had attended me. In transit to my *madrina*'s house, I wrote the following journal entry:

As I was buying water and chocolate at the airport kiosk, the clerk said to me, "My cousin did that; the whole white thing." I noticed her possibly Cuban appearance and I smiled. "But she's little," the clerk continued, gesturing to indicate a small child. Not knowing what to say, I smiled again and thought about how in some multi-generational communities today it's not uncommon for children to undergo the priestly initiation. I wondered how different my experience would have been with the year in white if I had been raised in the religion. I also noticed the careful way the cashier had spoken, choosing words that carried no stigma or even any cultural or religious reference easily identifiable to an outsider.

Such a positive interaction with a cultural insider was much more comfortable than most of my dealings with strangers who referred to my white attire. Only two days before, in the mechanic's shop, I endured a more typical exchange:

Holding a coupon, I stepped up to the guy with a name tag. "Are you a chef?" the mechanic labeled "Larry" queried enthusiastically. I hadn't yet come up with a good response for this common question. "No," I said. "I'd like the 75,000 mile service." I just wanted to get my car in the queue so I could complete my business in a timely fashion.

Or consider the interaction I had the morning before I left for the airport as I was leaving the laundromat in the basement of my building:

A middle-aged woman was already waiting for the elevator. "That's a lot of whites!" she exclaimed, waiving her hand towards the large laundry basket I set down. "Yes," I said. "I mean that's really a lot of whites!" she persisted enthusiastically. "I don't think I've ever had that many." I considered what and how much to tell her. I settled on: "It's all I wear lately." "Well it's a great time of year for it," she opined. I made some sort of noise indicating agreement and I wondered how things would change in the cooler months. Would I be noticed more because my fashion was out of season? Or would people around me have become used to my appearance by then?

Journal entries like these helped me process the everyday adventure and drudgery of the year in white.

In the Afro-Cuban religious traditions known alternately as Lukumi, Lucumí, Santería, and Regla de Ocha,[1] new initiates into the priesthood are referred to as "*iyawo*" for a year and a week. During the *iyawo* year in white, or *yaworaje*,[2] novices endure a host of prohibitions. Among others, they must wear only bright white clothing; cover their heads at all times; dress modestly; avoid going out at night; defer to their elders in the tradition; and, with few exceptions, forgo alcohol, parties, dancing, being photographed, touching adult non-initiates, and enjoying public spaces such as restaurants and movies. Although Cubans originally brought the practice of the year in white to the United States, the Lukumi religion—as is the case with many religious traditions in the contemporary globalizing, multicultural environment—is enacted now by people of many religious, ethnic, and national backgrounds. *Iyawos* in the United States today identify as Black, white, Asian, or mixed. They may or may not share Cuban ancestry, and they may or may not be Hispanic. They might have been raised in the Catholic, Jewish, Protestant, Vodou, Hindu, Buddhist, or Islamic traditions or without any religion. Some have been nourished from birth on lush and instructive stories about—and complex, reciprocal exchanges with—the *Orisha*[3] of "Yoruba"[4] religious traditions; some have not. In this book I draw upon a mix of qualitative data sources—in-depth interviews, a survey of *iyawos* and former *iyawos*, and auto-ethnographic observation and examination—to explore the year in white, especially (but not exclusively) as it is experienced among cultural newcomers to Orisha religions in the United States. I focus on the *yaworaje* as a strategic site for exploring issues of identity on the margins of contemporary pluralist society.

A BRIEF BACKGROUND

Having persisted and adapted through slavery, revolution, and migration, Lukumi religious traditions in the United States are variants of Orisha devotion that passed from people now called Yoruba in areas now known as Nigeria and Benin and were adapted in the Americas. Orisha-venerating variations include Cuban Lukumi and Ifa, Brazilian Candomble, Trinidadian Shango and Orisha worship, "Yoruba revivalism" and other traditions brought more recently to the United States directly from Nigeria, and (to some extent) Haitian *Vodou* (Olupona and Rey 2008, 4). Scholars offer varied guesses on the number of religious devotees of what they classify as "Orisha worship" or "Yoruba-derived religion" around the world.[5] Some project that they number up to 100 million, enough to declare these diverse devotees members of a "world religion" (Olupona and Rey 2008). Estimates of Orisha venerators in the United States range from 22,000 to five million (Ontario Consultants on Religious Tolerance 2005), and some suggest that there are "more practitioners of the Orisha traditions in the United States than in either Cuba or Nigeria" (Clark 2005, 8).

Unfortunately, Santería, a designation applied to Lukumi religion as early as the first decade of the twentieth century,[6] carries the popular connotation of dark sorcery. Such stigma should be understood as emerging in part as a means of social control over Blacks in Cuba after the abolishment of slavery (Clark 2007). For example, the criminological work *Los Negros Brujos* (The Black Witches) of Cuban folklorist Fernando Ortiz, whose subject was Lukumi and other Afro-Cuban religions, can easily be cast as racist (Brandon 1997). Whether derogatory associations with the religion of former slaves were the result of simple ethnocentrism or calculated efforts to maintain social hierarchies, Lukumi was repressed in Cuba for much of the twentieth century.

In the United States, where freedom of religion is both celebrated and debated, Lukumi religion continues to be plagued with historical stereotypes of sinister enchantment, leading "both the police and the media to describe any unusual or ritualistic crimes as involving 'voodoo or Santería'" (Clark 2007, 7). The association is strong enough that most scholars of the religion feel the need to address the stigma.[7] Ethnocentric and racist responses to these religions are exacerbated by their distinctness from U.S. American mainstream Abrahamic religions. Unlike most Christian, Jewish, and Islamic practices in the United States today, Orisha traditions include drumming, possession-trance, divination, and animal sacrifice. The latter, perhaps the most misunderstood religious custom in a post-agricultural society largely alienated from food production, was protected by a U.S. Supreme Court ruling in 1993.[8] Nevertheless, in the United States, both secrecy regarding the religion and suspicions of satanic involvement within it are tenacious.

Lukumi religious traditions in the United States—the main focus of this book—have diversified from their Cuban beginnings to welcome participants from many ethnic and religious backgrounds, including Latino/as from many national ancestries; African Americans who entered during the time of the Black nationalist movement and later (Brandon 1997); European Americans, many of whom were introduced through the "neo-pagan religious revival" (Pike 2001); and people of all ethnicities drawn to the music, art, divination, and ritual that play a central part in these religious traditions (Murphy 1988). Scholars commonly describe the diversification of Lukumi practitioners in the United States.[9] For example, Lukumi priest and scholar, Obá[10] Miguel "Willie" Ramos (2012) writes that given the great deal of heterogeneity in the religion today, "we can no longer refer to this as an Afro-Cuban religion" but must consider Lukumi an "international religion."

Because ethnicity often entwines with religion, racial, cultural, and national identities greatly shape participants' experiences within those sacralized practices. Lukumi traditions are intimately connected to both Cuban experience and African genesis. Indeed, practicing Lukumi can be a powerful way for Cubans and other Hispanics to assert and sustain their identities as Cubans or Latin American people: "the music, rituals, iconography and beliefs of Santería have become important media through which they experience and interpret the meaning of Latinidad or 'Latin-ness' as well as affirm the African contribution to Latin American cultures" (Gregory 1999, xi). Many who did not practice the religion in their country of origin have embraced the tradition after emigrating to the United States (Andrews 2004; Brandon 1997). The religion becomes a bulwark against cultural assimilation, a matter of ethnic pride, and a practical means of interacting with and creating and maintaining community with others from one's nation of birth. Likewise, African Americans have identified Lukumi religion as a way to connect with their African roots, honor their ancestors, and resist identification with—and distinguish themselves culturally from—the U.S. cultural mainstream (Gregory 1999; Lefever 2000). Orisha worshippers in the United States are predominantly members of minority ethnic groups and the religion carries a history that connects it to those groups. In the United States, both Cuban Americans and African Americans stake claims to the religion on the basis of ethnicity. Nevertheless, among most practitioners in the United States today, "initiatory genealogies reaching back to the African founders of these traditions in Cuba" have succeeded legitimation of religious participation based on birth and biological ancestry (Palmié 2013, 26). Lukumi participants trace their spiritual descent through the godparents who performed their *kario-cha* (priestly initiations). Kinships of stone[11] now trump those of blood. How identities, experiences, and practices in the traditions are affected as a result of ethnic diversification is an important question that may shed light on issues of religious identification within contemporary pluralism more generally.

CONSIDERING TERMS

In the rich tradition of Lukumi divination, Orisha devotees are often advised to be careful with their words. "From the lie shall the truth be born" (Ócha'ni Lele 2003), they may be told. The tongue can bring forth life or death, we are cautioned. Depending on how the cowries fall, clients of Orisha priests consulting with the oracle may be counseled to speak from their hearts, to avoid saying things in anger, to speak carefully, to remain silent, to eschew sharing secrets, to reveal only some of their plans, to dodge arguments, or to refrain from giving advice. Lukumi *oriaté* (diviners and ritual specialists) have long warned of the power of words that sociologists understand as the Thomas theorem (Thomas and Thomas [1928] 1970), which states that when something is defined as real it becomes real in its consequences. This particular variant of the social construction of reality (cf. Berger and Luckmann 1967) explains that our words, especially those repeated over time, have the power to affect what we understand to be true. The power of the tongue is a terrible burden for an author writing a book for multiple audiences, especially one whose allegiances straddle those of the social scientist and religious practitioner. The language I employ may affect the way people see Lukumi practice for years to come. My words may offend or confuse, legitimate or dismiss, distort or enlighten.

One terminological conundrum involves decisions between Spanish and Yoruba/Lukumi. When I refer to a religious house, do I say *ilé* or *casa de ocha*? Are godparents *madrinas* and *padrinos* or *iyaloshas* and *babaloshas*? Is divine energy and power *asé* or *aché*? Orisa or Oricha? In a diverse, historically divided, and ethnically healing Lukumi "community," these decisions may be seen as indicating allegiance to one side or another. My interview and survey participants varied in their language use. Some scorned Spanish terms and any mixing of Catholic understandings. Others relied more heavily on Spanish. Most drew freely from Spanish, English, and Yoruba/Lukumi. I attempt to honor the African and the Cuban within the language I use about Lukumi in the United States and at the same time reflect the diversity among my research participants.

Some of the Lukumi practitioners I interviewed pronounced the term *iyawo* as a three-syllable word and others dropped the first syllable, pronouncing it "yawo." The latter, less formal way of speaking, was more common and I am more comfortable with it. I have therefore decided to write about "a *iyawo*" rather than "an *iyawo*" when using my own voice.

Another problematic term is "Santería." If I use it, I may offend some Lukumi practitioners and scholars who understand the etic, pejorative, and inaccurate historical nature of the term. If I don't exploit it—even in the title—I risk losing readers for whom the less-recognized appellations for the religious practices are not known. Terms that describe initiated practitioners are similarly problematic. Among English-speaking scholars and practitioners in the United States, "priest" commonly denotes those who have undergone the *kariocha* ceremony. The Lukumi term *olorisha*—"owner of Orisha"—and the Spanish terms *santeras* and *santeros*—"from the Spanish santo, a person who deals with Santos (saints)"— existed before the English designation for the status (Clark 2007, 25–26). As a translation of previous labels, "priest" is a stretch and promotes an Abrahamic conception. However, like priestly ordination in Christendom, the *kariocha* empowers initiates to participate in ceremonies and perform certain rituals for the uninitiated. Also, as Obá Ernesto Pichardo contended (in a personal conversation), using the term claims religious legitimacy for a tradition that has long been stigmatized in Christian-dominant societies. If I choose "priest," I reify the English translation of a social scientist somewhere down the line, yet I support the political project of Lukumi who, in the struggle to have their (our) minority religion recognized as a legitimate and protected tradition in the United States, prefer mainstream and Christianized terms (church, priest, ordination, congregation) that help define what is acceptable from what is not in the socio-religious landscape of the twenty-first-century United States. There are good arguments for both using and abandoning the English term. Because it is commonly used and difficult to avoid, I will use it.

Similarly, using the term "Yoruba" to refer to the religious phenomenon I am studying is problematic, not only because of its troubled, socially constructed past (Palmié 2013) but also because of its seeming erasure of the Cuban environment in which Lukumi liturgy was created. Like a mother and her child, Lukumi is *of* but it is not *the same* as African tradition. "Afro-Cuban" honors cultural origins of the religion, yet it can be seen as a similarly problematic term that seems to simplify the history of the tradition (as if it arrived and was transmitted whole and singularly from Africa to Cuba) and racialize religious practices that are performed by diverse practitioners, many of whom are not "African" or "Cuban" and some of whom are not even Black or Hispanic (Palmié 2013). The problem with critiquing terminological objectification, of course, is that you have no common words left to identify for others what you study. Words have power and consequences both intended and unintended, but they are also necessary. As poet Adrienne Rich ([1971] 2002, 76) so deftly expressed in "The Burning of Paper Instead of Children," "this is the oppressor's language / yet I need it to talk to you." I endeavor to use words carefully, but use them I must.

STORYTELLING AND SOCIAL SCIENCE

This book is full of stories, "account[s] of incidents or events" (Webster's)—narratives related to me in person and over the phone by those who had not been raised in the traditions—by *iyawos*, former *iyawos*, and those who were considering one day becoming an initiated Lukumi *olorisha*; in communications that were digitally recorded and then transcribed; descriptions both cultural newcomers and those raised in Orisha traditions wrote in response to open-ended questions on surveys; and my own journal entries and memories of the year in white and the decisions and events leading up to it. Initiated devotees shared stories with me about how they decided to become *iyawos*; what were the best, worst, and most surprising parts of the year; victories and struggles with the many rules of the *yaworaje*; how they adjusted to everyday life as Lukumi novices in terms of their daily routines and relationships, their families, workplaces, schools, neighbors, friends, and more; and the internal and external changes they perceived during the year in white.

The story of how a work of research was created—the process by which its data are gathered—is central to understanding any book. As is generally the case, the present project was not cut from whole cloth. It emerged in pieces over a decade of work, study, and practice, during much of which I hadn't yet determined subsequent steps. Following the grounded theory approach (Strauss and Corbin 1990, 23), I did not set out to prove a particular theory. Instead, I began with a research site and allowed "what [was] relevant to . . . emerge," without having completed a literature review or defining a clear thesis or even a topic. At first I knew only that I was interested in issues of religious identification and practice. The territory I initially chose in 2005 was a neo-pagan campsite in the mid-Atlantic region of the United States. I soon discovered that on the fringe of the community of ritualists, seekers, healers, nature lovers, dancers, drummers, and partiers was an overlapping, smaller group that was performing invitation-only ritual that seemed much more interesting to me—richer and more grounded in highly structured tradition than most of what I had observed in the often anarchic creative world of modern-day witches, druids, faeries, ceremonial magicians, and Asatru. The group of Orisha devotees to which I was drawn was headed by a Cuban *babalawo* (a priest of Ifa)[12] and a Puerto Rican *olorisha* and Spiritist[13] who ran an Ifa-Lukumi house[14] in a nearby city. Their religious practices were very different from those I had encountered previously. Their religious world view was distinct, and I was intrigued.

At first I had no labels for what I experienced among the Orisha venerators. Religious participants referred to their practices simply as "the religion," initially making it difficult for me to investigate what others had written about it. Eventually I had words and understanding enough to plan a study that both expanded and narrowed my original focus on the neo-pagan site I visited. Both at that initial location and elsewhere, yet continuing with a grounded theory approach, I launched an interview project with cultural newcomers to Orisha veneration. I asked forty people—Hispanic and non-Hispanic; white, Black, and mixed race; and both initiated *olorishas* and *aleyos*[15]—general questions about their entry and their commitment to Orisha and to an Ocha house. I asked what attracted them to the Orisha and the practices that honored them and how they reconciled their new affinities with the religions in which they were raised. I requested information about how they gained entry into religious communities where historical habits of secrecy and wariness toward outsiders still often predominate, and I inquired whether their paths in the religion seemed difficult or easy. I probed about issues of gender, race, ethnicity, sexuality, and language and how they affected cultural newcomers' experiences with Orisha religion. In the narratives of my interview participants, I sought answers to my own questions: What attracted me so strongly to these practices and ideas that were so foreign to the ones I had been raised in? How could I reconcile my Jewish heritage with new practices that involved, among other things, divination with cowrie shells and honoring holiness within rocks? As a social scientist and a rational person, was it possible to maintain a religious world view that was so distinct from mainstream secular understandings? How could I reconcile my feminism with the gendered and hierarchical social structure of the religion? Why did I choose a religious path that required so much cultural adaptation, time, and money?

At the same time that I was beginning my research, I was also becoming more personally involved in and committed to Lukumi tradition. It wasn't until a couple of years later, in the early weeks of my year in white, that I narrowed the research emphasis further, using the new focus to commence an additional twelve in-depth interviews with *olorishas*. As is the custom for *iyawo* in the first few months of the *yaworaje* in my religious house, I was sleeping on a mat on the floor in front of the pots that contained my newly born Orisha. I awoke one morning with an answer to a research problem with which I had struggled for some time: How could I organize the voluminous interview data I had collected so far in a way that was sociologically interesting? I arose that morning with the inspiration I needed to refocus my research on the Lukumi year in white. What could be more sociologically interesting than the stories of the many *iyawos* who—despite their lives as pastry chefs, graduate students, construction workers, nail stylists, nurses, retail managers, lawyers, accountants, social workers, teachers, business owners, police officers, artists, librarians, bartenders, legal secretaries, interior designers, psychiatrists, and medical assistants in the postindustrial United States—were arising after nights spent sleeping on mats upon hard floors and taking their meals on those same mats, wearing white exclusively for an entire year, shunning the dark, spurning forks at meals, and keeping the rain from falling on their heads? What did such practices among people not raised in Lukumi tradition tell us about religious identification and practice in the United States today? What varied stories of triumph and toil, salvation and frustration were hiding beneath protective layers of white?

The present highly "storied" exploration of the *yaworaje* is informed by three social scientific methodologies, each working to enhance the others. The three methodological types are complementary, each offering distinct strengths to the project as a whole. The fifty-two in-depth interviews offer depth. The 197 survey responses bring breadth. And the auto-ethnographic fieldwork provides perspective.[16] I use the data from all three methodologies to explore the Lukumi year in white, especially as it is experienced by cultural newcomers to the tradition.

LIMINALITY AND THE CULTURAL NEWCOMER

At first glance it may seem that a book on the Lukumi year in white, especially one that emphasizes the everyday experiences of cultural newcomers to the tradition, is the study of the bizarre among the exotic, an examination of nongeneralizable oddities, a treatise on a curious identification at the periphery of U.S. society. Such a concern is troubling to the social scientist trained to generate generalizable knowledge. I believe a second look will show that a study of the *yaworaje* in the United States can be seen as more than an exercise in thick description. The *iyawo* is a distilled embodiment of identification on the margins. Not only is the *iyawo* considered to be and treated as inhabiting a liminal status in the Lukumi rite of passage, but the *iyawo*—like the Heinleinian "cat who walks through walls,"[17] regularly crossing the borders of religion, gender, ethnicity, minority and majority, mainstream and occult, sacred and profane—epitomizes the multiplicity and fragmentary nature of identification for many in contemporary pluralism.

In today's social environments of flux and flow, consumption, fragmentation, and diversification, borders multiply, as do the meaning systems they mark. Individual choices for identification expand. Increasingly in the West we are multinational, multicultural, multiethnic, multireligious persons engaged in the postindustrial project of self-creation.[18] In these dynamic times, we must attend to "religious borderlands," "spaces—geographical, cultural, psychological—in contemporary society where the boundaries of the religious are in question, if not openly challenged and contested." In religious borderlands, "symbols have emergent qualities; meaning is anything but fixed and arises out of the re-creation and reinterpretation of symbols" (Roof 1998, 1, 4). It is arguable that all religion (all culture, for that matter), can be seen in such a way—as in a continual state of negotiation and flux. Examining the year in white in the Lukumi religious tradition is one way to deeply consider the margins and peripheries. *Iyawos* are frontiersmen and women, forging identities across the boundaries. Yet Lukumi novices, epitomes of the liminal, may merely be models for increasingly common ways of experiencing and practicing religious identification in contemporary pluralism. In the case of "increased blending of the population" that we see in the United States today, border challenges "to the authority of descent-defined categories" (Roof 1998, 5) become even more prominent. The *yaworaje*, as an extended experiment in which religious and ethnic borders are amplified, may provide a "strong-case scenario" for understanding religious identification in the current era.

Most scholars have focused on the Orisha religious traditions, such as Lukumi and Ifa in the United States, as they are understood and practiced primarily by cultural "insiders" in Cuban and Puerto Rican ethnic centers (e.g., Brown 2003; Gregory 1999; Perez y Mena 1991). The "transformation of the religion" due to the entrance of "increasing numbers of non-Hispanics in American Santería . . . has received scant attention" (Canizares 1999, 125).[19] In contrast to this trend, the present project features the practices, experiences, and identifications of cultural "outsiders"—Black, white, Asian, mixed-race, Hispanic, and non-Hispanic English-speakers throughout the United States who were not raised within Orisha communities. It is my hope that emphasizing the year in white among cultural newcomers, like the Garfinkelian "breaching experiments,"[20] will highlight taken-for-granted processes within religious identification that are more fluid and less anchored to ethnic backgrounds perhaps than ever before.

As movements in, out of, and between religious identifications increase and as more people switch to or add new religious commitments derived from cultures in which they have not been raised, attending to the practices and experiences of cultural newcomers in religious groups becomes more important. As estimated by researchers for the Pew Forum on Religion and Public Life who examined the 2007 Religious Landscape Survey, religious traffic is high in the United States: "All groups are gaining and losing individual adherents." Indeed, approximately "44% of Americans now profess a religious affiliation that is different from the religion in which they were raised" (Pond et al. 2010, 3, 1). In the social scientific literature on religious joining, switching, and conversion, however, little attention has focused on differences in practice and experience between cultural newcomers and natives to religious traditions.

Questions concerning religious practice and identification on the margins are central for scholars of religion and society today. In an age of heterogeneity and pluralism, what happens to the traditional reliance on racial and ethnic categories for demarcating religious identification? When the margins are multiplied, who gets counted as an insider or outsider? In what ways do issues of power and privilege come to play when practitioners of varying ethnic groups pray together? Are cultural newcomers viewed as welcomed immigrants or as interlopers? How do individuals resolve the disparate beliefs, values, obligations and freedoms of minority religious world views and mainstream Christian-dominated secular society? In what ways do today's multireligious families bridge their religious differences? Can cultural newcomers to religious traditions reconcile their religious upbringing with their new religious practice, with their families of origin, and with the needs of their workplaces? And how do cultural "greenies" practice and understand their new religious traditions differently from cultural "veterans"?

The experiences of migrants to a religion may differ in many ways from those who were raised in and around a tradition. Cultural newcomers may have less comprehensive conceptions of a religious world view. They may have to work more consciously on entry and socialization into the religion. They may be less likely to take for granted some of the practices and beliefs of the tradition. Their cultural differences from previous members of the tradition may promote distinct practices and attitudes toward the religion, even if their liturgical practices are performed similarly. They may exhibit "convert's zeal," adhering more strictly to the letter of religious law than many of those who were raised in the religion. Or they may take some practices less seriously than cultural indigenes. Newcomers to a tradition may have less familial, peer, and community support for their religious pursuits. They may be less easily immersed in a religious world view. The experience of the year in white may differ for those who enter into the religion who were not raised in or around it and those who were born and bred in the religion with a multigenerational "insider" support system. Latecomers to a tradition who have ethnic or class statuses that differ from those of previous and already-existing inhabitants of the group may vary in their sense of entitlement and expectations. They may differ also in their access to material, social, symbolic, and cultural resources.

Some might call newcomers to Orisha traditions "converts." Scholars offer a wide variety of definitions for conversion, but the common denominator is that it involves religious change. There is no consensus, however, about the degree of modification required. Several researchers have proposed continua, reserving the label "conversion" for the most extreme levels of change (Snow and Machalek 1984, 169).[21] For example, one religious historian differentiates conversion ("reorientation of the soul") from "adhesion" (supplemental addition of new religions) (Snow and Machalek 1984, 169).

What is interesting in many of these definitions is that intensity of religious transformation is seen as dependent on the exclusivity with which the "convert" holds the new religious world view. Such description may be more relevant to relatively circumscribed mindsets such as those found in many iterations of Abrahamic religions than in the comparatively inclusive African-derived context. In addition, these distinctions may be mired in earlier modernist notions, such as the idea that religious identifications must be clearly bounded. To the extent that outmoded conceptions persist, our visions of religious "conversion," "switching," practicing, and belonging will exist within "a religious landscape that seems more like a fading oil painting hanging in a dark museum than a continually refreshing video stream from a live webcam" (Phillips and Kelner 2006, 18).[22] Within contemporary pluralism, practitioners continually create religious understandings and practices from multiple traditions: "More and more people can both claim some fairly conventional religious position and cheerfully add on other elements" (Lyon 2000, 74).

Unlike much of what is described as "conversion" in the sociological literature, entry into the service of the Orisha does not usually require one to abandon earlier religious identifications, beliefs, or commitments. It does not even require unquestioning belief. Despite the fact that in Christian-dominant society we often use the term "faith" as synonymous with religion, like many indigenous African religions, "Yoruba religion rests on practice more than faith" (Prothero 2010, 230; see also Brown [1991] 2011; Clark 2007). Practitioners of traditional Yoruba religion and its derivatives may also enjoy (or suffer) other religions. Entry into the service of the Orisha does not necessarily imply religious exclusivity.

In the social scientific literature on religious joining, switching, and conversion, however, little attention has focused on differences in practice and experience between cultural newcomers and natives to religious traditions. Some scholars have examined widespread assumptions of "convert's zeal," the idea that those who enter anew into religious groups tend to be more religious than those who remain in the religion in which they are raised, sometimes to the point of fanaticism. This could be because "switching requires a conscious decision and a certain amount of religious initiative, so that switchers tend to be persons with more religious motivation" (Hoge, Johnson, and Luidens 1995, 253). In some cases it can also be because some sociological definitions of "conversion" have been influenced by "Christian biblical conceptualizations of Saul's conversion on the road to Damascus" (Zinnbauer and Pargament 1998, 162). If true "converts" are those who, as in the story of the Apostle Paul, undergo sudden, radical transformations that involve new relationships to supernatural power(s), then intensity of devotion is almost predicted by the very definition of their religious status.

Research with findings of heightened religiosity of "converts" or "switchers" tend to be mostly limited to Christianity[23] and focused narrowly on church-centered definitions of religious practice—such as frequency of church attendance and prayer and identification as "born again" (Hadaway 1980; Hoge, Johnson and Luidens 1995). A number of studies have found that those who switch from one Christian denomination to another demonstrate higher religiosity than those who stay put (Hadaway 1980; Hadaway and Marler 1993; Hoge, Johnson and Luidens 1995; Roof and McKinney 1987). For example, one investigation of Christian university students found that "spiritual converts" (defined as those who "indicated that they had become more religious/spiritual in the last two years, had experienced a conversion to Jesus, God, a higher power, or a transcendent force in the last two years, and had not changed religious denomination in the last two years"), reported "more pre-conversion perceived stress, a greater sense of personal inadequacy and limitation before the conversion, greater pre-post improvement in sense of adequacy and competence, and a greater increase in post-conversion spiritual experiences" than those who did not report religious change (Zinnbauer and Pargament 1998, 167, 173). However, some find very modest differences. A survey of Utahans found that converts to Mormonism did not distinguish themselves much from lifelong Mormons. Only one practice yielded a statistically significant result in the study of religiosity, that of engaging in daily prayer (Albrecht and Bahr 1983).

Research that veers from Protestantism finds limited support for the "convert's zeal." Fieldwork from 1968 in a Japanese enclave in Bolivia—an admittedly unique and complex case—revealed that Catholic converts were less religious (defined as displaying religious artifacts, using Christian names, and attending mass) than those who were raised Catholic. The latter, the researcher explained, were "heirs of three centuries of intense religious persecution" in Japan who now found themselves able to worship freely in a Catholic nation (Thompson 1968, 207). A more recent study concluded that young people in the United States who joined a religious group or denomination or who switched religious affiliations were likely to have increased religious participation (defined narrowly as frequency of attendance at religious services) in the mostly Christian sample only if they were among the 23 percent who were "occasional attenders" (Petts 2009). And several researchers funded by the Pew Forum reported that "converts" (people with different religious affiliations from those in which they had been raised) evidenced "modest" yet significantly higher levels of religiosity than nonconverts. However the measures chosen—"religious salience, weekly worship attendance, absolute certainty of belief in God, daily prayer, regular sharing of faith, and assent with the statement that one's own faith 'is the one true faith leading to eternal life'"—seem to be largely "more applicable to Christianity than to other faiths." Conversion was not found to affect religiosity for people of non-Christian faiths (Pond et al. 2010, 14, 19).

Despite the increasing importance of conversion, little scholarship has examined differences in practice and experience between cultural newcomers and natives to religious traditions. The scholarship that exists tends to focus on Christianity and even, at times, to employ definitions of central variables (such as "conversion" and "religiosity") that are based on Christian presumptions. Much of this scholarship tends to focus on a narrow set of traditional church-based practices rather than on the great variety of everyday experiences that constitute lived religion. This leaves many interesting questions left unanswered (and unasked). I will examine some of these in the pages that follow.

LUKUMI CULTURAL NEWCOMERS TO THE *YAWORAJE*

In the contemporary U.S. environment of intensifying cultural and religious pluralism, the liminal status of *iyawos* among Lukumi cultural newcomers offers an intriguing site for the study of everyday coping strategies, privileges, and problems involved in traversing cultural, religious, and ethnic boundaries. *Iyawos* in the United States—especially those living outside Cuban ethnic centers—must inhabit two worlds. Such duality may be exacerbated for *iyawos* who are cultural outsiders, as their ability to find respite within in-group space may be severely limited. At the same time, the class, racial, ethnic, national, gender, sexual, and linguistic privileges and disadvantages of diverse newcomers may provide ease and hardship in complex, intersecting ways. Using the lens of the "year in white," this project examines everyday religious identification as it is experienced in an increasingly dynamic multicultural social context. It asks specifically about the religious lives of cultural newcomers and makes some initial comparisons to cultural natives, who, due to their largely minority status in the United States, must also walk in two worlds.

In Chapter 1, "Situating the *Iyawo*," I explain the status of *iyawos* and discuss the year in white in terms of three main themes: transformation, socialization, and seclusion. I then situate this examination of the *yaworaje* among cultural newcomers within the growing body of research that views religion as lived every day. From this perspective, I examine each of my data sources regarding the question of why people enter the year in white, seeking similarities and differences among cultural newcomers and veterans and among religious practitioners of different ethnicities.

In Chapter 2, "*Iyawo* Experience," I discuss experiences of the year in white in the United States. What was most difficult and rewarding about the year? How did *iyawos* and former *iyawos* characterize the year generally? Some of the most common themes in response to general questions about *iyawo* experience concerned transformation, seclusion, emotional turbulence, and visibility. Many respondents spoke of loving and hating the very same aspects of their year. In addition, I examine differences between cultural newcomers and natives in their experiences of the year in white and among those of various ethnic backgrounds.

The third chapter, "*Iyawo* Rules," highlights religious practitioners' interactions with the rules of the year in white. I discuss the rules *iyawos* must follow and how they were experienced by a diverse group of cultural newcomers and natives in the United States with a focus on consequences for our understandings of contemporary religious identification and practice. The rules participants found most difficult were those concerning dress, covering, and carrying and those prohibiting touch and exchange.

In Chapter 4, "*Iyawo* Social Relations," I cover some of the social structures that affect experiences of the year in white, including participants' discussions of connections and conflicts with family and friends, at work, and within their respective Ocha houses and communities. Survey and interview participants spoke most frequently of bonds and breakages in their religious "houses." *Iyawos* and former *iyawos* generally saw godparents and their religious houses as sources of support, family, and training. A smaller number described negative relations in their *ilés* (religious houses), ranging from arguments to abandonment and racial, ethnic, or sexual discrimination. It is here that I discuss some of the tensions accompanying diversity—ethnic, racial, gender, and sexual–within the religious communities I study.

Chapter 5, "Relating to the Orisha," examines how increasing religious commitments, including to the year in white, are generally made in the context of a growing relationship to the Orisha. Broadening the language of "conversion," I suggest that these relationships occur in the context of religious socialization processes.

In the concluding chapter I summarize what study of cultural newcomers to the Lukumi year in white teaches us about religious identification in contemporary pluralism, especially concerning questions discussed earlier in the book. These include issues of insider/outsider status, the resolution of disparate beliefs and norms in pluralist society, and reconciling religious difference.

1 • SITUATING THE *IYAWO*

Lukumi is an initiatory religion in the United States. In contrast to the emphasis placed on belief or faith in the Christian tradition or on submission in Islam (Prothero 2010), "it is participation in ritual and ceremonial activities . . . that is the focus of religiosity" in this "Afro-Cuban" religious tradition (Clark 2005, 73). Initiations are a primary source of one's status in Lukumi culture; they determine the practices one is obligated and privileged to perform and the religious knowledge one is permitted to receive. The *kariocha* ceremony is a particularly important one in Lukumi culture; it is the ticket to entrance "behind the sheet," the area the uninitiated are not permitted to see. Thus, in many Lukumi houses in the United States, priestly status is more common than the term "priest" generally suggests in Abrahamic traditions.[1]

In many communities, children are commonly initiated via the *kariocha*. Some *ilés* consist of extended families in which priests outnumber those who have not undergone the *kariocha* ceremony. Children may be initiated as priests because of a promise a parent has made to an Orisha, because there is a health problem the family wants to avoid or overcome, because the parents have been advised in divinatory consultation to do so, or simply because it is now seen as advantageous in some Ocha communities to initiate children as early as possible. I was recently at a Lukumi ceremony where I spoke to an *olorisha* who told me that all her young grandchildren had undergone priestly ordination already. "People initiate their children as soon as they can afford to do so," she said. "It's easier that way." The perceived advantages of initiating children are that the discipline of the *yaworaje* is seen as less difficult for very young children, the children's lives are expected to have fewer obstacles, and the extensive divination that accompanies the initiation is believed to be of great assistance to parents in bringing up their children. Despite the increased popularity of initiation, the process, for both children and adults, is neither simple nor casual.

In the Lukumi tradition, for a year after the *kariocha* ceremony—alternately called *asiento, ocha,* crowning, coronation, making *santo,* making *ocha,* or having one's head made—*iyawos* are encumbered by scores of rules and regulations that encompass most daily and many occasional behaviors and social situations:

> He must always dress in white; must not visit bars, jails, cemeteries, hospitals, or other places of contamination; must not drink alcohol or use recreational drugs; must not use profane language; must not shake hands or eat with a knife and fork. A female iyawo may not wear makeup or curl, cut, or dye her hair; a male must be clean shaven. All iyawo must keep their heads covered and may wear no jewelry except their Santería necklaces and bracelets. For the first three months after the initiation, the iyawo may not use a mirror, even to shave. In addition, during that initial period he must eat all meals while seated on a mat on the floor using only a spoon and his own set of dishes. During the entire year, the iyawo loses his name and is simply addressed as "iyawo" by his family and friends (Clark 2005, 77).

This list includes behavioral guidelines regarding dress and adornment, grooming and hygiene, eating and drinking, social interactions, and prohibited areas and activities. Yet that inventory is only partial.[2] In addition, *iyawos* are often told to avoid physical contact with other people unless those others are Lukumi priests or children. They are not to take things directly handed to them from others. In the first three months or longer, *iyawos* must keep their bodies mostly covered, except for the hands, neck, and face, even in the heat of summer. They should not allow rain to fall on their heads, and (with few exceptions) they must avoid going out after dark. Although the rules vary among houses of Ocha and even sometimes within the same *ilé, iyawo* life is highly regulated. And lest they seek freedom on the sly, *iyawos* are traditionally monitored by community members, including those belonging to other religious houses, and are subject to disciplinary penalties for breaking rules.

While allowances are often made for conduct in the workplace, *iyawos* generally must wear only white. They are even required to use white bags, purses, and umbrellas. But why white? There are several reasons. "White . . . is the color of orí, embodies the purity of the creator and metaowner of this head, Obatalá, and is consistent with the spiritual protection and evolution of the iyawó. White clothes are also consonant with the iyawó's regimen of spiritual hygiene and regulated program of behavior during the obligatory yaworage, or 'year of white'" (Brown 2003, 196).[3] The multiple associations of white include the clarity of *orí,* the wholesomeness of Obatalá, and general cleanliness. Yet white dress may be a relatively new addition for *iyawos,* perhaps chosen for its associations with "the sanitary customs of medical practice—particularly in the context of childbirth," given the metaphor of birth and rebirth of the priestly initiation ceremony that precedes the *yaworaje*. White is also associated with "the purity of a woman's bridal status," which accords with the theme of sacred marriage in the *kariocha* (Brown 2003, 354).

In contrast with the detailed accounts and analyses of the Lukumi priestly initiation, scholars have written little about the year in white that follows.[4] The focus on the seven-day *ocha* ceremony at the expense of the 365-day ritual that follows privileges the spectacular over the ordinary and risks missing much of the sociological and religious import of this transformative religious practice in which the extraordinary and the everyday merge. The existing scholarly analyses of the *yaworaje* can be grouped into three basic sociological themes. First, the year in white is part of a process of identity change that begins in the priestly initiation ceremony to realign the *iyawo*'s personal and social identification with the Orisha to whom the novice has been dedicated. Second, during the *yaworaje*, new priests learn to subordinate themselves to the needs of the Orisha and the religious community. Third, the *iyawo* year is a time when "newborn" initiates are sheltered as children by their "parents" and are viewed as being in need of special protection.

TRANSFORMATION

The *yaworaje* can be seen as part of a process of identity death and rebirth that begins with the seven-day priestly initiation ceremony. The *kariocha* generally proceeds in a manner consistent with rites of passage (van Gennep [1909] 1961) that consist of three basic stages: separation, liminality, and reintegration (Clark 2005; Mason 2002). During the week-long initiation the novice is removed from her home, work, and daily routine and is confined to a single room. In part of the ritual, the initiate is considered "symbolically dead" and "icons of the initiate's old life and identity" are removed (Mason 2002, 79). The initiate sheds important signifiers of self and status: name, hair, and clothing. This is separation. "During the rest of the year the iyawo's status is ambiguous" (Clark 2005, 74). During this time, his or her previous name is not supposed to be spoken; s/he is referred to only as "*iyawó*," further "distancing her even more from her previous identity and reinforcing the agency of the oricha" (Mason 2002, 79). This is liminality. "As the year progresses, the restrictions that surround him are loosened or lifted," and the process of reintegration begins (Clark 2005, 74). Thus, the year in white continues a journey of change that begins in the *kariocha* ceremony. Through a sequence of initiatory phases, the novice is transformed.

Iyawos are encouraged to leave their old selves behind and gradually align their sense of self with particular Orisha. As *iyawos* are separated from their previous identities, they are encouraged to identify with the Orisha who is said to "own their heads," or to "crown" them. They are given a ritual name associated with that Orisha, and over time there is a "slow merging of their personalities" (Mason 2002, 81).

A wealth of material culture—intricate costumery and ritual—is used in the *asiento* (initiation) as symbolic power to affect change in the initiate: "A series of clothing changes, physical modifications, and body adornments over the course of twenty-four hours registers a person's transformation from an uninitiated state (*aleyo*), to the highly liminal and symbolically dead condition of abokú . . . to the living vessel of an oricha's *aché*:[5] the iyawó, the newborn condition that begins after the mounting of the oricha on the head and for a period of one year afterward" (Brown 2003, 195). During the *kariocha* ceremony, initiates are stripped of the clothing and hair that helped identify them to others and to themselves. They are dressed in elaborate attire in the colors associated with the particular Orisha to whom they have been assigned. The removal of the material signs of former life (a symbolic death) is followed by symbolic "rebirth" and identification with an aspect of divinity. One day after losing former markers of identity— hair, name, colored clothing—the *iyawo* is dressed in elaborate ceremonial dress that includes the symbols of office that correspond with the Orisha to whom he or she has been assigned in prior divination. At the same time, these *iyawos* are not permitted to view themselves in mirrors: "Seen by an 'audience,' they cannot (fully) 'see themselves.' Indeed, the absence of self-reflection—in a mirror, for example—discourages reversion of identification to the former 'self' (is it 'me' in these clothes?), leaving the elders and audience to recognize and constitute the object of their gaze as an oricha king, queen, or warrior" (Brown 2003, 198– 199).[6] When one is denied a mirror, s/he relies much more heavily on the eyes of others. Beginning in the initiation ceremony and continuing throughout the first few months of the *yaworaje, iyawos* become accustomed to seeing themselves as their community views them: as children, as new brides of the Orisha, and as embodiments of the Ocha who "rule their heads."

The year in white is a continuation of the transformative process of identity shedding and renewal begun in the *kariocha* ceremony. This theme is highly present in the narratives of *iyawos* and former *iyawos*.

SOCIALIZATION

The *yaworaje* is also a socialization process. Socialization is an induction into a social world. Through socialization we learn fundamental things such as language, meaning, norms, values, and what constitutes "sense" and "nonsense" (Berger and Luckmann 1967). Over the course of a year, *iyawos* learn to subordinate themselves to the needs of the Orisha and the religious community. The term "*iyawo*" is a designation of status, specifically gendered and ranked status. In the context of precolonial, patrilocal Yoruba culture, "*iyawo*" originally referred to a new wife, a woman who had recently married in to a community.[7] This was a low-status position: "Among the Yoruba a newly married *iyawo* has the lowest status in her husband's household, since she is considered younger than even the youngest child. By calling new priests *iyawo*, Orisha worshippers are subjecting them to the status loss experienced by every new bride". In this way, *iyawo*, whether male or female, are "*subordinate* new wives," to both the Orisha and to other religious community members who have already completed the *iyawo* year (Clark 2005, 44).

To the extent that the Lukumi priestly initiation involves a temporary loss of status, the *kariocha* ritual may be seen as a "degradation ceremony" (Garfinkel 1956), a ritual in which an individual's identity or status is stripped away so that it can be replaced by another. Degradation ceremonies often accompany resocialization, as in the case of mental patients, prisoners, and military recruits (Goffman 1961), and can be seen as one form of a "commitment ritual," as in the case of Christian baptism, which reinforces "the rejection of old patterns and behaviors and the incorporation of new behaviors into one's life" (Rambo 1995, 127).

Iyawos are expected to perform "wifely" duties for the community, such as cleaning and cooking, maintaining Orisha shrines, and caring for animals (Clark 2005, 79). In return for this loss of status, *iyawos* are ranked above *aleyos*, those in the religious household who have not undergone priestly initiation. Thus, from a sociological perspective, the year in white can be seen as resocialization. This theme frequently arose in the accounts of *iyawos* and former *iyawos*, especially with regard to relationships with the Orisha and relationships with families, friends, and co-workers.

SECLUSION

The year in white is a time when newborn *iyawos* are sheltered like children by their parents:

> During this time, often referred to as the Year of White, he [the iyawo] lives surrounded by cool, peaceful white, and encumbered with an array of restrictions on his behavior. . . . These rules are designed to protect the iyawo, who is considered especially sensitive, from places and situations that are physically, emotionally, or spiritually dangerous. They teach the iyawo to remain cool, calm, and clear-headed, in control of himself and aware of his environment. They help him to solidify his understanding of himself as both the priest and the embodiment of his Orisha. His ongoing adherence to these rules helps to establish and maintain his commitment to his Orisha and the practices they demand (Clark 2007, 129).

The *yaworaje* is a time when susceptible *iyawos* are secluded from many ordinary worldly things (such as darkness, mirrors, forests, revelry, rain, the uncleanliness of the uninitiated, and forks and table knives) that might cause them to lose their "cool" heads or bring upon them physical or spiritual harm.

The view that *iyawos* are vulnerable has at least three interrelated aspects. First, in a continuation of the metaphor of rebirth, new initiates are viewed as infants, especially during their first three months. (It is common for Lukumi priests to reckon their "age" as beginning with initiation.) As babes, these infant priests are forbidden to eat with forks and knives, are required to be home by dark, and must subordinate themselves to the authority of their godparents regarding a range of everyday activities. Especially in the first three months of the *yaworaje*, they may be pampered by their godparents and other priests, for example by being served food before most "adults" partake. Second, *iyawos* are newborn specifically with regard to Orisha. As Clark (2005, 76) explains, novices are encouraged to understand specific Orisha as parents. Through divination, for each *iyawo*, a "father" and a "mother" Orisha is determined. Thus, "the initiate's first relationship to the Orisha . . . is that of a child to a loving parent." Third, *iyawos* are seen as open and therefore at risk because of the exposure of their heads during the *kariocha*. At the *asiento*, when the head is shaved, the tutelary Orisha is said to be "seated" in the head of the initiate. As a result, the newly consecrated *iyawo* becomes "a walking temple" whose head is "a mobile sacred site" (Clark 2005, 76) that must be kept clean from the defilement of the world.

Thus, in various ways, *iyawos* are seen to be in need of protective seclusion. This is a theme *iyawos* and former *iyawos* spoke of frequently, especially when discussing their experiences with the year in white and the rules of the year.

RELIGIOUS IDENTIFICATION IN PRACTICE

Religion and the study of religion are influenced by ever-changing, complex sociocultural and sociohistorical contexts. Practices associated with contemporary religions may be affected by trends in rationalization, consumer capitalism, individualism, geographic mobility, uncertainty and risk, improvements in communication and information technologies, pluralism, urbanization, and egalitarianism (e.g., Bruce 2002; Giddens 1991; Hervieu-Leger [1993] 2000; Lyon 2000; Wuthnow 2007). Social hierarchies and institutions particular to late nineteenth- and early twentieth-century Cuba, forged in relation to racial politics, socialism, and Catholicism influenced the development of Lukumi (see Brown 2003; Brandon 1997). Scientism, capitalism, and the dominance of Christianity affect the way Lukumi is understood, enacted, and has changed in the United States. Individualism, increasing attention to technical proficiency and professionalism, competition between *babalawos* and *oriatés*, Afrocentrism, and the environment of increasing openness afforded by the 1993 U.S. Supreme Court decision confirming the legality of animal sacrifice in Lukumi (Sandoval 2006) now shape the way adherents understand and practice the religion in the United States.

Dynamic social contexts also affect the questions researchers find interesting and relevant, sometimes in ways that are so fundamental that they seem invisible. To what extent, for example, do Western liberal assumptions about the nature of religion and its distinction from the secular affect how we conceive of the religious? In what ways does the social scientific focus on the symbolic aspects of religion cause us to neglect the ways that religion is embedded in the activities of everyday life (see Asad 1993)? For example, the predominance of Christianity in Western culture may lead us to define religion in Christian-centric ways such that religious expression that differs from Christian custom is seen as aberrant and cultish and not quite in the realm of religion.[8] Scientism and rationalization may lead us to dismiss religious understandings in favor of a reductive functionalism (see Gregory 1999). Today, when more and more scholars are becoming religious practitioners and more religious practitioners are becoming scholars, the "ethnographic interface," in which ethnographies shape their ethnographic objects and vice versa (Palmié 2013), is another social influence on the religion. Today's scholarly interpretations may become tomorrow's Lukumi praxis (for good or for ill).

New times lead to new ways of being religious. The prodigious pluralism brought about by the wave of new immigrants after 1965 produced expanded options for religious practice in the United States (Eck 2001). When social scientists go beyond records of church attendance and the study of traditional religious beliefs, they find evidence of surging spirituality in the West that is not necessarily limited to old-fashioned religion (see Ammerman 2007; Hall 1997; Lyon 2000; McGuire 2008; Partridge 2004). Scholars of the late twentieth and early twenty-first centuries have described a new "spirituality of seeking" (Wuthnow 1998), a "spiritual marketplace" (Roof 2001) that is characterized as being spiritual rather than religious, and an "occulture" that is constituted of religiosities based on a variety of alternative religious movements and the diffusion of Eastern spiritual beliefs and norms into everyday life, such as alternative healing modalities and yoga (Partridge 2004). If we base sociological understanding of religious identification and practice primarily on the examination of what Christians do inside their churches, our knowledge will be limited.[9]

The transformations in religion have led scholars to view and study religion differently than they used to. A number of scholars have moved beyond the study of church attendance to focus on lived religion. These interdisciplinary approaches emphasize religion as it is performed in "everyday thinking and doing" (Hall 1997). One example of the insights that can be gained from the study of lived religion can be found in examination of "Golden Rule

Christianity," possibly "the dominant form of religiosity among middle-class suburban Americans." It is best understood as practices "of doing good and caring for others" rather than ideology (Ammerman 1997, 199, 197). Sociologist Nancy Tatom Ammerman (1997) argues that instead of seeing this as diluted evangelism, this common form of religious identification in the United States is worthy of study in its own right. Examining the religious activities and beliefs of non-experts in both public and private life may yield different views from those seen in studies of what the influential sociologist Max Weber might describe as religion in its "ideal-typical" (pure and hypothetical) form. For example, Italians and Spaniards may skip church on Sundays and abstain from confession, but "they still think of themselves as Catholic." Similarly, "many American Jews are Jewish in the way Italians are Catholic"; they retain their identification as Jewish yet choose from among the traditional observances that were once viewed as obligatory (Ammerman 2007, 220).

This move away from the study of religion in its ideal-typical forms requires a basic reconsideration of what constitutes the religious. It may not be completely separable from the "profane"; it shares "an ongoing dynamic relationship with the realities of everyday life" (Orsi 1997, 8). A focus on lived or everyday religion recognizes the importance of religion as it is understood and experienced both by those who study religion and those who are being studied. Attending to everyday religion demonstrates that "religious identities are often maintained and negotiated in surprising places." If we focus only on attendance at worship services and traditional expressions of belief and church membership we may underestimate the strength of contemporary religious life (Ammerman 2007, 221). If we limit study of Lukumi religious practice to the "ethnographically relevant" situations (Palmié 2001, 15) of drum ceremonies, possession experiences, and liturgical "syncretism" our knowledge of the lives of religious practitioners will be confined to those realms. Religious expression happens at home, on the streets, at work and school, in artistic performances, in financial dealings, at the playground and the gym, and in the grocery. When scholars expand their notion of the spiritual and religious, they discover that religious identification is tenacious and adaptive. In a pluralist cultural environment, where religious identification is increasingly achieved rather than ascribed, we can no longer be content to examine religious movements only among their ethnic originators. We must include the diverse members of any religious group. Many traditional sociological conceptions of the religious are no longer useful. The sacred cannot be easily separated from the mundane, religion may merge with magic, and various traditions believed to be "pure" contain slips and slices from a variety of places (McGuire 2008).

Focusing on religion as experienced in the lives of real persons requires us to take seriously the stories people tell about their religious lives, understandings, and behaviors. We don't have to measure what they tell us against some ideal religious form or model of what religion should be. We don't need to justify their beliefs and experiences by reducing them to theorized social or psychological functions. Instead, we are free to accept religious narratives as examples of the many ways religion can be practiced and understood. Gathering stories about the *yaworaje* told in interviews, surveys, and autoethnographic reflections allows us to explore how cultural newcomers and natives thought, felt, and acted during the year.

WHY "MAKE *OCHA*"? DIFFERENCES AND SIMILARITIES

No description of the *yaworaje* would be complete without some discussion of what brings people to the year.[10] Individuals enter the Lukumi religion via multiple pathways and for a variety of reasons (Clark 2007, 8). Some are raised in families or communities that practice Orisha worship. Some are not. Some "know someone who knows someone who is a devotee and seek their aid when their physical, mental, or emotional problems seem intractable. . . . Others learn about these traditions in classrooms and dance studios where dedicated teachers provide instruction into the cultures of Africa. For some people their first introduction to the world of the Orisha is scary, as everything seems alien and unsettling; for others there is a sense of coming home to the religious tradition of their forbears or of their own heart" (Clark 2007, 8). The fifty-two religious practitioners who spoke to me in formal interviews and the 197 who completed surveys shared the entire range of experience described above and more. Most of those I interviewed narrated a process that began with their first awareness of the Orisha or Orisha religion and continued with their attraction to the tradition and the ways they overcame barriers to entry. Awareness and feelings of being drawn generally fueled active seeking, which culminated with increasing levels of religious participation and/or initiation (Carr 2010).

The decision to undergo Lukumi ordination and participate in the year in white is often bound up with the many reasons people first enter the religion as *aleyo*.[11] The path requires too much commitment to be taken lightly. In the survey, *iyawos* and former *iyawos* offered many reasons for this important decision. Of the 183 responses to the open-ended question "Why did you make Ocha/Saint?" seventy-three shared multiple reasons, despite the constraints of a written survey.

The largest number (n = 51; 28 percent) said that they were instructed to do so by a Lukumi priest performing divination with cowrie shells or a priest of Ifa using the *opele* divining chain or *ikin* palm nuts.[12] Given that these types of divination are commonly viewed as the ultimate (and necessary) legitimation for undergoing the priestly initiation, it is likely that most underwent them while determining whether or not they would make *ocha*, even if they did not mention it. Some in this category described being told they must undergo the *kariocha* ceremony by priests who were possessed by Orisha in a drum ceremony. Many (n = 48; 26 percent) reported undergoing priestly initiation because they felt called to do so and/or they believed it was their destiny. Some wrote of dreams and intuitive knowledge to buttress these assertions. Forty-two (23 percent) claimed to have surrendered themselves to the *kariocha* to deepen their connection with the divine or out of love for the Orisha and a desire to connect with them (or a specific aspect of divinity) more closely or offer something back for all they believed the Orisha had given them. A large number (n = 37; 20 percent) reported making *ocha* for reasons related to their mental or physical health. They believed the sacrifice involved in the ceremony would save their lives or the lives of family members. Others (n = 32; 17 percent) felt that the initiation would change their lives or circumstances or bring them stability, personal or spiritual growth, or needed guidance. Still others (n = 26; 14 percent) spoke of falling in love with the religion. Many who answered in this way offered comparisons to other religions and chose Lukumi as the religion that made the most sense or felt best to them or called to them most strongly. For some, this included a desire to deepen their connection to African roots. Twenty-one (11 percent) mentioned their families or ancestors as their reason for undergoing the *kariocha*; they felt that their *egun* (ancestors) or blood demanded the sacrifice from them. Or they were raised in the tradition and felt drawn to undergo initiation because of family expectations or because they wanted to connect more strongly with kin who practiced Lukumi. A smaller number (n = 7; 4 percent) claimed that they made *ocha* in order to obtain the knowledge, privileges, and responsibilities of the priesthood. Only 3 (2 percent) reported that they underwent the ceremony to connect more strongly with their religious godparents or their godfamily. (See Figure 1.)

Despite the information a quantitative analysis of survey data provides, categorizing multifaceted and often knotty reasons for such important decisions diminishes their complexity and threatens to neglect the diversity of survey participants. We risk reducing a multidimensional choice to a flat, two-dimensional rendering. Much of our lives are not easily categorized and do not fit snugly into a researcher's boxes. More in-depth examination of people's reasons for undergoing the *kariocha* uncovers similarities within diversity. As examples, I offer two responses from open-ended survey questions about a respondent's "calling." María[13] answered:

> I want to say that I made this decision, but I really didn't *make* the decision to make Ocha/Saint. It was just the most natural thing in the world to me when I discovered Ocha. It became apparent to me when I began to understand and learn

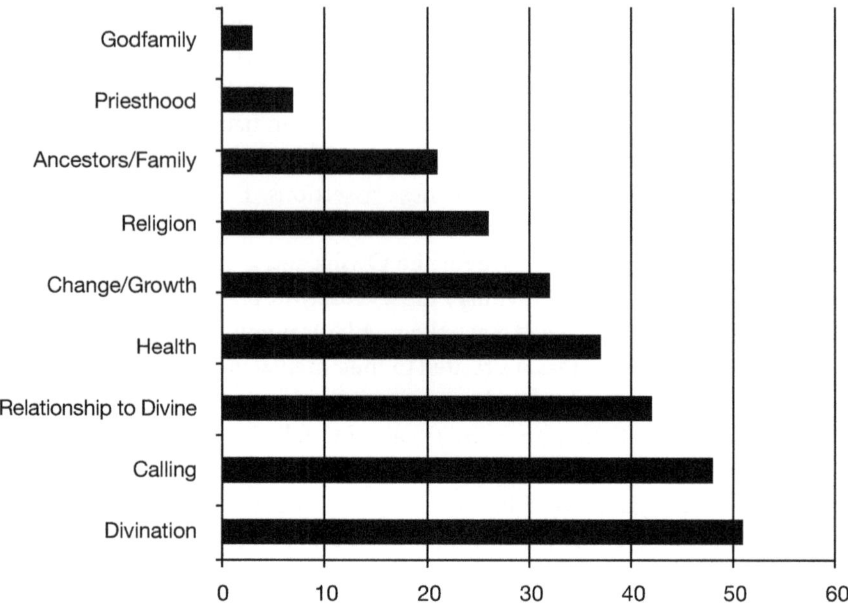

FIGURE 1. Survey Respondents' Reasons for "Making Ocha"

about Ocha that I was born to be in this religion, even though I was brought up by devout Catholics. As a child I worshiped as a Catholic, but even at the age of 8 years old, sitting in that church listening to mass on Holy Thursday, Good Friday, and Easter Sunday, I knew Catholicism was not for me. Since my introduction to Ocha in 1988, my life has progressed by leaps and bounds. I went from being a lost soul, to a whole new person. *Maferefun*[14] Obatalá and my Ocha every day!

For this cultural "native" who grew up in a community that worshipped Orisha, the draw to the priesthood was destiny, affirmed as such because it felt "natural," as if she was "born" to it. Comparing Lukumi to the Catholic religion in which she was raised, María chose the former.

Douglas similarly described his entrance into the Lukumi priesthood as a "calling," but in a different way:

I was introduced to the Yoruba culture in college (U of IL) through an African Rites of Passage Group. I established my first Egun [ancestor's] altar at that time. Long after I left the organization, I was still being called to and was curious about the culture and becoming a priest. I was unable to find anyone for a long time but that was in divine order. I eventually found . . . [a priest] who began teaching me. . . . After she moved to Florida, some of us began looking for *ilés* . . . . Why did I initiate to Orisa? My Orí told me to; it was a calling.

For this second respondent, who was drawn to connect to his African roots, his Orí, his spiritual head, guided him to find an *ilé*, a religious house, and eventually guided him to the year in white. It is instructive to see that while cultural indigenes and newcomers have different backgrounds and different associations with the religion, they may enter the priesthood for the similar reason that they felt it was their "destiny" or "calling." Although survey respondents (and interview participants) gave a wide range of answers to the question of why they entered the Lukumi priesthood, most of them would probably agree that they felt called to the priestly path. It is generally accepted that the Orisha choose their children and that "few are chosen," despite the increasing popularity of the *kariocha*.

Interviews with cultural newcomers also explored the reasons people entered the *kariocha* ceremony that launches the year in white. Iyawo Eduardo offered a moving story that interweaves many of the reasons listed above for undergoing priestly initiation:

> I always kept asking every time he [Iyawo Eduardo's godfather, an Ifa priest] would read me [through divination], "Would I get crowned this year?" Meanwhile I don't have any money; I live below poverty level. My wife and I live on less than $9,000 a year. . . . He says to me "Play your number here or there." And every time I would ask, "Will I get crowned this year?" [The answer was always] "No." . . . In the meantime, I am already 61 years old. I am thinking by the time I get crowned, just crown me and get the [coffin] box!. . . . In the meantime for like two months, I was so sick—physically, mentally, emotionally. I was so sick I thought I was going to die. . . . The day I felt the worst in my life is the day I hit [the lottery] for $10,000. My Godfather comes over and he reads me again. And I go "Padrino, I have . . . $7500." (You have to pay taxes.) . . . "But I don't know. Madrina has never quoted me a price [for the *ocha* ceremony]." He goes "She won't do it for that. She charges at least $13,000." . . . So I became discouraged. . . . [My Godfather] says "You have to do *ocha* immediately, because your health is really getting worse and worse."

Iyawo Eduardo explained that when his *madrina* returned from traveling she agreed to do the ceremony with the funds Eduardo had available.

> The most beautiful thing out of this is that she says to me . . . "I am going to do something I have never done in my life. . . . I am going to do your crowning in my house [i.e., her own home]. I have done 19 saints and you will be my first Oshun." . . . I felt so privileged. That was the most beautiful thing I ever heard in my life. And . . . I know she put money of her own, because this was like one of the most beautiful coronations—rituals, drum, everything you could ever

imagine—that she has ever done. When I was being crowned, there was not a dry tear in the house. Everybody just broke down. . . . Of course, when Oshun cries it is like joy. So I felt so blessed. . . . And every time anybody that came to the throne and would salute the throne and me, they would break down in tears. So the blessings have been incredible. I guess I had to wait this long to feel this blessed.

Iyawo Eduardo told an emotional tale of finally undergoing *kariocha* after decades of waiting. The lengthy deferral of the initiation was not his choice. Even though he deeply desired to make *ocha*, his faith was strong, and he believed the ritual would improve his health and situation, his lack of funds made it impossible for him to experience ordination for many years.

The financial barriers to ceremony are neither arbitrary nor necessarily reducible to the greed of religious practitioners. The *kariocha* requires a wealth of material culture and specialized skills, all of which initiates must purchase. The necessary materials include cloth, food, animals, special herbs, and dozens of ritual supplies. Services must also be purchased, including that of the *oriaté*, cooks, drummers, and all the *olorishas* who provide the labor, knowledge, artistry, and *ashé* needed to create the elaborate seven-day ritual. Despite what may seem like a high expense, much of the work that is done for the *kariocha* is unpaid labor or is compensated nominally. The *aleyos* who cook and clean and collect and tend animals in advance and during the ritual are generally volunteers. Each Lukumi priest who attends the *asiento* is paid a token sum—five to twenty dollars, perhaps—for a full day (or more) of often very physical labor. Although the primary godparent and a secondary godparent (called the *ayubona)* may receive *derecho* of several hundred dollars for their labor, this is small compensation for their effort. The godparent generally works for weeks before the ceremony to arrange a location suitable for the event; organize priests, drummers, cooks, seamstresses, and ritual specialists; purchase herbs, cloth, and specialty items; and perform preparatory rites with the initiate. The *ayubona* is responsible for tending to the initiate's physical and spiritual needs, day and night, for an entire week. If Eduardo's ceremony seemed lavish, it may very well have been that his *madrina* paid for some of it out of her own pocket.

Eduardo and his *madrina* were both marked in divination to Oshun, the Orisha associated with rivers, tears, honey, and all that makes life sweet (such as love and art). During the *ocha* ceremony, initiates reside on a "throne" for much of the seven day ritual. It is customary for community members to pay their respects by "saluting" (prostrating) themselves before the throne during an initiation to honor the Orisha represented on the throne. The fact that Eduardo had waited so long for the ordination increased the emotional intensity of the experience both for him and for the people around him.

Star shared a very different story about her road to *kariocha*:

S: I had picked up a statue for *La Diosa Del Mar* [The Goddess of the Sea, viewed as corresponding to the Orisha Yemaya] years and years ago and I had no idea why it seemed important. . . . And the weekend that I received my *kofa* and my Warriors[15] I was told . . . that I had to make *ocha* very quickly after that. And seven months later—almost exactly seven months later—I was in Cuba making *ocha* . . . . They told me that Yemaya was going to open the way for you and just everything—boom, boom, boom—just happened.

C: So what made you decide to go along with that?

S: There is a rhythm in certain people and in certain traditions that resonates well with me.

C: So you say there is a rhythm. Were there things happening? How was it that you—

S: My entire life had pretty much fallen apart that year. In June I had—my relationship had fallen apart. And consequently I lost my place to live. My car broke down shortly thereafter. I lost my job. I mean everything just fell apart, for lack of a better word. And it felt very much like there was a hand in it. You know, there was a hand going "Okay. This is all just crap you don't need to worry about." You now need to focus on, you know—put your eyes forward; stop looking back.

In contrast to Iyawo Eduardo, whose story unfolded over decades, Star's experience occurred in a period of under a year. Despite the fact that everything was "falling apart," Star retained the economic means to pay for the ceremonies she hoped would help put her life back together again. Finances for *ocha* weren't a salient part of the story she told, though she was far from wealthy. Star and Eduardo were both cultural newcomers, and they shared the same *madrina*. However, they differed in ethnicity and class status, and these differences were part of what shaped their paths to the year in white.

Star's reference to the saint's statue she had for years and her emphasis on the length of time between her *ikofa* and her *kariocha* ceremony indicated that her affinity to (and possible relationship with) Yemaya extended much longer than a year. (Both the statue and the number seven are associated with Yemaya). When she became ordained as a priest, it was Yemaya to whom she was ordained. During the first Ifa ceremony Star underwent, a *babalawo* divined that she needed to undergo the *kariocha* ceremony quickly. The fact that Star's life had "disintegrated" and her resonance with the religion pushed her to take the leap to *ocha* so she could refashion her life.

These responses enrich our understanding of why both cultural newcomers and cultural adepts commit to something as costly and consequential—in terms not only of wallets but also of identity, freedom, and everyday routines—as Lukumi priestly initiation. An excerpt from my autoethnographic fieldwork further exemplifies the "messiness" and multifaceted nature of the decision to undergo the Lukumi priestly initiation, and indeed, of lived religion itself.

I was taking a break from cleaning the kitchen at the end of a *bembe*[16] drum ceremony for an *ocha* initiation in California in August 2006. Many people had left already. It had been two long days of work at the *ocha* for me—the second of two weekends in a row stuffed full of intense experiences. The week before I had undergone a profound ceremony for my health in which I was said to have "received Olokun," the Orisha who embodies the depth and mystery of the ocean floor. Afterwards, I faced a divinatory reading from Madrina Julia that still had my head spinning. I was only a few weeks into synthroid therapy following a complete thyroidectomy and radioiodine ablation therapy; I was physically exhausted and emotionally overwhelmed.

As I sank into a chair on my godmother's back porch, Madrina Julia, a priest of Ogun, the Orisha of iron and knives, technology, hard work, and surgery, passed me carrying a plate of food. "Is this your first *ocha*?" she asked. I greeted her with the expected honorific, "*Bendicion*" and I admitted that it was my first. It was also the first time that she had initiated conversation with me. I had been waiting ten days for such an opportunity.

I asked her if she had considered my request for an interview. "Yes," she said. She questioned me about the purpose of my interviews: A thesis? A dissertation? I told her I had my Ph.D. already; I was writing a book. I explained that I was a sociologist, that I was talking to people in the religion because it was a subject I found interesting, and because I hoped it would help me figure out my own relationship to the religion.

Madrina Julia quizzed me about the books I had read concerning the religion. She was familiar with many of them. Some priests came to speak to her, interrupting our conversation. I waited uneasily.

When the priests left, Madrina Julia told me she would agree to speak with me, but she didn't want to be recorded. I asked what bothered her about being recorded. She responded firmly that those were her conditions, indicating that this was not a negotiation. More people came to speak with her. I waited again.

When the others left, Madrina Julia explained that she would speak with me because she was a priest. She would help me understand myself and my place in the religion. But she wasn't interested in helping me with my book. There were enough academic books on the religion already, she insisted.

We talked about her understandings of the religion, gender, and priests who she believed were reinterpreting *odu*[17] to suit their narrow views. She discussed the proper way of treating sacrifice as a sacred act, and of her respect for the drums. She explained that the debates about gender in the religion were as old as Oyo, as old as Ilé Ife.[18] "The religion is riddled with power struggles between men and women, *babalawos* and *santeras*," she told me. She declared that she didn't have time for it. She was too busy saving people's lives. "That's what the religion is about. That's what sacrifice is about. This is *real*. When I perform sacred ceremony I'm saving people's lives. I'm making their lives better."

I gathered my courage to ask about what most concerned me. Madrina Julia's divinatory reading from the week before remained heavy on my mind. My inner skeptic was troubled that her advice was similar to counsel I had received in my first reading in the religion, 18 months prior, by a different priest. Either the repetition validated the truth of the readings, or it was customary for diviners to tell newcomers such things. It felt urgently important that I know which. In particular, I had been told twice now in divination—first by a *babalawo* and then by an *olorisha*, Madrina Julia—that I needed to become initiated as a priest in the religion. If I didn't make *ocha*, I would never fulfill my proper destiny or feel complete, I had been told. Complicating matters, I knew others who had been told they needed to become Orisha priests. But how to ask the question that would dispel or confirm my doubts without offending? I asked Madrina Julia if there were many *odu* that instructed the recipient to "make *ocha*."

"There are only three *odus* that tell you that you have to make *ocha*," Madrina Julia explained. The *odu* I had received was not the most dire, she continued, but she expected that if I didn't make *ocha* in a few years the more insistent *odu* might arise. "I hate telling *unle meji*[19] people, people like you, that you need to make *ocha*," she said. "What kind of person is that?" I asked. "People who think they're just passing through the religion," she responded sharply.

Her words seemed to cut me. I felt exposed. She had laid bare my unspoken conflict. On the one hand I felt deeply drawn. On the other, I remained unconvinced about the religion as an enduring truth in my life. How could I be assured that my engagement with the Orisha was genuine and deep-rooted?

"You *unle meji* people are all the same," she pronounced. "You want to wrap your mind around things. You want to understand things before you experience them. But religion often needs to be experienced before it's understood. One day you'll just let go and really experience things. Then things will be different for you." She paused and continued, "Sixteen times sixteen *odus* and only three tell you that you need to make *ocha*. And you received one of them." And with that, I knew the conversation was finished.

I thanked Madrina Julia again for speaking with me. And then, exhausted, overwhelmed and numb, I fled the *ocha* house for my hotel room.

This excerpt illustrates a moment early in my interaction with Lukumi culture that was characterized by struggles over belief and commitment, conscious consideration of the dueling expectations and interests of participant and researcher, concerns about religious gender roles, tensions between respect for and suspicion of religious hierarchy, and attraction to and curiosity about the rich Lukumi religious tradition. To reduce this excerpt to that of a person coming to *ocha* because she was told to in divination would not only be a loss of the richness and complexity of lived religious practice, it would also be a distortion of the untidy truth as I lived it. (Indeed, the story of why I chose to undergo the *kariocha* is even more complicated than this. I will share more about this choice later in the book.)

NATIVES, NEWCOMERS, AND ETHNICITY

Each story of the road to *kariocha* and the year in white is unique. Social statuses of race, ethnicity, class, gender, sexuality, and cultural newcomer and native affect our religious experiences and identifications in complex ways. Many tell of years spent as seekers while they found their way into Orisha communities and/or the year in white. Some described going from initial divinatory reading to *igbodu*[20] in mere months.

Yet sociologists seek patterns of practice based on group membership and social structures. The diversification of religions in the United States raises a question: Do cultural newcomers and indigenes to the Lukumi priesthood differ in their reasons for undergoing the *kariocha* and the year in white? And what is the salience of ethnicity? Many scholars have noted the draw of Lukumi for those seeking to honor their African heritage and disassociate themselves from a Christianity implicated in the enslavement of their ancestors (e.g., Curry 1997; Falola and Genova 2006; Gregory 1999; Hucks 2012; Lefever 2000). Obá Miguel "Willie" Ramos[21] says that in his experience, Cubans and Puerto Ricans generally come to the religion to find *solutions* while cultural newcomers come to find *religion*. Cultural natives, he believes, often interact with Lukumi priests and participate in ritual to address problems with health, money, the law, and personal relationships, but because of their Catholicism, "they don't fully convert," preferring to see themselves as "good Christians." In contrast, he believes, cultural newcomers seek conversion. Another scholar (Pérez 2012, 361) proposes that Espiritismo, one of the most popular "religious formations to have crystallized during the transatlantic slave trade," can serve as a "theater of conversion," preparing participants—especially in Cuban and Puerto Rican communities—for entry into Lukumi practice: "Spiritist ceremonies have instructed participants in the reality of superhuman entities; the normative conditions for access to them; and the benefits of proper intercourse with the divine in Yorùbá- and Kongo-inspired initiatory traditions." These are some of the ways scholars have theorized that culture and ethnicity may affect an individual's reasons for entering the Lukumi religion.

To begin to see if it mattered that a person was raised in or around the religion, I identified "cultural natives" as the forty-three survey respondents who answered that they were raised in Orisha-worshipping families or communities or were ordained as children. I then performed chi-square statistical analyses of each of the reasons people gave for entering the religion. This type of computation allows for quantitative comparisons of how we would expect cultural neophytes and "natives" to answer questions if the distinction between them wasn't important and compare those results to how the two groups actually answered. When a chi-square test is found to be statistically significant, the distinction between the two groups seems to have affected their answers, provided certain mathematical assumptions are met related to size of sample and the distribution of answers.[22]

Analysis of my survey data did not yield differences in the reasons cultural natives and cultural newcomers gave for entering the Lukumi priesthood and the *yaworaje*. It's possible that the data or my analysis of it was not sufficient to tease out significant results. I grouped raw qualitative survey data into categories of reasons for making *ocha* to render them quantifiable (e.g., divination, having a calling, relationship to the Divine). There may be too much diversity within the categories to distinguish between responses of cultural veterans and newcomers. It's also possible that the short answers most survey participants shared in response to this question were not sufficient to elicit differences among them. And it's probable that natives and newcomers overlap more than they differ in their broad reasons for undergoing the *kariocha*.

But what about the effect of ethnicity? Hispanic status did not predict in a statistically significant way whether respondents reported that they had undergone *kariocha* because of divination, destiny, health, as a preferred religion, knowledge or status of the priesthood, ancestry or family, personal or spiritual growth, or desire for change or growth or a godfamily. Similarly, a comparison of the reasons for undergoing the *kariocha* of those who indicated that their racial or ethnic status was Black, African American, African, or Yoruba, with those who did not identify themselves in these ways did not yield statistically significant results. The same was true for those who indicated that they were white, Caucasian, or of European ancestry, regardless of Hispanic status. One significant difference emerged when I compared those who reported Hispanic ethnicity with those who did not, however.[23] Those who claimed Hispanic heritage were statistically more likely than those who did not to mention love of the Orisha or desire for connection to the divine as a reason for making *ocha* ($X^2 = 3.94$, $df = 1$, $p = .047$; $N = 154$). That is not to say that most Hispanic respondents mentioned this as a reason or that most non-Hispanics did not. Only 31 percent of Hispanics made statements that I characterized as falling in this category, compared to 17 percent of non-Hispanics who did so.

In contrast to the minimal quantitative evidence on the effect of ethnic identities on the reasons people came to the *kariocha*, inductive analyses offer more promise. While all may enter the traditions for health reasons, because of a desire for change, because they love the Orisha, and because they have a sense that they were called, non-Hispanics are much less likely than Hispanics to join for reasons of familial pressure. In addition, African Americans are more likely than those who are not Black to be drawn to the Africanicity of the religion, to choose a religion that is less implicated in the slavery of their forebears, and to select a tradition that honors their African ancestors. Hispanics are more likely than non-Hispanics to join to celebrate Latinidad and the religion of their kin. In addition, racial and ethnic identities affect which types of claims to authentic participation cultural newcomers to Orisha traditions may make. These include those made on the basis of origins (ancestry, roots, and "blood"), perceived personal destiny, direct or strongly felt connections to divinity, and comparisons with less authentic participants (Carr 2011).

Motives for committing to the *kariocha* are multifaceted and manifold. Cultural newcomers and natives share many reasons, yet broad patterns can be seen based on ethnicity.

2 • *IYAWO* EXPERIENCE

It was my third *ocha* birthday, the anniversary of my initiation into the Lukumi priesthood. I had worked long hours for three days to prepare an elaborate *trono* (throne or altar) to honor and celebrate my "father," the Orisha Chango, and all the rest of my Orisha. I had ironed and draped fabric on the walls and ceiling in a corner of my study, shopped for food and flowers, created a separate altar for the *egun* (ancestral spirits), cooked special foods for ten different Orisha and dinner for human guests, cleaned and dressed my Orisha, draped each of them with specially made colorful *pañuelos* (cloths) and piled fruit and candy on and around them. Finally I had performed divination with *obi* (pieces of coconut) to my *egun* and each of my Orisha, asking for their blessings for the year. A small group of friends had come to pay their respects to the Orisha and share the celebration with me.

Having discovered that one of my former students, Solana, was initiated in the religion, I had invited her as well. She arrived along with her mother, Yadra, who spoke little English. I asked if they were Cuban and Solana said that they had both been born on the island and had grown up around the worship of *los santos*. Solana explained that her godparents in the religion—whom I had also invited through her—had sent their blessings and their regrets for not being able to attend. I knew that Solana had been recently initiated, so I asked about Yadra's "age" in the religion. I needed to know who had been initiated first to decide who must salute whom according to the formal Lukumi protocol. Solana informed me that both she and her mother were *iyawo*; Yadra had been initiated into the religion the day before Solana.

Hearing my guests' *iyawo* status surprised me and left me in a quandary. I had known there was a possibility that Solana might still be in her year in white, which was why I had made sure to invite her godparents too. When I heard that Solana was bringing her mother, who was also initiated, I had assumed her mother was a full-fledged *olorisha*, someone who was permitted to escort a *iyawo* to a religious event such as my *ocha* birthday.

Solana and Yadra's appearance offered no clue that they were *iyawos*. They had full, long heads of hair. They were wearing business-casual clothes. Solana was even wearing fashionable black strappy heels and stud earrings. Solana did not wear any *elekes* (ceremonially consecrated beads, also called *collares*), although she wore the green and yellow Ifa bracelet. Yadra wore only the Ifa bracelet and an *eleke*. Both were in pants; Yadra's were a dark brown. They wore nothing white and carried no whites to change into, not even a white skirt, and no mats and dishes on which to eat. I must have been staring because Solana took it upon herself to explain that they had both come straight from work, where their godparents permitted them to wear light colors.

Part of the confusion came from what may be a larger trend—at least in my area of the United States—of loosening religious restrictions. It is very common, even in my stricter *ilé* (religious house), for *iyawos* to be permitted accommodations so that their year in white does not adversely affect their jobs. These *iyawos* are generally allowed to wear light colors to work—off-white, beige, maybe pastels—and sometimes even wigs. (I was offered this option, but with the exception of a bit of off-white during the coldest months, I decided in consultation with my *madrina* that it was not necessary for my job. However, unlike the practice in some religious houses that are even stricter than mine, I was permitted to wear standard white underclothing and white pants to work. In my experience, *iyawos* who were permitted to wear light colors to work are generally expected to go home immediately afterward to change into whites and those *iyawos* are still held to all other restrictions. Certainly they would be required to wear white and bring mats and dishes to a religious event (such as my *ocha* birthday), where protocol tends to be more formal. (Later, when I told an elder about the situation, I was instructed firmly that in the future, if *iyawos* dressed in colors showed up at my door for a religious event, I should not let them enter.)

Knowing Yadra and Solana's status as *iyawos* put me in a difficult position. According to the highly structured religious protocol with which I was familiar, several rules had been broken. When *iyawos* visit a Lukumi priest's house, the priest should know in advance so she might gift them with a special plate. I had prepared no plate to give the *iyawos*. Worse, I was in the uncomfortable position of being an "elder," obliged to defend tradition. Being only three years initiated and having no true elders around, it was a difficult position indeed. Another friend of mine, Celeste, the only other *olorisha* in attendance, who was also three, took me aside and told me how uncomfortable the breach of protocol made her. Oddly, when I had originally met Celeste at her workplace, she had been what I have come to call an "incognito *iyawo*" herself! Yet although Celeste had been permitted (via divination) to keep most of her hair and wear light colors to work, she had gone home after work each day, donned her whites, avoided the dark, and eaten on a mat on the floor.

Later, while cleaning the dishes she had offered to wash, Solana told me a bit about her *iyawo* restrictions (and lack thereof). She had her own special set of dishes that she used when she was at home. She had her own plate, bowl, cup, spoon and fork. (I was not permitted to use a fork during my entire year in white.) She was forbidden to look in the mirror for a whole week. (*Iyawo* in my house are generally prohibited from viewing themselves in mirrors for about three months.) As they were leaving, Yadra reminded Solana to collect the umbrella they were sharing. I winced when I noticed that it was black. Solana gestured to the umbrella and gave a little laugh, "Yes, we're supposed to keep the rain from touching our heads, but I'm a bit rebellious." Solana demonstrated an easy dismissal of traditions that I had struggled with such difficulty to keep. White umbrellas are not easy to find, they are not cheap when you do find them, and they rarely last long. How much time and exertion had I expended to keep myself armed with serviceable white umbrellas every time I left home during my year in white?

But the umbrella was just a small symbol of the differences in my *iyawo* year and that of my incognito *iyawo* visitors. It occurred to me that in contrast with my much stricter *yaworaje*, Solana and Yadra were experiencing a version of "Lukumi lite." As a social constructionist and sometimes postmodernist, I was surprised to find myself having strong feelings in defense of tradition. The great number of restrictions I endured during my *yaworaje* three years before had required great effort and caused me much frustration. I struggled against what I perceived as scores of shackles. For me it was a year of discomfort, social awkwardness, boredom, and obstructions. It was also a year that forced me to confront my fears, learn to embrace quietude, and connect to strength and knowledge within myself. The requirement that I avoid mirrors for almost three months obliged me to face my vanity. Sleeping on a mat on the floor with my Orisha for several months was both humbling and empowering. Forgoing crowds, restaurants, movie theaters, and being out after dark required me to accept silence, simplicity, and solitude. Covering my head for an entire year was a daily, hourly remembrance of the ceremony of initiation that I had undergone, one in which my head was specially blessed with an aspect of divinity. My head no longer belonged only to me. Wearing whites for a year was a constant reminder that I had chosen to commit myself to a spiritual path of service. And as soon as I took these things for granted, the people with whom I interacted daily—strangers, friends, co-workers, and family, in my apartment building, at work, at synagogue, and at the grocery—reminded me of them again and again as they remarked upon my white clothing, shoes, bag, and umbrella. What, I wondered, were incognito *iyawo* missing from their experience of the year in white? What, in the name of convenience, assimilation, and/or secrecy, did "Lukumi lite" sacrifice from the rich, potent yearlong ritual?

DIVERSITY OF EXPERIENCE

Although their practice is probably not typical of the *yaworaje* in the United States, Solana and Yadra represent a trend among some U.S. Lukumi in which *iyawos* are permitted great leniency during their year. Because there is no centralized authority, there is enormous variety within Orisha communities in the United States, even if we confine our comparisons to those whose religious practice shares Cuban heritage. Individual godparents choose the rules to share with their godchildren and whether and how to enforce them. Some religious houses are very strict and others are comparatively lax. A *madrina* or a *padrino* may treat his or her godchildren differently, being more lenient with some and more exacting with others. Some of the diversity can also be attributed to *itá*[1] divination. As part of the *kariocha* ceremony, each *iyawo* receives substantial instruction from each of the Orisha they receive as part of the initiation, usually six or seven. This is meant to shape their year in white and guide the rest of their lives. In addition, some of the diversity is due to the inexact nature of socialization into a mostly oral tradition. The rules of the *yaworaje* are rarely written down; instead they are given orally to each *iyawo*. Because of this, *iyalosha* and *babalosha*[2] may instruct each *iyawo* differently in the rules of the *yaworaje*, forgetting some restrictions while remembering others.

In addition, as with any contemporary religion in the United States, Lukumi evinces great diversity in terms of religious commitment, orthodoxy, and assimilation into mainstream, secular culture. Some religious houses practice in strict accordance with Cuban tradition. Others are flavored more with African customs. Some *ilé* make accommodations for the workplace only. Others have loosened restrictions related to gender. In the name of secrecy, some modify the year in white so it is undetectable by outsiders.

Drawing on the contributions of *iyawos* and former *iyawos*—cultural newcomers and natives who completed my survey and cultural newcomers who interviewed with me—as well as my own stories, in this chapter I discuss the experiences of *iyawo* with the year in white. What was most difficult and rewarding about the year? How did *iyawos* and former *iyawos* characterize the year generally?

BLESSINGS AND STRUGGLES

Large majorities of survey respondents spoke of the *yaworaje* positively. Fully 94 percent said that the year in white had changed them for the better. Most recalled feeling protected and safe and experiencing deep feelings of gratitude during the year. Many checked "agree" or "somewhat agree" next to the statement "I loved being *iyawo*." A majority said the year in white helped them improve their health, deal with emotional issues from the past, and fix what was wrong in their lives. Just over half missed being *iyawo* when the year in white was over. (See Table 1.)

Although the scaled responses tended toward the positive, small majorities or large minorities of respondents hinted at the hazards of the *yaworaje*. Just over half of the respondents claimed to have gained weight during the year in white. Large minorities recalled worrying a lot about money, frequently feeling vulnerable, being lonely a lot, and experiencing depression during the year. Forty-one percent wished they had been given more information about the year in white before their initiation. And almost half agreed with the statement that they "could barely wait" for the year in white to end. Nevertheless, 77 percent agreed somewhat or strongly with the statement that "all the hardships I endured as *iyawo* were worth it. I would do it again."

When elaborating on their experiences with the *yaworaje* in response to open-ended questions, many wrote about the year in glowing terms. Health problems decreased. Relationships improved. Families united. Money came easily. Contentment increased. New jobs were gained. Houses were bought. Bad habits were jettisoned. Many believed the year in white to have been a wonderful opportunity for spiritual and personal growth. Valentina, who had undergone the *kariocha* for health reasons two years before, exclaimed that it was the "best thing I have ever done." Bianca was told in divinatory readings that she should become ordained. Nine years after becoming a priest of Oshun, she remembered it as "one of the best years of . . . [her] life." Iyawo Cristal, who made *ocha* because she felt called to do so, described her year as best characterized by gratitude and happiness. Santiago "discovered Orisha . . . during a difficult time." Recollecting a practice he had begun three years before, Santiago characterized his *yaworaje* as involving "a lot of self-reflection and having the time to put things in my life into perspective." Because he had the time to take care of himself by "eating right," resting, and abstaining from alcohol, his health improved and he lost ninety pounds. Camila knew "for years" that she would "eventually give . . . [her] "head to . . . Ocha" but didn't actually do it until after "devastating" things occurred to her family and her. Despite her initial reluctance, she recalled that during the year in white, "you are sent into the inner you" and given spiritual guidance. Mariana, who underwent the *kariocha* "out of love for Orisha," especially Oshun, objected to my use of the word "hardship" in one of the survey questions: "I don't feel that I went through hardships during my *iyawo* year. I felt blessed every minute of every day and I was so grateful." Many spoke of the blessings they believed they received as a result of making *ocha* and going through the year in white.

TABLE 1   General Experience of *Iyawo*

	Disagreed	Agreed	N
I love/d being iyawo!	20% (n = 36)	79% (n = 140)	177
During my year in white my health improved.	15 (27)	68 (120)	176
I worried a lot about money during my year in white.	62 (108)	43 (76)	175
During my year in white I usually felt protected and safe.	11 (20)	86 (149)	174
I wished I had been given more information about the year in white before my initiation.	52 (92)	41 (72)	175
My year in white changed me for the better.	4 (6)	94 (161)	171
My year in white helped me to deal with emotional issues from my past.	20 (35)	68 (118)	173
During my year in white I often felt deep feelings of gratitude.	11 (20)	85 (148)	174
After my year in white I missed being iyawo.	28 (48)	55 (96)	173
During my iyawo year I was often depressed.	64 (112)	31 (55)	175
My year in white helped me to fix what was wrong in my life.	26 (46)	66 (116)	175
I gained weight during my year in white.	46 (80)	51 (88)	173
During my year in white I often felt vulnerable.	50 (87)	48 (84)	174
I can/could barely wait for my year in white to be over.	42 (73)	47 (82)	173
During my year in white I felt lonely a lot.	55 (95)	42 (74)	173
All the hardships I endured as iyawo were worth it. I would do it again.	14 (24)	77 (134)	173

In my reporting of scaled responses, I merged "strongly agree" with "somewhat agree" and "strongly disagree" with "somewhat disagree." Not every participant responded to every survey item, so I calculated percentages based on the number of responses for each given item. Percentages do not total 100 due to rounding and because some individuals checked N/A for some statements.

Others spoke of struggles during the year. They felt isolated and depressed. They had difficulties with their families. They resented *iyawo* rules as if they were straitjackets. They had such problems with their godparents that they had to leave their *ilé*. They experienced violence in their communities or they faced discrimination at work or on the street. In contrast to the rosy portraits of the *yaworaje* many respondents painted, Mía drew a different picture. Although she had been "marked for Ocha" by an Orisha priest, she pointed out that it was her choice to undergo the ceremony since there was no urgent reason to do so. She "longed for a deeper unity with" the Orisha Yemaya, who "promised to be . . . [her] salvation." After the initiation, however, Mía developed problems: "My mental health declined considerably. I was diagnosed with severe depression. . . . The experience brought a lot of repressed emotional/spiritual issues front and forward, coupled with feelings of loneliness, vulnerability and neglect. . . . I almost had a complete breakdown." Regina was told in several Ifa divinatory readings that she needed to offer herself as a priest to the Orisha. However, her year in white was not easy. She complained that she lost the vessels consecrated to her Orishas on her way home from her *kariocha* ceremony, was mugged during the year, and had many problems at work.

Some *iyawos* and former *iyawos* attributed the struggles they endured during their year in white to normal everyday life. Estevan—who made *ocha* because he "was repeatedly advised" to do so via the oracles of *diloggun* and Ifa and because of his love of Orisha—explained that he suffered painful changes that were foretold in divination but were not caused by the *yaworaje*. Diane, who undertook the *kariocha* for health reasons, believed her difficulties during the year were mostly due to a "tough marriage." Others specifically connected their problems to the *yaworaje* and its challenges. They spoke of tense relationships with their godparents or within their *ilé*. Or they wrote of internal growing pains they believed were brought about by the year in white. Zoe, who was ordained out of love for her mother and the Orisha, attributed her troubles during the *iyawo* year to her "rebellious, questioning" personality. Knowing that elders in the religion withheld information—"I need to know why I do anything" she wrote—she admitted to feeling "left out and treated like an inferior." Thus, while some *iyawo* challenges were attributed to the normal pains of life, others were linked to the *yaworaje* itself.

Iyawo and Orisha priests shared many different stories about the year in white. Some recalled counting the days until it would end. Some wished it were possible to do it again once it was complete. The year was different for each *iyawo*. However there were also many commonalities in the stories they told. I asked several open-ended questions in the survey about experiences with the *yaworaje*: How would you describe your year in white? What were the best parts about your year? What were the worst parts? Excluding discussions of *iyawo* rules and social, spiritual, and familial relationships (which I detail in subsequent chapters), the most common themes in response to general questions about the *iyawo* experience concerned transformation (N = 67; 44 percent), seclusion (N = 66; 43 percent), emotional turbulence (N = 34; 22 percent), and markedness/visibility (N = 32; 21 percent).[3] (See Figure 2.)

TRANSFORMATION

The most frequent general descriptions of the year in white referred to self-discovery, change, healing, and growth. As a yearlong rite of passage (van Gennep [1909] 1961), the year in white is launched by the intense seven-day *kariocha* ceremony, during which the uninitiated *aleyo* transforms several times, first into the symbolically dead *abokú*,[4] then into a vessel for the Orisha, and then into the newborn *iyawo* (Brown 2003). The liminal period of the *yaworaje* follows the "separation" of the *kariocha* rite of passage. A gradual loosening of restrictions during the year in white allows for reintegration, an incremental movement from the marginality of the *iyawo* to full *olorisha* status (Clark 2005). As a continuation of the *kariocha*, the *yaworaje* is meant to be a process during which the changes wrought in the ordination rite are gradually integrated into the initiate's new life.

In open-ended survey questions, sixty-seven (44 percent) wrote that the *yaworaje* changed them for the better, provided them with important lessons for growth, and/or improved their health. Respondents frequently described the

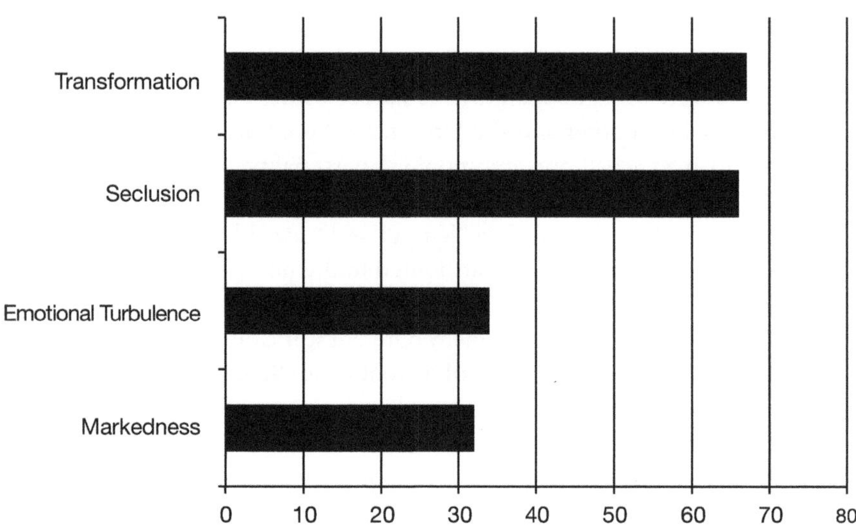

FIGURE 2. General characteristics of the Year in White by frequency of mention in survey

year in white as bringing "many changes for the better" such as transforming their attitudes or making them wiser or more mature. Orisha priests reported becoming more reflective and thoughtful during the year in white due to increased time alone. They spent less time doing and more time resting and being still. They were forced to let go of habits that they believed may have kept them from progressing, such as drinking, taking recreational drugs, gambling, or engaging in casual sexual encounters. Some found themselves getting rid of the people in their lives who were not good for them. Elsa, who had undergone Lukumi ordination "because Obatalá wanted . . . [her] head," described the year in white as "a wonderful period of self-reflection, growth, and learning."

María, who felt that she "was born to be in this religion," explained that her year in white "was about discovering who would really be there with . . . [her] when things got tough." Some believed the year in white strengthened their character. Iyawo Faith, whose path to *ocha* included a dramatic tale of being chosen by Orisha in a drum ceremony, health problems, and dreams that contained messages from the world of spirit, felt that the *yaworaje* helped her to "build . . . courage and confidence." Ana underwent the *kariocha* because she believed it was time for her "to stop running" and make positive changes in her life. She felt that the year in white gave her the "voice to say 'no' or 'yes' in any situation." Some mentioned experiencing a deepened sense of spirituality that pervaded their daily existence. "It took many years" and a series of adversities that befell Eugene and his family before he agreed to "surrender" himself to the will of the Orisha. Once he became ordained, he gained "knowledge and appreciation of . . . [his] limitations as a human being in relationship to the planet and those things within and without the natural plane." Others told of relief from spiritual or psychological terrors. Carmen—who made *ocha* for her health and that of her unborn child—related that during her *yaworaje* she "finally felt peace from all the nightmares and spiritual intruders that would not let" her sleep. In addition, she experienced "deep peace and reassurance . . . thanks to Obatalá," that she "would deliver a healthy baby." Still others wrote of the year in white as assisting with acquiring deep inner knowledge. Gavin undertook the *asiento* ceremony and the *yaworaje* purely out of love for the religion and for Obatalá. He characterized the year as one in which he frequently meditated, prayed, and wrote in his journal. As a result, he detailed, "I got to know myself better than I've known myself all my life."

Similarly, interview participants attributed many changes to the *kariocha* ceremony and the discipline of the *yaworaje*. Iyawo Emma—a quick-tempered young adult who "was made" to Chango in California—believed she had a newfound serenity. Iyawo Kenneth was introduced to Orisha at a time when he really "needed religion." Having just left a "violent barrio" and struggling with drug addiction, he stumbled across Orisha music in the public library. Hearing the traditional call-and-response praises chanted to traditional rhythms of the *bata* drums, he felt a connection as if the Orisha Yemaya had "wrapped her arms around" him. Following the *kariocha* several years later, he reported that he was healed from post-traumatic stress during his year in white. Silvia asserted that her ancestors demanded that she make *ocha* and that Orisha chased her in her dreams until she complied. Although she used to drink a gallon of wine a week, she was instructed in *itá* divination that she must avoid intoxication from that time forward; she "had to stop drinking wine immediately." Years later, she drinks only beer. Vincent, who underwent the *asiento* to heighten the embrace and guidance of Orisha in his life, likened his year in white to a "detoxification," during which he "got rid of a lot of junk." He claimed he let go of habits and attitudes that no longer served him and gained new ones, emerging as a stronger and more sensitive man. Opal was initially drawn to the religion to connect with her African roots, although she decided to undergo the *kariocha* because she was told to in divination, her friends were becoming ordained, and it felt right. She believed the experience made her "more connected to God, his emissaries, the earth, what was going on around me." She claimed to now experience divinity in a more concrete manner than she had previously: "God is in rocks and herbs and all these different elements that you see and touch, and it is part of your life. . . . So it changed my approach or my view of the world and everything that is in it." Bea came to Lukumi ordination through a strong feeling that she was "called" and from messages through divinatory oracles, including a dramatic "fight" over her head by two Orishas. When asked if the *yaworaje* changed her, she exclaimed that it was a "coming to Jesus moment." She said that because it changes a person's perspective, requiring the *iyawo* to interact "in the world with . . . a long-handled spoon," the *yaworaje* encouraged her to cultivate accountability and humility. Lincoln was pulled into Lukumi at first through a feeling of connection to the drums. When his sister made *ocha*, she was told that her entire family needed to do the same. He did not comply until years later, when, after being involved in Lukumi culture for about thirty years, he was told again that he needed to undertake the *kariocha* or face death. Lincoln believed that the transformations of the year in white required his active participation. He had to stop telling himself lies: "There is magic but that magic isn't going to change [you] until you change who you are, not until you shift who you are, until you become ready." But, he continued, the Orisha help *iyawos* do this hard work, help make it less painful. *Iyawos* and former *iyawos* frequently described the year as one in which they "found themselves," connected with their innermost selves, learned a lot about who they really were, became stronger, developed character, and became more spiritual, humble, grateful, peaceful, successful, balanced, stable, healthy, tranquil, disciplined, thoughtful, compassionate, and/or patient.

Like many *iyawos* and former *iyawos*, I too found the *yaworaje* to be transformative. To be fair, I came to the *kariocha* with aspirations of radical change. I wish I could say that I made *ocha* for the pure motives of love for the Orisha and desire for service, but like many of those who commit to the expensive, time-consuming process, I had ulterior motives. An adept worrier, I found the notion of making *ocha* frightening on many levels. I was concerned about gaining weight because I would be subject to a curfew and social restrictions. I feared the financial expenses involved. I was apprehensive about what I might be asked to sacrifice in the elaborate *itá* divination that accompanies the *ocha* ceremony. I was concerned that the rules of the *yaworaje* would increase my feelings of isolation. I troubled about losing my freedom to my godmother and the Orisha. Most of all, perhaps, I worried that after going through the all the trouble of the elaborate ceremony, that it would not make the difference I needed in my life.

I overcame my apprehensions about making *ocha* in large part because I feared more what would happen if I did not make major alterations in my life. In the year or two before I decided to commit to *ocha*, I had experienced a series of losses that left me feeling broken and alone. I lost my thyroid to cancer. I lost a significant relationship. More important, I lost hope in the future and confidence in myself. Depressed, heartbroken, beset with fears about an upcoming academic tenure application process, and feeling as if I had lost joy in life and reason for being, I eventually decided that I had lost the right to determine my life course on my own. If I couldn't find contentment and meaning, perhaps *ocha* could help me find a way. I had been told in divinatory sessions that Chango wanted me as his priest and that only by making *ocha* would my life be complete. I had been instructed that the *kariocha* ceremony would seat a spark of the vibrant Orisha in me; I would share my "head" with him. Thus, I would never be alone again. I understood that Chango, the fiery king, was said to exude confidence, passion for life, leadership, and dynamism. It was with hopes for sharing in the strengths of Chango, for healing change, that I made *ocha*.

And change is what I received. In the sense that one is what one does, the *yaworaje* cannot help but affect an initiate. Almost all of one's regular activities are altered after making *ocha*, at least for a few months following the initiation ceremony. *Iyawos* are commonly required to change how they eat, drink, sleep, socialize, exercise, and speak. Some *iyawos* are even instructed to change the way they think; they are told to maintain "cool" heads and avoid worrying. With such modifications of everyday behaviors, how could one not experience transformation? But I found even deeper healing than mere alteration of routines. In the *itá* divination I received at my *kariocha*, the Orisha Yemaya told me I needed to release pain from the past, and the realities of being a *iyawo* often confronted me with feelings from my early life in surprising and visceral ways. Besides gratitude, calmness, and optimism, being treated as a child by my religious god family triggered within me gut feelings of powerlessness, unrealistic expectations of my elders, resentment, abandonment, and rebellion.

Midway through my year in white, I entered therapy. It seemed like the perfect thing to do during my year in white, especially given Yemaya's message. I had already said my goodbyes to a decade of hair growth; I thought I might as well clean up whatever garbage I could that still littered my psyche. I chose to undergo Eye Movement Desensitization and Reprocessing (EMDR) therapy with my good friend (and professional therapist) Susan Menahem. I chose EMDR because it claims to heal the past without retraumatizing the client, and because I believed I needed a method that transcended the intellect in a way that talking therapy might not. In my sessions, Susan would begin by having me recall a significant memory. I would soon find my consciousness drifting to associated feelings, images, and thoughts. Meanwhile, intermittent (bilateral) pulsing in my hands would calm me. The pulsing, I was told, was supposed to help integrate traumatic episodes into my normal memory, removing them from the "trauma network."

What follows is an excerpt from my journal that I wrote about ten months into my year in white, describing what felt to me to be an intense healing that occurred during my *yaworaje* that was infused with imagery of the Orisha:

I had been through EMDR sessions over several months when I ran into difficulty. I kept returning to the image of an inconsolable, crying baby whose depths of despair, loss, and futility seemed endless and unendurable. Because of the work I'd done in previous sessions, I understood that the memory was significant. I knew it was at the root of my tendency to protect myself from others. And I felt the pain of the babe as if it were my own current reality.

"It's not fair," I whispered through tears.

The utterance sent me in a flash to a realization of the affective origins of my deep concerns for justice. Yet the emotions were so overwhelming I feared I would not be able to handle them. I thought they might consume me, leaving me unable to function, unable to leave my therapist's couch and drive home at the end of the hour. The feelings didn't move as they had in past sessions. I began to despair that I was stuck in a hole of sadness in which I might drown.

"What do you know about yourself when you see the child?" Susan asked.

"She is alone," I replied. "I am alone."

And then, with a renewed flood of emotion, I whispered "She is me."

Susan guided me to put the baby and the feelings into a mental container and then to imagine myself in my safe place (by the ocean) with my nurturer (the Orisha Yemaya). The session was so powerful and disturbing that Susan asked if I could return the next day, something she had never asked me before. Unfortunately I couldn't.

In session the following week, we began with the distressed baby. I closed my eyes, bilateral stimulation pulsing in each hand. I began carefully, tentatively, hoping to avoid being overwhelmed: I saw the infant. She was wailing a deep sadness. She had been abandoned. No one was there for her. There was no comforting her.

I saw an image of my mother, young and breastfeeding. I looked up at her face. It showed sorrow and resignation. I felt for her. Unable to give what the child needed, she resented its need. She was feeding the nursling her bitterness and disgust! I felt the rejection deep in my stomach.

"I'm not wanted," the baby seemed to say. "I don't want to be here."

The profundity of the statement shook me. Tears rolled down my face.

"I don't want to be here," I whispered aloud.

"If I'm not wanted, I don't want to exist," I heard echoing in myself. "I did not choose this life. I don't want to be here." Suddenly I understood the depths of my depression after my breakup a couple years before. And I understood the feelings of unfairness, the lack of consent I had experienced in parts of my *yaworaje*. The *iyawo*-me did not choose many of the rules that were surprises to her, just as the baby-me didn't choose to be born to parents not capable of caring for a newborn. They were the same feelings, speaking from the same hole in my middle.

Despite the insights, the anguish did not diminish. If anything it gained strength. Like waves at rising tide it rolled in and out, increasing and increasing. Yet I had the idea that though I was in over my head, I remained in shallows. I had no idea what to do.

Overwhelmed, I opened wet eyes, looking to Susan for help.

"Go to Yemaya," she said. "Ask her what you need to take from this." Susan guided me to close my eyes again and connect with the child, and then to feel Yemaya and ask my question.

I saw salt water on sand and rock. I felt the comfort I have always felt when I spoke to her, and I focused on the sounds of the waves. I attempted to listen and wait. Soon I heard what seemed like an answer. It made me cry more. I waited and heard another one. Were they real answers or just my own mind's manufacture? I wasn't sure, but I was tired of crying. I wanted this to be over.

"I'm supposed to be strong" I said, opening my eyes. "And I'm supposed to know compassion." I felt awful—queasy and defeated.

"Is that all?" Susan asked. She sounded unconvinced. "Did you ask if there was anything more?"

Susan was right. The messages certainly hadn't made me feel any better; they didn't give me any sense of closure. Was I likely to get more if I waited longer? The situation seemed insoluble. The feelings ran too deep. They had been there too long. I felt exhausted. I didn't want to do this anymore. It was just too much. But I wanted to never have to do this again. I wanted to not have to drag a damaged infant through all my adult relationships. I had to try.

I closed my eyes and heard the waves again. I felt the suffering of the child. Bottomless, crushing sorrow. How was I to live with this much pain? How could I possibly carry it all? It was far too large a burden.

I saw myself on the beach, calling to my Mother of the ocean as I had so many times—since long before I called her "Yemaya." I remembered what the oriaté had said in my *itá* divination about her: "She is your mother. She loves you. She will always take your side."

"Mother!" I called out to the waves.

"Mother, help me" I cried.

I did not have to wait long. She was there.

"Give her to me," She said, opening her arms.

The offer astounded me. Yes, that was the answer! Of course that was the solution. Why hadn't I seen it before? It was so obvious I felt stupid. Yemaya, the Great Mother who raises unwanted children—She would take the babe I could not comfort—the child my own biological mother could not nurture. She had taken her—me—already.

I covered my mouth with my hand as I began to cry convulsively—big heaving belly sobs—and I handed the squalling infant to Yemaya. Standing in the surf, she was the Madonna. She was la Virgen del Mar. She was the Universal Mother. Cradling the babe in her strong arms, inexhaustible love sated immeasurable need in a manner not possible from human embrace. The child quieted.

Stunned with gratitude, I opened my eyes.

As in my case, many turn to *ocha* initiation for salvation or healing. While *iyawos* and former *iyawos* often list several reasons for this important decision, of the 183 responses to the open-ended question "Why did you make Ocha/ Saint?" in my survey, thirty-seven mentioned physical or mental health reasons and thirty-two discussed a variety of other motives related to change and spiritual and personal growth. Iyawo Lucy explained that she had "taken the plunge" to the priesthood to heal from grief: "I went through drastic life changes due to the loss of my mother ten months prior, and I felt no peace with[in] me. One day I was passing the river on my way to get my hair done and I heard Oshun's voice clear in my head: 'It is your time.' . . . At this point I had no reservation in my mind and heart to do santo. I crowned about four months later." Henry— who didn't share much about himself—also became initiated in order to enact healing change in his life: "I did Ocha to better my life. It saved me from a tough time with drugs." Some are pulled to *ocha* for emotional healing, while others are drawn for physical healing. When she answered my survey in her early thirties, Gloria believed that making *ocha* had literally saved her life: "I been sick of Hodgkin's disease since I was twenty-five years old. And at the time I made osha I was in a critical moment of my sickness. No treatment was really responding. I was getting deteriorated as my blood counts were so low due to the treatments. So I deposited all my expectations in[to] making osha, hoping for a miracle. And you know what? The miracle happened." Only seven months later, she found a marrow donor who saved her life. This, she believed, was due to the healing miracle of the *kariocha*.

Some surrendered themselves to the *asiento* and *yaworaje* because of previous healings they attributed to the Orisha. When Gillian came to the religion she was suffering emotionally. She was advised by the oracle to undergo a ceremony to "receive" Olokun. Gillian's subsequent healing made her feel that she owed Orisha a debt of gratitude which only the *kariocha* could repay. As with the *promesas* to *los santos* in folk Catholicism, Gillian had prayed for healing and then believed she was required to make up for it with service (cf. Savastano n.d.).

Several became initiated in the hope of general change or progress in their lives. Eugene wrote: "I made *ocha* because I wanted my life to be different than it had been." Similarly, Iyawo Halie wrote that she was "compelled [to initiate] by divination and a personal desire for spiritual elevation." Many explained that they underwent Lukumi ordination to deepen their spirituality, improve their lives, or seek the fulfillment of a promise for their own continued health or the healing of someone they loved. Combining these expectations with the focus on transformation in the *kariocha* ceremony, it is not surprising that change, growth, and healing were the most popular general characterizations of the year in white by survey respondents.

Speaking of how the *yaworaje* had changed them for the better, *iyawo* and former *iyawo* frequently noted that the growth was uncomfortable or difficult at the time. Zoe "chafed against the restrictions and relative subordination" of the *iyawo*: "I was la niña linda, but still a child, and struggled to accept my status. . . . Still, I am glad I did it. It has brought me closer to truth and deep happiness than any time since I was a child." Most expressions of hardship were moderated with descriptions of lessons learned. Matías noted that the year was "difficult" because he was forced to "deal with [himself] and [his] own issues." Douglas, a priest of Ogun, spoke of family and marital problems, explaining that without those experiences, he would have never learned lessons about "working with the people in my family and community." Others also focused on the positive aspects of the trials they faced. Harmony, who came to the year in white after multiple divinatory consultations with her godmother and through a desire for protection, described the *yaworaje* as "the most challenging and most rewarding thing I've done so far." In responses to different questions in the survey, Hunter spoke of becoming ordained because of a combination of coercion and desire. Although he had difficulty at first connecting to an *ilé*, he told of being warned by a mounted priest[5] that "the Orisha . . . [were] getting tired of waiting" for him to make *ocha* and that if he didn't soon they would see him in the cemetery. During the year in white, which he described as "a journey that led inside myself," he spoke of having to "'wrassel' with . . . [himself] about things . . . like being obedient to the rules." Yet "always it came back to one fact: I chose to do this because it was what I wanted and I love the Orisha; it is they that ask it of me." At the end of the year he felt transformed:

> Now I don't feel as if I need nearly as much human contact as I did before my year; I feel more confident and self-sufficient; I am healthier . . . I am much more happy. I don't feel the need to get a relationship going like I did. If it happens it's alright but I am not looking for one. I seem to not be nearly as interested in sex. . . . My life has changed; I am better and a better person. . . . I think a little differently and things don't bother me nearly so much. I am a lot more laid back and my priorities have changed.

Ivy, who initially felt the religion was "too much work" for her but was told otherwise by a mounted Yemaya, believed that though the year was difficult, it and her new connection to the Orisha Oshun "gave [her] the strength to finally do what needed to be done and make the necessary changes in" her life. Many Orisha priests said that they believed that changes and challenges, growing pains, and specific issues they were forced to encounter had transformed them for the better during the year in white.

SECLUSION

The next most common theme *iyawos* and former *iyawos* discussed in general characterizations of the year in white centered on notions of cleansing, quietude, serenity, and protection. These discussions were most consonant with the third of three themes of the *yaworaje* discussed in scholarly literature: seclusion. An important ritual function of the year in white is for the "newborn" to be protected. *Iyawos* are believed to be especially vulnerable to otherworldly pollution due to the exposure of their heads during the priestly initiation ceremony. Many of the rules of the *yaworaje* are designed to protect the initiates spiritually (see Clark 2007). Being fully covered in white garb; being inside when it is dark and during the (potentially phantasmal) liminal times of noon and midnight; avoiding cemeteries, parties, movies, restaurants and crowded spaces; forgoing touching non-initiated adults or even taking items from them; eating only from one's own special dishes; wearing a white shawl when one cannot avoid being out at night—all these restrictions (and more) are enacted, at least in part, to shield Lukumi novices from darkness and evil. *Iyawos* are understood to have experienced an intense spiritual cleansing during the *kariocha*, and they are instructed to avoid many ordinary worldly things to protect themselves from otherworldly forces that might do them harm and to maintain the great light that was placed within them when they were initiated.

Sixty-six survey respondents (43 percent) made remarks that I placed in this category, almost as many as described transformation. They spoke of the *yaworaje* as a time of quiet enjoyment, relaxing at home with the pots that contained their new Orisha, focusing inward, and engendering "peace of mind" and spiritual progress through contemplation of life and the divinatory instructions they received at their *kariocha*. Many recalled their year as an interlude in their lives when they were able to leave many troubles behind and instead focus on caring for themselves and their new relationships with Orisha and their godfamily. Some described the *yaworaje* as like living in a bubble or a cocoon, as getting to enjoy "me time," or as feeling cleansed, renewed, and reborn. Many recalled the year in white as generally peaceful, serene, and introspective.

Iyawos and former *iyawos* commonly appreciated the opportunity for solitude and reflection. Diane said, "That was the most peace I ever had in my life." Zoe felt that "the relative remove from society" helped her "to reflect on . . . [her] life and choose . . . priorities more carefully." The *yaworaje* was often remembered as a time when one could look inward. Iyawo Faith, who was ordained to Ochosi, the master hunter Orisha and enactor of justice, wrote that she "love[d] having an excuse not to go out at night." Instead, she kept herself busy at home: "I am home before sundown. I decided to wash all my clothes by hand . . . and hang them out on the line. I love this ritual." *Iyawos* often find projects such as this to keep them busy at home. Routinized domestic or crafty tasks can free the mind to meditate and provide a sense of "groundedness." In "Reflections on My Iyawo Year," an article on a Web site from the Orisa Community Development Corporation, Iyawo Omo Ase (2011) writes that although she was told not to socialize much during her *yaworaje*, she wasn't sure what she was supposed to do with her time until later in the year. It didn't make sense to her "to replace social time with becoming a couch potato or sleeping all day." As she expresses, "What would be the purpose of that? Surely that can't really improve one's life and help one grow in understanding of the orisas." Instead, Omo Ase suggests that the *iyawo*'s focus should be on spiritual endeavors and self-improvement: 1) "Focusing on connecting with the energies of the orisas"; 2) "Focus[ing] on growing with ancestral energy"; 3) "Focus[ing] on learning the religious philosophy, language, prayers, songs, and rituals"; and 4) "Creat[ing] a life of discipline, uprightness, accountability, and balance." Along the same lines, Gavin—who declared his love for his tutelary Orisha Obatalá, who is often associated with clarity, deliberation, and thoughtfulness—explained how his simple daily routine granted him freedom of mind:

> My year was very simple, and having lived a busy life for decades, it was refreshing. Every day, I would wake up, refresh my front door [with cool water], pray and salute to my orishas, and go to work. At the end of my shift, I'd come home. . . . When the sun was down and I was on what I lovingly called "*iyawo*-lockdown," I was in my *ocha* room, meditating in front of my orishas. I spent a lot of time writing and journaling, and for those reasons alone I think my iyaboraje was one of self-reflection and self-knowledge.

Thus, some *iyawos* felt that seclusion combined with structure offered possibilities for greater inward movement than unstructured solitude.

Although my routines varied throughout the year, I too experienced peacefulness and introspection within the *yaworaje*, though I would not characterize the year primarily in those ways. I wasn't able to turn life off for a year; I still had to deal with work, car troubles, money worries, and family events and dramas. But like many *iyawos*, I found that forgoing most social and evening activities freed up quite a bit of time and energy. I used some of the newfound time to write regularly in my journal, begin psychotherapy, contemplate my new Orisha, attend synagogue services and classes regularly, and take care of myself through cooking, laundering my clothes, and exercising. Although I appreciated the opportunities for prayer, quiet reflection, and domesticity, instead of taking baths and enjoying nights at home, I spent a good portion of the year feeling bored, wishing I was able to go out more, and distracting myself with endless hours of *Buffy the Vampire Slayer*, *Six Feet Under*, and *Star Trek: Voyager*. Yet there were times when I enjoyed the "excuse" of the *yaworaje* to stay at home, reading and contemplating instead of socializing. And it is perhaps because of my impatience and preference for doing rather than simply being that quietude was most beneficial for my personal growth.

Many of the same people who described the benefits of being away from the hustle and bustle also spoke of difficulties with stillness. As I did, many *iyawos* and former *iyawos*, at least at times, focused on the tight bonds of the *yaworaje*'s figurative swaddling. Thirty-four respondents reported experiencing struggles with curfews and social restrictions; the curfew was the third most frequently mentioned category of rule that people experienced as most difficult. Many recalled wrestling with the "serenity" of seclusion, viewing it as both blessing and battle.

Iyawos and former *iyawos* often described themselves as feeling clean and purified. As a symbol of their inner housekeeping, they are commonly instructed to maintain perfect exterior cleanliness in dress and hygiene. Several respondents noted that they enjoyed the feeling of being clean outside and inside and took special care to maintain a pristine presentation. Some described being told by others they had the *iyawo* "glow," a visible manifestation of the inner radiance it is believed that *iyawos* achieve through the *kariocha* ceremony. Nicolás—who first entered Lukumi via the sometimes related practice of Espiritismo—recalled enjoying the wholesomeness and effulgence of *iyawo* life: "My year in white was comforting; it was like being always in a clean bed with new and fresh sheets. I felt innocent and people said I was glowing." Similarly, when I was a *iyawo*, especially in the first three months, when I was not permitted to see myself in the mirror, I was told I had "the glow" almost every time I encountered members of my extended *ilé* or other *olorisha*. Some believed that *iyawo* radiance might be felt even by cultural outsiders. Iyawo Eduardo, a "child of" Oshun, expressed a not-uncommon belief that when he was a *iyawo*, strangers were drawn to him without knowing why because of his inner radiance.

Jorge, who was ordained because of his love for the religion in which he was raised, recalled feeling "young and reborn again" during his year in white. For him (and others), this meant the joy of being able to leave behind former pain and struggle and have a new start in life. Magdalena, who became a Lukumi priest out of love for her "mother" Yemaya and other Ocha, described "feeling new," as if she had "a second chance." Others spoke of a change in attitude or a renewed sense of innocence. Mark—who believed he had been "born to be a priest"—found that the year allowed him to see "the world through new eyes." Ursa—a priest of Obatalá who claimed to have been "pretty atheist" when she first encountered Lukumi—described the feeling of newness she experienced as a *iyawo*: "I felt like I had this new energy and vulnerability as well. . . . It just felt like a huge opening up in the initiation. And prior to that it is kind of a dismantling, cutting off the old clothes. . . . You are basically losing your old ways and your old person, kind of dying sort of in a way. . . . Everything is so new; you are encountering everything freshly." For Ursa, the combination of the feelings of renewal and the vulnerability she experienced was strong enough that she appreciated the protective measures of the *yaworaje*; she even felt that she "needed to go slower and quieter" in order to assimilate new experiences properly and carefully. Lincoln, a priest of Oshun, spoke of having a new outlook when he was a *iyawo*: "It was just a wonder. Everything was just beautiful; everything was new. It was like [I was] a baby." Thus, *iyawos*, who are treated ritually as "babies" by members of their godfamily, often described feeling reborn and enjoying the potential and wonder of a fresh start.

Others focused on feelings of being sheltered. Like Kendra—who underwent the *kariocha* because she was instructed to do so in a divinatory reading—they felt they were "pure, special, and protected." Just over 86 percent of respondents agreed with the statement "During my year in white I usually felt protected and safe." Iyawo Ashley—who made *ocha* out of a desire to give back to Oshun—explained: "I definitely do feel like I'm in a little cocoon with my Ochas. I feel protected and loved by them whether I am in the house or outside." Similarly,

Leslie—who became a priest for health reasons—shared that she "felt special and strangely untouchable." Ted—a priest of Oshun who first encountered the Orisha in a black studies course—liked the feeling that "you could walk the world blindly and there was a force of protection over you, as if God Himself held your hand as you did anything, and nothing would harm you. The very day I wore colored clothing [once the year in white was complete], was the day that protection left and I felt that now I had to learn how to defend myself against a cold cruel world." Another priest of Oshun, Vincent, offered an interesting metaphor for the feelings of safety he recalled experiencing nine years before during his year in white. The metaphor came from a television cartoon from his boyhood:

> Mister Magoo was this blind man with thick glasses. . . . I felt just like him. An *iyawo* could walk in the street, cars going 90 miles an hour, but because I was so protected by Orisha gods and I felt immaculate in this white; I just felt protected wherever I went. There could be a shoot-out in the street but bullets would avoid me, because I was protected. . . . That is how it felt, like Mister Magoo walking [in a] straight line and everybody crashing their cars [around him]—except he is okay. . . . That is exactly how I felt; everything was okay while I was in my white.

Iyawos are believed to inhabit an insulated space, spiritually shielded by white cloth and the grace of Orisha. In a variety of ways, Orisha priests and *iyawos* illustrated the year in white as one of quietude, cleanliness, protection, inner peace and reflection.

EMOTIONAL TURBULENCE

While many characterized the year in white as overwhelmingly peaceful, others described it as unsettling. A sense of unrest often accompanies transformation. Deep alteration of identity, involving the stripping of an old self to make way for a new one (see Garfinkel 1956), is bound to be emotional. The quietude of the year in white, including the elimination of potential emotional crutches such as consumption of drugs or alcohol, casual sex, eating routines, the use of cosmetics, and potentially addictive behaviors such as exercise or socializing may force a person to confront her inner demons. Iyawo Lola—who underwent the *kariocha* for her health—characterized the *yaworaje* as "an up-and-down emotional rollercoaster." Nyesha—who made *ocha* because the "cosmology made sense" to her—described the year in white as a generally "horrible" experience that she looked back upon years later as having been "necessary" to her "growth and development." She explained: "As an Iyawo you are pretty much forced to deal with your emotional baggage. I was not ready to deal with a lot of things but because of the solitude, I was put in that space." In an interview, Lincoln elaborated about the emotional process of adapting to the inner changes wrought by the *kariocha*: "In my *iyawo* year I could feel the change. I was very emotional. I cried a lot. I was very moved by a lot of things in my *iyawo* year: people, incidents. [It was] a very moving period for me. And I got better, but it was very eye opening, my *iyawo* year; I could see things that I couldn't before, the face behind the face . . . when you can really see who [people] . . . are." Lincoln described an emotional accompaniment of transformation: far from being a smooth passage, the ripples underneath made for choppy sailing. Similarly, Lily, a priest of the oceanic Yemaya, used watery metaphors to explain that one must deal with buried emotional wounds as part of the process of healing: "I [had] to look into what cause[d] me pain and learn . . . how to let that go. I cry a lot that year. It's about healing and learning how to trust Orisha. . . . The best metaphor is like riding . . . big waves. At first you feel like the waves (your problems) are so big and it's going to drown you. Just when you feel you are going under, somehow you always survive." Indeed, the year in white can be seen as a healing journey that unfolds over time, and that is not always comfortable.

Many respondents pointed to agitated feelings as their primary memory of their year in white. Some understood emotional turbulence as a necessary part of a healing process. Approximately 68 percent of survey respondents agreed somewhat or strongly with the statement "My year in white helped me to deal with emotional issues from my past," 48 percent reported that "During my year in white I often felt vulnerable," and 42 percent recalled that "During my year in white I often felt lonely." In the open-ended survey questions, thirty-four *iyawos* and former *iyawos* (22 percent) described the year in white as generally being emotionally turbulent.

Emotional upheaval was most commonly (though not exclusively) attributed to the first three months of the *yaworaje*. Leslie explained that the year in white was "very up and down emotionally. The first three months were the worst." Similarly, Iyawo Lucy, who is ordained to Oshun, wrote that the "first set of three months were hard and I felt very cranky," but during subsequent months "I was feeling emotionally much better." Iyawo Matías also found the first quarter of the year to be especially difficult: "The first three months, my body was all out of whack and my mental state had changed. I had lost my ability to control my anger and I couldn't keep my patience for even the shortest amount of time." Hunter began the year feeling "isolated and lonely," but his emotions eventually "gave way to solitude and being self-contained and serene." Iyawo Monette, who underwent the *kariocha* because she felt it was "important to" her "bloodline," described the year as "a mixed bag. The first three months were a tremendous adjustment. . . . I battled feeling imprisoned and at times felt unconsidered. . . . After the first three months, I began to become more accustomed to the ways of being an *iyawo* and I opened myself up more to the experience and let go of a lot of the frustrations that plagued me." For some, the first three months were more difficult emotionally than the rest of the year. Several *iyawos* described initial emotional troubles followed by a transition that led to acceptance.

Among those who felt that the first three months of the *yaworaje* differed substantially from the rest of the year, some saw it as the first year in a longer healing journey. These *olorishas* described the time following the *kariocha* as a multiyear process of unfolding. Iyawo Ronna, who understood Lukumi initiation as "an opportunity to fulfill not only" her own destiny but that of her ancestors, explained: "I believe the *iyawo* year to be a process and a beginning." Tino, who made *ocha* "to better ... [his] life and give service to Oshun," recalled that "it was not until my year itself ended that my life truly started to change." He saw the *yaworaje* as "more of a stasis year," followed by "real changes" once he began wearing colors again: "I became a completely new person and it took approximately two years after my year ended for the dust to start to settle, for everything ... to start to heal and for me to find myself on the other side of the province pursuing new education and new career options." The emotional turbulence of the year in white can be seen in a larger context of maturation.

Some shared emotional challenges that lasted throughout the year in white. Tomás, who made *ocha* "mostly for health reasons," explained that although he found the year to be reflective and transformative and although his physical health improved, psychologically, he was a mess: "I was a wreck. My mind got much stronger but emotionally I was a roller coaster." For these *iyawos* the bumpy ride lasted longer than three months. Ivy complained about a very difficult year, in large part because of lack of acceptance from her family and friends, especially lack of acceptance from her husband about her decision to make *ocha*. As a result, she found herself "often bitchy and depressed."

Several attributed their emotional troubles to their appearance and their visibility as *iyawo*. Teresa, a priest of Oshun who had observed her *yaworaje* when she was a child in order "to save ... [her] life," explained that the cruelty of both kids and grownups provoked feelings of shame about her appearance: "During my iyaworaje, I was enrolled in public school. I wasn't so self-conscious about my all white dress attire as much as I was about being bald and having to wear a head cover. Being that I was a little girl, not having my hair made me feel less than pretty. Unfortunately I was taunted a lot during my year, not only by kids my age, but by many ignorant adults as well." The way *iyawo* must present themselves breaks norms, marking them as deviant. To the extent that girls are evaluated by their appearance and by conventional markers of femininity that generally are not allowed during the year in white, the *iyawo* is out of luck. But adults too find that compliance with *iyawo* rules related to wardrobe and grooming can affect their sense of self. Serena, who was ordained to "deepen" her "relationship with the Divine," found that the *yaworaje* exacerbated body issues: "I was . . . somewhat vain prior to my *iyawo* year but when I got into my year my vanity escalated and I got very depressed about my looks. I spent many days and nights in tears because I felt ugly." To the extent that self-conceptions are located in physical presentation, the *iyawo* uniform can be disturbing.

I also found it challenging to switch from a practically all-black wardrobe that I believed to be slimming to all-white clothing that allowed for absolutely no concealment. My friend and therapist Susan thought the year was almost designed for confronting vanity and body acceptance: "So they take away your hair that you put a lot of your identity into," she said, gesturing to indicate the mid-back length of my former glorious mane. "And then they put you in bright white clothes so you can't hide. And in the winter you *really* can't hide. You stand out. You're really visible. It sounds like a setup for appearance issues. They've set things up so you will have to deal with this." I can't say that I was cured of all my body issues during my year in white, but I certainly had plenty to process in psychotherapy.

A number of survey respondents described feeling isolated and/or depressed during the year in white. Approximately 31 percent agreed with the statement "During my *iyawo* year I was often depressed." A large minority of respondents described the year in white as a time when they felt isolated and lonely. In the open-ended survey questions, twenty-three mentioned feeling lonely during their year in white. Vanessa, who underwent the *yaworaje* because the Orisha Orula indicated through his oracle that initiation would improve her health, fought with loneliness, humiliation, and feelings of alienation throughout the year: "It was very lonely. . . . I frequently came home and cried all the stress and hurt out." Mía, whose *ilé* was in the process of a meltdown during much of her *iyawo* year, wrote: "I did have some 'nice' moments but they were overshadowed by my struggles with depression and feelings of isolation." Tiffany, who was advised multiple times to make *ocha* in divinatory readings during the decade she spent as an *aleyo,* attributed her sense of isolation and boredom to spending her *yaworaje* in a small town in North Carolina. Faye, who lived over seven hours away from her *ilé,* similarly complained of a lonely *yaworaje. Iyawos* who were separated from their godparents or their *ilé* because of geography or because of schisms and drama were especially likely to describe feeling isolated during their year in white.

In many traditional houses of Ocha, *iyawos* are expected to balance the social probation of the *yaworaje* with regular and active involvement in their *ilé.* During religious occasions, such as *ocha* birthday celebrations and religious ceremonies, some of the social restrictions of the *yaworaje,* such as the curfew, are often relaxed. Religious contexts may be the only real socializing for *iyawos,* especially in the first three months. And in a very active *ilé, iyawos* may visit their godparents monthly, weekly, or even more often. In some houses, especially after the first three months, godparents will permit *iyawos* to attend religious events in other houses and will even allow them to go to normally forbidden locations such as restaurants or movie theaters when they are escorted by a godparent or another priest in the house. Thus, *iyawos* who do not have the social outlet of an active *ilé* may have been at the greatest risk of feeling socially isolated. This is what Nyesha experienced: "It was very difficult. I was deeply depressed and I felt very alone. My godparents lived in another city so I did not get to see them much." Occasionally those who lived near their godfamily also described experiencing feelings of alienation. Regina, a white non-Hispanic priest of Yemaya, felt that racial differences were the cause of her feelings of isolation during her year in white: "The worst parts were loneliness. Only three people from my godmother's spiritual house visited me. . . . I was not accepted by the Latino community and very few African Americans, even those I considered my godbrothers and godsisters." Some *iyawos* who lived near their godparents and maintained good relations with them complained of loneliness and isolation if their godparents were not active religiously, thus denying them an escort and opportunities to attend the religious events that many *iyawos* cling to as social lifelines.

Emotional turbulence was a major aspect of the year in white for a large minority of respondents. *Iyawos* and former *iyawos* described feeling cranky, confused, frustrated, panicky, angry, sad, lonely, depressed, alienated, and isolated or simply emotionally unsteady during the first three months of the *yaworaje*, while they adapted to new routines and identifications, or sometimes for much of the year in white. They shared stories of shame and embarrassment attached to lack of acceptance of their bodies and appearance—the shame produced by others' judgments and also by their own. And they recalled feeling depressed and isolated, mostly, though not always, when they lacked support from a strong Ocha family that was nearby.

MARKED STATUS

Another very common theme in survey respondents' general descriptions of the year was the experience of being a person with a marked status. Living as a *iyawo* in the United States is like a yearlong experiment in deviance. As Clark (2005, 72) notes, "The *iyawo* becomes wholly (holy) other while continuing to participate in the world of work, school, shopping, and all the other minutiae of daily life." As is often true for members of groups in the minority—whether ethnic, racial, sexual, or religious—*iyawos* must pass through spaces every day in which they are visibly deviant in order to work, attend school, exercise, bank, attend religious events and doctor's appointments, transport their children, and shop. The appearance of *iyawos* makes them stand out from others, often bringing attention—both desired and unwanted—from insiders and outsiders alike.

Most *iyawos*, depending on what their godparents require, must dress completely in white; even belts, shoes, umbrellas, and bags must be white. At the beginning of the year they have generally been shaved bald and must wear head coverings. In the first three months they may also be seen wearing white shawls. In the heat of the summer, especially in their first three months, *iyawos* will generally be covered almost head to toe. In the coldest parts of the winter, *iyawos* will commonly be dressed unfashionably in white. The appearance of a *iyawo* is different enough from U.S. social norms to mark novices (see Shapiro 1982; Waugh 1982). Unless one lives in a tight community where *iyawo* status is understood and *iyawos* do not have to often interact with outsiders, being a *iyawo* makes the interruption of taken-for-granted normalcy—what sociologist Garfinkel (1967) would have called a breaching experiment—an everyday experience.

Whether they enjoyed the feeling that they were ambassadors to the world from the year in white, radiating purity and tranquility to all they met, or they liked getting attention from strangers due to their unconventional dress or they experienced ill will from others because of their appearance or they felt embarrassed and awkward and didn't want to leave home because of their appearance and garb, thirty-two survey respondents (21 percent) spoke of visibility as being particularly memorable or characteristic of the *yaworaje* in open-ended survey questions. Twenty-one wrote that it was the worst part of their year in white. Indeed, many of the most detailed stories survey respondents told about the year in white had to do with reactions from others because of their increased visibility in the *yaworaje*. Respondents recalled being asked about their religion a lot by curious strangers, co-workers, students, teachers, and sometimes friends and family. They became accustomed to stares. They had to decide whether and how much to reveal about their status to outsiders who might have negative associations with the religion.

Several respondents spoke of the increased visibility of the *yaworaje* in neutral or mixed terms. Zelda, a priest of Oshun who had been told by a *babalawo* at the age of twelve that she would make *ocha*, liked "gaining recognition on the street for being a *iyawo*" but also spoke of having "to deal with the stares." Iyawo Ronna, who lives in a part of Florida where *iyawos* are rare, spoke of coming to the realization that her appearance made her stand out from others around her: "At a certain point it occurred to me that I am different—wearing the white in itself sets me apart—and it's not a bad thing, it's just a thing." Victor, who spent most of his *iyawo* year in New York, recalled feeling such calmness and connection to the Orisha Obatalá that he didn't mind the constant inquiries from strangers: "Even when people would look and stare, ask me if I was at a seminary or studying for the priesthood (for the latter of course the answer was yes!), I felt calm, comfortable and at peace." Bianca felt particularly visible "in the winter where most people seem to wear black coats." It made her "feel . . . conspicuous." Nevertheless, she wrote, living "in the San Francisco Bay area . . . people here are mostly nonchalant about things like people dressed head to toe in white." *Iyawos* often found easy ways of adapting to their visible deviance in mainstream society.

Others described struggling with their visibility. Iyawo Allison, who made *ocha* because of her faith in the Orisha, wrote about her embarrassment "at being dressed all in white in public." Harmony, who became ordained because of her godmother's divination and from a perceived need for greater "grounding and centering," felt that "standing out so much all the time was difficult." And Sergio, who had received beads and minor ceremonies as a teen but didn't undergo the *kariocha* until many years later after being told to do so in divinatory *consultas,* felt "uncomfortable when . . . stared at." He also disliked "having unnecessary comments made indirectly" about him. Vanessa, who experienced the year in white as a self-conscious adolescent, recalled, "I felt like I stuck out like a sore thumb a lot." Valentina, a priest of Oshun, didn't like the way people at her workplace stared at her and whispered. Joan, who underwent the *kariocha* to improve her mental health and to learn more about the Orisha, disliked being the center of attention before her *yaworaje.* Afterward, of course, this was something she had difficulty avoiding: "I knew that my headscarf covering my new head with its lack of hair and my white shawl and dress must have caused curiosity at work. . . . Trying to explain the why and the process was daunting or I felt I would be considered a cult nut. I had to learn to render irrelevant that fact that I was in bright white in the middle of winter on the U.S. East Coast." In these ways, respondents described the social discomfort of their noticeable religious status. They explained that for many reasons it's not easy being a *iyawo* among those who don't understand the yearlong religious rite.

For some, the heightened visibility as a member of a minority religion seemed to invite awkward and sometimes hostile reactions from others. Kirstin, who had been "claimed" by the Orisha Oya in a ceremony and "always knew" that making *ocha* was her "destiny," alluded to difficult encounters with judgmental Christians during her year in white. Adriana, a priest of Yemaya in Brooklyn, felt that "people looked like they were afraid to sit next to me on the train because they thought I was going to do something to them, or maybe they were going to get bad luck." Iyawo Rebecca, who found that strangers often interpreted her white attire as nurse's garb, nevertheless believed that her unconventional appearance affected the people around her in unexpected ways: "I am a mirror for the world right now. I often sense that my action makes people see things that they may or may not be internally comfortable with. For some close to the religion, it might be a realization that they aren't ready to make the life-changing step of *ocha.* For others it might be that they are too afraid of breaking society's rules to make such an obvious personal statement." This *iyawo* took a sociopsychological approach to her social interactions, understanding that the awkward reactions she experienced from people around her were influenced by each person's unique history. The *iyawo* can symbolize many things to the people with whom she or he interacts, including spirituality, weirdness, disease, and religion, especially since their understandings of the *yaworaje* vary widely. Some people's "readings" of the polysemous *iyawo* may be surprising. Daniela, who became ordained immediately after her sister because of dire warnings in a divination, related an incident at a mall in which "a lady got out of a car to give me a pamphlet stating [that] the [Orisha] Elegua, Ogun and Oshosi were demon[s]." In this case, an onlooker interpreted the *iyawo* as evil. Although she was glad she did it, Elena "made santo" because it was expected of her in her Lukumi family. While her kin were supportive, she remembers being discriminated against in school: "One of my teachers who was an animal protector had a hard time with me being in his class. He would always make comments like 'religion is no reason to kill animals.' He even dropped me from his class . . . [and] I really needed this class to transfer." In this case, the teacher reduced a young *iyawo* to an animal sacrificer. Teresa told of being harassed when she was a child *iyawo*: "I remember walking down the street. . . . A man was riding on a bike passing us and I was dressed in my little white dress, with my white shawl and head cover, and the man was shouting very hurtful things to me. At nine years old I couldn't understand how someone can be so vile and mean when I was just a little girl walking down the street." In this case it's difficult to know just what the child represented to the villain in the story. *Iyawos* shared many accounts of times when their prominent difference made them targets for whatever associations the people they encountered made about them.

Because *iyawos* tend to begin the year bald and wearing head coverings, the people they encounter often assume they are ill. Many *iyawos* and former *iyawos* wrote that they were believed to be cancer patients. Though she felt connected to the religion through her Puerto Rican roots, Michelle came to *ocha* via a road that wound through Catholicism and Wicca. She wrote that her co-workers thought she "was sick" because her "head was shaved and . . . covered with a white scarf." To those who wanted to avoid having discussions about the religion with outsiders, being thought to be undergoing chemotherapy or radiation may sometimes have been preferable. Carmen, a priest of Obatalá, was also mistakenly seen as diseased: "Most people would look at us when we were out as if we were aliens from another planet. . . . I attracted a lot of attention everywhere I went. Some people would turn away from us as if we might be carriers of an infectious disease. Sometimes it was funny, and at other times it was very discriminating." Teresa, who was initiated as a child, recalled having to deal with taunts at school from both children and adults, many of whom assumed she was sick: "At school, the nurses would follow me all over the school grounds inquiring if I was a cancer patient or whether I had a terminal disease. They were going to have me segregated from the rest of my classmates, which made me feel more isolated." Elena found it difficult to be thought to have cancer: "The first few months were the hardest. Everyone in school would ask me 'Why are you always wearing white?' or 'Are you sick or what?' I would always try to explain but some people didn't really understand. . . . People would ask me 'Do you have cancer?' or 'Why are you doing this?' This comment always made me feel so bad." Some respondents told of allowing the people around them to believe they were unwell. Others corrected those who inquired. Having to deal with people who thought they were ill was an ordinary experience among *iyawos*. It was also common for people they encountered to assume *iyawos* were Muslim, nuns, cooks, and nurses.

Markedness was a big part of the year for me and I noted often in my journal the varied responses I received from others because of my appearance. One entry from my field notes marveled about the frequency of "nurse mistakings" and my perplexity about the aggressiveness with which some people inquired about my status:

> Strangers keep coming up to me and asking if I'm a nurse. It must have happened three times today. Some shop clerk followed me around the department store in order to ask me. She was literally out of breath from running after me to ask that same question. I'm not sure what to think about that. What motivates people to go out of their way to break the stranger barrier, to risk awkwardness, and to hunt me down in the store? I've seen lots of odd and interesting strangers but I don't think I've ever gone out of my way to interrogate them. And why "nurse"? I feel like I should say, "No, I'm a doctor." (Actually, I've got a doctorate. Maybe I should.) Lately I haven't felt much like having extended conversations in elevators and department stores or whatever. So they ask me and I just say "no" and move on.

At different times in the year, probably because of my head coverings, I was told I looked like a chef or a sailor. I was aware that many of my students thought I was sick with cancer. A neighbor once asked me if I were a missionary. A synagogue member thought I had become ultrareligious, honoring the Sabbath by dressing all in white. Once, when I had to be outside briefly at night, I wore my protective white shawl over my head. A car passed and I heard, "A ghost?" Then the car swerved, and there was a yell: "Ghost!!!" Perhaps my favorite moment of being labeled by a stranger occurred when I was walking on a New Jersey boardwalk in the summer with a friend:

> Adrienne and I walked the boards for an hour and a half from Ocean Grove through Bradley Beach and Avon on the Sea to the Belmar Bridge. I was dressed all-out *iyawo* (ankle-length pants; skirt below my knee; roomy, long-sleeved, high-necked top; floppy brim hat; and all-white sneakers). Adrienne thought I looked like an Orthodox Jewish married woman. Some elderly guy passing us on

the boards had a different idea. "Are you advocating suffrage?" he asked. I thought that was pretty darned funny.

The encounters I've described thus far were mostly quick exchanges with strangers. But markedness can become more difficult (and interesting) with prolonged interactions and with some of the same people over time: consider dealings with co-workers, neighbors on the elevator in a high-rise building, or members of one's church or synagogue. Most of the reactions I encountered because of my *iyawo* dress were of the amusing or slightly annoying type. If I felt more comfortable I might tell the stranger I was undergoing a spiritual cleanse. And occasionally these brief contacts would initiate deeper conversations. Infrequently I found myself recognized as *iyawo* by strangers, a bright beacon of *la religión*.

Some described learning to carry themselves with dignity during their *yaworaje*. Cantrice, who came to *ocha* initially for the sense of connection to God she experienced through the Orisha and through pan-Africanism, explained how embarrassment about her appearance was transformed into pride: "I didn't want to go out because people on the street would stare or say '*Asalaam alekum*.' My Godfather asked me to go to the store one day, and I said 'dressed like this?' My Godfather was disappointed and said 'You should be able [to be] happy, proud, and not ashamed of your status. You should be proud to show and tell people who [and] what . . . you are.' After that 'discussion,' I was never afraid to be out wearing my white." Thus, some *iyawos* found that the markedness of the *yaworaje* was an important lesson. Daniela, a priest of Obatalá, related a story from the playground: "At the time my son was five and it was summer so I had to take him out to play. I had my shawl on and one of my neighbors always had something to say until I explained that I had gone bald and would be wearing white for at least nine more months. Needless to say she never said anything else to me." Another child of Obatalá, María, also recalled having to adapt to the attentions of strangers: "Even though I live in a city where iyawos are a common thing to see, people can be cruel and indiscreet. But I held my head high wherever I went and ignored the ignoranc[e] of others." Similarly, Iyawo Faith wrote, "I love discovering that I can go into public places dress[ed] all in white and not mind it—even when people stare." Thus, *iyawos* can learn to turn the awkwardness of conspicuousness into a process of learning to be proudly different.

Several respondents spoke of the positive aspects of *iyawo* visibility. Going out into the world dressed as a *iyawo* may draw encouragement from members of one's tradition. Because of his association with (and dependence upon) a godparent who was increasingly isolated from her Ocha community, Nicolás was particularly grateful for the times when his distinct appearance engendered Lukumi connections, even if they were fleeting: "I think the best parts [of the year] were meeting other brothers and sisters in the tradition. Being an *iyawo* is an instant beacon for others in the religion to notice you. . . . As an *iyawo* . . . you had no choice but to tell the world who you were." Just as *iyawo* garb may hold negative associations for some outsiders, it carries positive associations for cultural insiders and may draw them to interact enthusiastically with a *iyawo*, reveling at times in the knowledge that they share a secret. Phoebe, who underwent the *kariocha* sooner than she would have otherwise because of health concerns, enjoyed the interest from the people around her: "Being all in white, I became a beacon. Some people wanted to talk to me more than they ever had before, some people clammed up, but everyone noticed. Now that I'm back in color, everyone is noticing that, too. I like the attention, because it's been positive." Although she suffered from discrimination because of her visibility, Elena also enjoyed the positive attention from many people she encountered: "People would come up to me and tell me 'You look so beautiful,' or 'You look like an angel.' . . . I felt so happy when I would meet someone that understood the religion. I felt I wasn't alone in this process." *Iyawos* and former *iyawos* described markedness—for good and ill—as an important part of their experience of the year in white.

NATIVES, NEWCOMERS, AND ETHNICITY

The survey on the year in white offers an opportunity to ask if cultural newcomers practice and understand their new religious traditions differently from cultural indigenes. Were newcomers more or less likely to report that they followed the rules of the *yaworaje*? To recall enjoying the experience? To report that their health improved during the year? To complain about gaining weight or worrying often about money? Were those who were not brought up in the religion more or less likely to recount feeling depressed during the year in white? Feeling protected? Lonely? Vulnerable? Grateful?

To assess if and how it mattered that a person was raised in or around the religion, I compared survey respondents I classified as cultural natives with cultural newcomers in chi-square analyses on each of the ordinal variables.[6] For most questions I asked in the survey, lifelong and relatively recent Lukumi practitioners did not offer answers that differed enough from each other to be statistically significant. For example, newcomers and natives were generally equally as likely to say that they loved the year in white, that they felt that the *yaworaje* changed them for the better, that they were lonely during the year, and that the hardships of the year in white were worth it.

However, in a handful of survey questions, Lukumi upbringing affected answers enough to be statistically significant (see Table 2). Cultural natives (57 percent) were more likely than cultural newcomers (34 percent) to "strongly agree" that they missed the year in white once it was over. Although just over half of respondents recalled gaining weight during the *yaworaje*,

TABLE 2.   Chi-Square Tests Comparing Cultural Natives and Newcomers

Survey Statements	Chi Square	Significance
After my year in white I missed being iyawo.	$X^2 = 9.56$, df = 3; N = 144	$p = .02$
I gained weight during my year in white.	$X^2 = 8.19$, df = 3; N = 168	$p = .04$
During my year in white I often felt vulnerable.	$X^2 = 4.72$, df = 1; N = 170	$p = .03$
I can/could barely wait for my year in white to be over.	$X^2 = 10.06$, df = 3; N = 164	$p = .02$

approximately 43 percent of cultural natives agreed strongly that they did so compared to 33 percent of newcomers. Those who were cultural newcomers were more likely (54 percent) than cultural indigenes (33 percent) to agree somewhat or strongly that they felt vulnerable during the year. Cultural natives were more likely (47 percent) than cultural newcomers (22 percent) to strongly disagree with the statement that they "could barely wait" for the year in white to end.

Given the suggestion that Hispanic heritage may also affect experiences with the year in white (Pérez 2012; Ramos, personal communication), either as an alternate operationalization of "cultural native," or because of the confluence between saint adoration popular in some Hispanic groups and Lukumi Orisha devotion, or for some other reason(s), I also ran chi-square analyses that compared the seventy-eight survey respondents who described themselves as "Latina/o," "Hispanic," "Puerto Rican," "Cuban," or "Mexican" to those who did not for each of the ordinal variables. Like "cultural natives," with whom they overlapped, Hispanic respondents were less likely than non-Hispanic survey respondents to report feeling vulnerable during the year in white. Only 41 percent of Hispanics remembered feeling vulnerable during the year compared to 58 percent of non-Hispanics ($X^2 = 4.52$, df = 1, $p = .034$; N = 150).

Results from ethnic analyses of other groups were similarly minimal, but they do provide some insights. Those who claimed African heritage were less likely (36 percent) than those who were not (57 percent) to recall gaining weight during the year in white ($X^2 = 4.86$, df = 1, $p = .027$; N = 168). Comparing those who reported they were "white," "Caucasian," or of European ancestry (regardless of Hispanic status) to those who did not, I found only one statistically significant result. The former were more likely to remember often feeling vulnerable (61 percent) during the year in white than those who did not claim white or European identities (43 percent) ($X^2 = 4.05$, df = 1, $p = .044$; N = 148).[7]

In general, although both cultural newcomers and natives were mostly positive about the year in white, there were some significant differences in their responses. Either newcomers to Lukumi seemed to have recalled the year as more difficult in a handful of specific ways or they were more likely than lifelong practitioners to discuss certain negative aspects of their experiences in an online survey. I found few ethnic distinctions from quantitative analyses of survey data. It is very possible that additional differences exist that I might have picked up upon had I asked different questions or had I asked them in different ways. Nevertheless, the modest results here do suggest that whether or not an individual has been raised around the traditions and an individual's ethnic and racial status may cause people to experience the year in white differently but that similarities outweigh differences in experiences, at least as far as present quantitative analyses can determine.

CONCLUSION

The people who enjoy and endure the blessings and struggles of the year in white in the United States are diverse. They experience the *yaworaje* in many different U.S. states. They come from many ethnic and religious backgrounds and have many different personal histories. Interestingly, many things that some discussed as struggles in the *yaworaje* others described as great blessings of the year in white. While many felt that the worst thing about the *yaworaje* was the solitude, it was also common for them to write that "quiet time for reflection" or "me time" was the best thing about the year. Where some wrestled with feelings of dependence when being served at religious events, others recalled being babied or pampered as one of their favorite parts of the year. Just as certain former *iyawos* listed internal growing pains as the most difficult part of the year, for others (and even for some of the same respondents), spiritual growth and its attendant conflicts were the most memorable part of their *yaworaje*. Many *iyawos* and former *iyawos* spoke of loving and hating the very same aspects of their year. Finally, a few results hint that cultural natives and newcomers and members of different ethnic groups may experience aspects of the year in white differently, despite great overlap.

Those who shared with me about their experience of the year in white offered a great variety of stories about a special time in their lives. Nevertheless, there were commonalities. While a great many survey respondents told stories of transformation, healing, and growth; serenity, solitude, and safety; emotional ups and downs; and the challenges of visibility, a variety of other stories were also told. These include themes of struggle, acceptance, and victories related to the rules of the year in white; social support and social rejection; and connections with the Orisha. These other themes will be taken up in the following chapters.

3 • *IYAWO* RULES

Standing at the podium of the small lecture hall between classes, I checked my e-mail as my Introduction to Sociology students left and my Social Inequalities students began to file in. The e-mail from my godmother was titled "*Iyawo* Rules." I hesitated before opening it and checked the clock. I had about eight or nine minutes before I would begin my next class. But the urge was irresistible. I had been waiting five days for a response to an e-mail to my godmother asking if ivory was acceptable for me to wear. (I knew that white was preferable but I had been unable thus far to find anything warmer than cotton in bright white, and winter was coming.) I had been concerned because I hadn't yet heard back from her.

I couldn't resist. The e-mail threatened to complicate my life beyond the question of off-white coats and sweaters. I clicked and began to read. There was a short note from my godmother to me and her other *iyawos* explaining that the attached list was particular to our house and that we shouldn't share it. I scanned through the extremely long list that followed, consisting of statement after statement of what "the *iyawo* must know," "the *iyawo* must realize" and "the *iyawo* cannot." It was thirteen pages long. Overwhelming! I paused, realizing I was showing signs of anxiety. My chest felt tight. My stomach churned. I took deep breaths and put aside the document to ready myself for class.

As soon as I arrived home after work I turned on the laptop again. While I waited for it to boot up, I considered my very physical reaction to the e-mail I hadn't had time to finish. Why was I reacting so strongly? It was true that the e-mail was sure to burden me further on a daily basis. But more than that was the feeling of unfairness. It seemed unfair to be held to rules—and so many rules—after the fact. Unfair that I was expected to live up to strictures I had not known about when I committed to make *ocha*. It seemed wrong.

I realized that my reaction was probably extreme. I didn't think most *iyawo* reacted this way. Perhaps *iyawos* raised in Lukumi culture understood the rules and the reasons for those rules in a way I did not. Perhaps *iyawos* with happy childhoods accepted their deprivations with an acceptance nurtured from past experience of having their needs met. But the hierarchical Lukumi house structure had put me in a position I had not experienced since I was a child, when I was subjected to the arbitrary and changing rules of a violent, patriarchal household. What I remember most from that time—and I've thankfully forgotten much of it—was frustration about the fact that it was impossible to negotiate the dizzying array of shifting rules unscathed. My situation as a *iyawo* was exposing deep issues from my youth.

At the beginning of the year in white, *iyawos* are treated as children. They eat on a mat on the floor with only spoons for utensils. They are told not to speak once food is placed before them. They are not to move or change posture until their plates are taken away and then returned. They must ask permission before satisfying many of their ordinary needs. Is it any surprise that such a situation would trigger emotional baggage from childhood? It seems *designed* to do so.

DIVERSITY OF RULES

Iyawos vary in how rigorously they follow the rules, how they feel about them, and how they react to them. There were some, like myself, who kept the regulations to the best of their ability, despite chafing at the restrictions. Others were obedient and uncomplaining. Some understood the reasons for the rules. Some didn't understand but trusted their godparents enough to endure. Some enjoyed many of the limits placed upon them. Some struggled with them. In this chapter I will discuss the rules for *iyawos* and how they were experienced by those who shared their stories with me.

ENUMERATING THE RULES

The Lukumi tradition in the United States is organized through a lineage-based, decentralized structure of *ilés, or* "houses." Members of the religion belong to the house of the person who initiated them, who is also described as their godparent, their *madrina* or *padrino*. They may also consider themselves to be a part of a larger *ilé* composed of the original initiator in a particular geographical area (Brandon 2002; Curry 1997). Despite the absence of a centralized Lukumi authority, many *iyawos* in the United States share general rules. Obá Miguel "Willie" Ramos (2008) lists the "Iyawó's behavior and dress code during the first three months":

> An iyawó is expected to be well dressed, and the iyawó's clothes are expected to be immaculately white, clean and never torn or mended. . . . Men must wear sleeved

undershirts, boxer shorts, long-sleeved shirts, loose-fitting pants, and socks at all times. Women must wear loose-fitting skirts and blouses or dresses—never pants—with minimum elbow length sleeves and a high neckline, brassieres, slips, panties, petite-pants—a boxer-like panty—knee-high socks, and a shawl. Neither can wear sandals other than house slippers to be at home, nor can they wear shoes that do not fully enclose the foot. . . .

Both men and women must wear a hat, cap, headscarf, or head covering of some sort during the entire period, removing it only to bathe and sleep. Under the head covering, a piece of cotton is also required for the first three months. . . .

The novice is also expected to practice proper hygiene. . . . An iyawó is not allowed to use perfumes or cosmetics of any sort, including perfumed soap, though exceptions are made for deodorant. . . . Men must be well shaved and groomed, and after the third month may visit a barbershop to keep their hair at a reasonable length. Some *ilés* forbid growing a beard and moustache for the entire year. Though women are not forbidden to cut their hair, they must not style, dye, or submit their hair to any unnecessary beauty treatments. Still, iyawó must be conscious of his/her appearance and personal hygiene at all times.

Thus, especially in the first three months of the year in white, *iyawos* are expected to dress flawlessly in white, modest clothing, including skirts for women and specific underclothing generally not worn in contemporary American society. They must keep their entire body covered in white—including their heads—with the exception of hands and faces. (One respondent mentioned wearing white gloves throughout her year in white, though this is not standard.) Ramos specifies that most aspects of beauty regimens associated with femininity are forbidden. *Iyawos* are not to "pluck their eyebrows, [or] paint their nails," and in many *ilés* they are not supposed to shave their "legs and underarms." They are not permitted to wear jewelry, including watches, with the exception of necklaces and bracelets consecrated to their Orisha, which they are required to wear. Although they must keep themselves clean, they are not permitted to use scented hygiene products and may not wear makeup or jewelry except for specific religious items that they may be required to wear. They are often told to sleep in white clothing with a small light on.

Iyawos are given similarly detailed rules for eating:

The iyawó must eat on a mat on the floor, and never at a table. Iyáwó is provided with a plate, cup—usually enameled tin—and spoon with which he or she is expected to eat and drink for the entire year. For the entire year the iyawó must not use a fork or knife to eat. In modern society where most iyawós must work, most godparents give them permission to eat at a table or a counter during the workday as it would be awkward, and probably unacceptable at most restaurants for an iyawó to walk in carrying their mat, plate, spoon and cup to eat on.

For the first few months, *iyawos* eat on a mat on the floor using a special set of dishes they must carry everywhere.

Ramos ends with a list of additional prohibitions and requirements for *iyawos* that illustrates the extent to which the rules pervade the daily routines of the Lukumi novice. *Iyawos* must avoid using mirrors, eating with knives and forks, getting rain on their heads, eating at restaurants, being outdoors at noon or midnight, going to the movies, swimming, attending social gatherings that are not religious and have not been approved by their godparents, enjoying alcohol or recreational drugs or even being in places where they are served, being photographed, touching or taking objects (such as money) directly from the hands of someone who has not been initiated, and going out at night.

Iyawos are generally required to sleep on white sheets and use white towels that they don't share with other members of their households. They are frequently instructed to refrain from recreational travel; from visiting bars, marketplaces, jails, hospitals, crowded areas, parties, cemeteries, and forests; from dancing, walking over holes such as sewer grates, waiting in lines, standing on street corners, participating in illegal activities; and to avoid being outside during inclement weather. *Iyawos* may be instructed to respect their elders and to avoid arguing, cursing, swearing, gossiping, and speaking negatively. At religious events they must defer to and "salute" those who were initiated before them, greeting those "elders" by prostrating themselves on the floor.

Sexual restrictions vary. In some houses *iyawos* must abstain from sexual activity for sixteen days or three months after initiation and must not engage in sexual activity with more than one person. Others seem to have a "don't ask, don't tell" policy concerning sexuality. Still others are told they are not permitted sexual activity outside marriage or a committed partnership for the entire year, and such relationships are not to be begun during the year.

Some *ilés* have even more stringent rules. For example, they may not allow *iyawos* to shop at all or leave their homes without an escort after 6 PM. In one house in which I inquired about the *iyawo* dress code recently, novices were told that they should try to wear natural fibers only, especially on their heads. However, the women were required to wear stockings (pantyhose), which are generally synthetic. *Iyawos* may be required to wear two white head coverings (generally a bandana-sized head scarf and a hat or larger head scarf) plus a piece of cotton on the head for the first three months and only one head covering for the remainder of the year. It is also common for *iyawos* to not cover their heads after the first three months.

Most *ilés* loosen rules that conflict with a person's work. For example, a nurse may use a watch at work, a police officer may wear a uniform, and a business executive may don a wig to cover her shaven head. Many *iyawos* are allowed or instructed to wear light colors to work to avoid detection as a *iyawo*. Some houses of Ocha loosen restrictions regarding gender. For example, when not at a religious ceremony, women may not have to wear skirts or may not have to wear all of the undergarments generally required at more formal events. Indeed, in the first open-ended comments section of the online survey, most responses noted the adjustments to the rules that were allowed in their house or to them individually. Perhaps the most common was the wearing of light colors or uniforms to work and eating at a desk or table (instead of on a mat on the floor) when on the job.

Respondents varied in the rules they kept. Only 60 percent said that they were celibate for the first three months (or more) of the year in white. (Since rules vary by house, this does not necessarily indicate they were breaking them.) Fifty-five percent wore only white to work during the *iyawo* year. Twenty-three percent slept on a mat on the floor for the first three months or more during their year. (The latter practice, while common in my house of Ocha, is not mentioned in Ramos's list above or in some of the other lists I have seen. Nevertheless, I found the practice to be a comforting and humbling aspect of my *yaworaje* that I was reluctant to give up once I was given permission to do so.) While there is great variation in *iyawo* rules, a core experience of the *yaworaje* does seem to exist. (See Table 3.)

TABLE 3.   *Iyawo* Rules and Practices

	Disagreed	Agreed	N
I followed iyawo rules completely.	10% (N = 18)	89% (N = 156)	175
I wore only white to work during my iyawo year.	36 (63)	55 (97)	174
I often felt the iyawo rules were unfair.	70 (121)	27 (47)	173
I slept on a mat on the floor for 3 months (or more) during my year in white.	64 (112)	23 (40)	174
I was celibate for the first 3 months (or more) of my year in white.	30 (51)	60 (104)	172
Many of the iyawo rules didn't make sense to me.	71 (122)	28 (49)	173

FOLLOWING THE RULES

Most survey respondents (89 percent) agreed somewhat or strongly with the statement they followed the regulations of the year in white completely. Although many explained that certain restrictions or prescriptions were waived or modified for them, few admitted to carelessly disobeying the instructions of their elders in the tradition or to intentionally breaking rules. A handful described defiant episodes that were followed first by consequences and then by compliance. Tiffany, a priest of Oshun, illustrated this pattern: "It was wonderful for the first 3 months. Then I became disobedient and I did not follow the *iyawo* rules. Things began to fall apart, [and] as a result I had a difficult time with employment and I lost my apartment. This also caused my godmother to increase my *iyawo* time by three months as a 'discipline measure.' . . . Toward the end I did not want to end my *iyawo* period; it had become a comfort zone and the norm for me." Similarly, although he was raised in a large Lukumi community, Xavier "lashed out" against the restraints of the *yaworaje*. His *babalawo padrino* explained the reasons for the expectations, after which he was more observant and deferent, viewing the *yaworaje* as an important "year of sacrifice." The few respondents who admitted to disregarding the rules of the *yaworaje* tended to tell stories of redemption and lessons learned.

Iyawos and former *iyawos* commonly said that they "tried to follow the rules," kept *iyawo* rules "by the book," or were "good *iyawos*." Rosa, who underwent the *kariocha* for health reasons, reported that despite being "tested by the Orishas," she "was able to follow all *iyawo* rules." Estevan, a priest of Yemaya, mentioned that beyond the several accommodations that were made for him because of his work, he "followed what the Orisha laid down for" him "to the letter." Such descriptions of attempted adherence were common.

Sixteen participants responded to the online survey question "What *iyawo* rules did you find most difficult to keep?" with "nothing" or "none." Some explained that they were proud to be *iyawo* or added that the regulations were part of the sacrifice expected of the year in return for so much more. Others wrote that the regimen was simple or easy to follow. Still others noted the temporary nature of the year in white, listing this as the reason they found the proscriptions and prescriptions to be rather easy. Leon, a priest of Obatalá who underwent *kariocha* for "personal reasons," recalled that the constraints were not "really hard" for him because he "knew it was for only a year." Oluwo[1] Antonio replied: "Rules are rules. And you just follow them." Beatriz, who promised to make *ocha* "to save" her father when he underwent open heart surgery, answered: "When one respects, one has to do all as they say. If not, why do it?" In her interview, Shango priest Silvia expressed a similar notion: "People want to change the religion to suit themselves. If you didn't like the rules of the religion, don't get in it." Thus, some found nothing difficult about the extensive guidelines for *iyawo* behavior and may have even felt that the question in my survey or interview bordered on disrespect.

Iyawos comply with the rules of the *yaworaje* for many reasons. Large-scale conformity is partially explainable by the fact that 70 percent of the participants believed that the rules were fair and 71 percent felt that they were understandable. *Iyawos* followed their assigned protocol because it made sense. Fawn, who undertook the initiation because she "fell in sync" with the religion and wanted the change in her life she believed it would provide, theorized that experience with the religion may account for some of the variations in how *iyawos* handled the rules: "I had been involved in the religion for 13 years before I was initiated so I knew very well what to expect and what to do." In her experience it was "people who are only involved a short time" who "do not know what to expect and are usually the ones to find the rules hard to live by." Likewise, Adriana told me that though she counted the days until she would be free from *iyawo* restraints, she "understood the whys of the rules of *yaworaje*." These respondents linked compliance to comprehension.

The limitations *iyawos* face are generally justified using one or more of the three basic themes of the *yaworaje*: transformation, socialization, and seclusion. Many regulations are legitimated by referring to the liminal status of the *iyawo*, a position of becoming. They are in between the people they were before and the fully "crowned" people they will be. *Iyawos* are separated from their previous identities and are encouraged to identify with the Orisha who are said to "own their heads." They are supported in experiencing their initiation as a rebirth. Some of the prescriptions of the year, such as wearing white clothes rather than the colors associated with one's former life, avoiding seeing oneself in mirrors, and eschewing habits perhaps associated with negative outcomes in one's former life such as drinking, drugs, gossiping, swearing, and promiscuity, can be seen (at least in part) as fostering the transformative process. *Iyawos* must learn during the *yaworaje* to subordinate themselves to the needs of the Orisha and the religious community. The norms for *iyawos* regarding submission in the community, such as deferring to one's elders, can be justified in this way. Finally, most of the constraints of the *yaworaje* can be explained by the fact that the year in white is viewed as a time when newborn *iyawos* are sheltered as children by their parents. *Iyawos* must be guarded from the seen and the unseen. Because mirrors are "considered portals to other realms" (Ramos 2008), they are a potential spiritual threat to vulnerable new initiates. It is believed that people who have not been initiated can transmit negativity to the pure, "newborn" *iyawo* through touch or even by the exchange of objects. Apparitional activity, which is believed to exist more strongly in the liminal periods of noon and midnight and in liminal places such as forests and cemeteries, must be avoided. Like children, *iyawos* must not use knives and forks or be out after nightfall. Vulnerable *iyawos* must be sheltered spiritually by covering their bodies in the comforting coolness of white cloth.

Whether or not they understood all the rules completely, many *iyawos* kept them as best as they could out of respect for their godparents, the Orisha, or the commitment they had made to the process. They were "good *iyawos*" because they loved or feared Ocha, because they felt it was their responsibility or their path, because they expected a particular outcome for their efforts, or because they wanted to make their godparents proud. Helen explained that she "tried very hard to be a good *iyawo* and generally succeeded." Despite experiencing "some resistance to all the rules a *iyawo* must follow," she attempted to do her best: "Having made the decision to follow this path, it didn't make sense to 'cheat' on the experience." Sacrifice and reciprocity is another big reason for following the rules of the year in white. Commenting on celibacy in particular, Fawn felt that the effort made of the *yaworaje* was reciprocated: "I feel if you ask the Orishas to sacrifice for you then you can sacrifice at least that for them." Most who undergo the elaborate and often expensive *ocha* initiation have made substantial sacrifices of time and money to do so. Why make such a large offering if one did not intend to complete the process? In addition, many "crown" for compelling reasons in their lives: to assure the healthy birth of a child, to overcome medical or spiritual dangers, or to rise above their present circumstances. *Kariocha* is often seen in a way that is similar to the way the Catholic folk practice of making a promise to a saint is viewed (see Savastano n.d.). In these cases, the devotion of initiation is performed as part of a bargain in exchange for the blessings of life, health, safety, or peace for oneself or family members.

A final reason for following the rules of the *yaworaje* is to avoid a *multa* (penalty or fine). One *olorisha* told the story of an abusive godmother who used the threat of a *multa* to gain her compliance to many regulations that did not make sense to her. My *madrina* periodically threatened me and her other *iyawos* with *multas*, generally as a joke, for some pretended violation of *iyawo* behavior. For example, when my godmother asked my godsister about what she had been doing with her time while she was a *iyawo*, my godsister might tease, "Nothing much. I've just been hanging out at cemeteries around midnight and then drinking at the neighborhood bar." Another godsister would up the ante, adding "And didn't you tell me, *Iyawo*, that you were lying on the gravestones and smoking pot?" Despite the jesting, I was aware that my godmother had given a *multa* to one of her other godchildren for a drug-related incident during the year in white. Although it is discussed less frequently than the other reasons for compliance with the rules, it is important to note that there is a "stick" as well as "honey" associated with the *iyawo* regimen.

Traditionally, I have been told, *iyawos* were monitored by community members, including those who belonged to other houses. *Iyawos* were viewed as subject to inspection by elders in the community, even those who did not belong to one's direct line in Ocha. My second godfather in the religion, the late Afolabi (aka Clay Keck or Shloma Rosenberg), told me a story once about encountering a *iyawo* in the street dressed in tight blue jeans, no head coverings, and no white clothes. Although my former *padrino* was not the *iyawo's* godparent, he claimed to have exacted a *multa* from the *iyawo* that both the *iyawo* and his godparent honored. Vestiges of this tradition persist, even in today's more scattered, anonymous society. Many Orisha communities remain small enough that if someone in the tradition doesn't know you, they may at least know of your godparent or her godparent. Whether or not this is the case, *iyawos* are often told and frequently believe that they may be subject to scrutiny by others and held to account for expected conduct at any time, if not by nearby *ilé* members, then by a stranger who will recognize them. Being all lit up in whites creates a situation for *iyawos* like the surveillance within Foucault's (1979) panopticon. In such a situation where one is always capable of being seen but is never certain of when, inmates learn to internalize the discipline of the institution. Similarly, the visibility of *iyawos* causes many Lukumi novices to accept the regimen as if they were constantly monitored. For this reason, I generally found *iyawos* to be some of the least interesting interviewees. They are instructed to avoid arguments, gossip, negative and harsh language, and sometimes, speaking unless spoken to.

Despite being philosophical about them, I too internalized *iyawo* protocols. About two months into my *yaworaje*, my *madrina's* godmother surprised me by calling me on the phone to set up a visit while she was in town. I wrote a short entry about the encounter in my journal:

Madrina Julia scared the crap out of me by calling while I was on the other line with my Mom. I didn't expect to hear her voice over the wires. She showed up as an "unknown caller" so I didn't [say] "bendicion" until she identified herself. I [then quickly] looked around and inventoried myself to make sure I wasn't breaking any rules. (Isn't that ridiculous?! As if she could see me over the phone drinking a beer in a black bathing suit.)

The latter was sarcasm, of course. (The most I would have dared to depart from *iyawo* rules was to go bare-armed and sockless while in my own apartment alone.) *Iyawos* internalize the discipline of the *yaworaje* and its many rules in order to enjoy protections that come from following the *iyawo* regulations; to respect godparents, tradition, and the Orisha; to obtain the benefits they made *ocha* to receive; and/or to avoid punishment.

ENDURING THE RULES

Despite the reluctance of a handful of survey and interview participants to speak of difficulties with *iyawo* standards, most were willing to talk about a variety of rules they had trouble with. Even for those who have great respect for Orisha and their godparents and for those who want to be "good *iyawos*," the year in white is not always easy. For those in more orthodox houses, the dictates of the *yaworaje* are so all-encompassing that it would be strange if *iyawo* expressed no discomfort about following them. One hundred twenty-eight survey respondents (89 percent) answered the question "What *iyawo* rules did you find most difficult to keep?" with minor or major complaints. Many of the same people discussed specific *iyawo* restrictions or prescriptions in answer to the open-ended question, "What were the worst parts about your year in white?" and occasionally in answer to the question "What were the best parts of your year in white?" *Iyawos* and former *iyawos* most commonly cited policies about dress, keeping covered, and carrying things everywhere (N = 51; 35 percent). The second on the list of issues that were mentioned as difficult (N = 43) concerned prohibitions against touching, shaking hands, and exchanging objects with those who have not been initiated; 30 percent wrote about such issues. Next were rules about going to social functions and being out at night (N = 34; 24 percent), avoiding mirrors and regulations concerning grooming and accessorizing (N = 26; 18 percent), miscellaneous prohibitions (N = 23; 16 percent), instructions about eating on the mat (N = 17; 12 percent), protocol concerning subordinate status (N = 13; 9 percent), norms concerning celibacy and sleeping on the mat (N = 11; 8 percent), and general complaints about *iyawo* requirements (N = 8; 6 percent).[2] (See Figure 3.)

Dress, Covering, and Carrying. The rules that *iyawos* and former *iyawos* described most frequently as difficult to observe were those involving dress, covering, and carrying. These are the standards of behavior that are the most visible about the *yaworaje*; they are the regimen that (along with rules of grooming) shape what sociologist Erving Goffman ([1959] 1990) called "the presentation of self in everyday life." These norms most obviously identify a *iyawo* to others and are most likely to be considered as reflections on the godparents of the *iyawo*. The visibility of these guidelines makes them more highly susceptible than many others to "policing" by godparents, community members, and by *iyawos* themselves. For example, Roger, who was an *aleyo* for twenty-five years before entering the year in white, confessed in the online survey that he worried a great deal about keeping clean while he was a *iyawo* because he "didn't want to bring a 'bad name' to the religion or to" his house of Ocha. In my experience, this attitude is common among *iyawos*. Protocol concerning dress and covering the body are numerous and detailed. According to the Web site of the Ilé Osha Oló Obatalá Oshagrinan Adé Yeri Temple (Jane 2007):

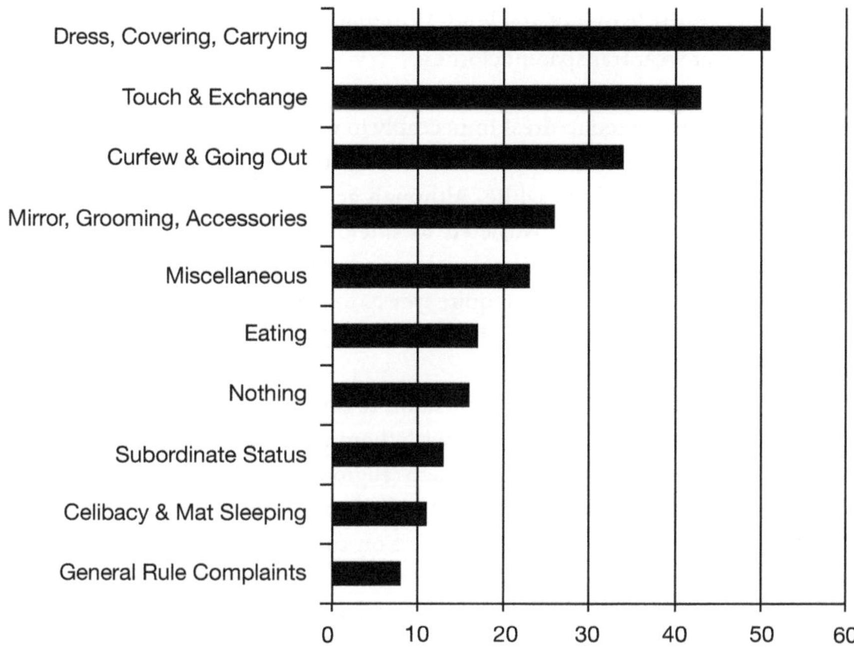

FIGURE 3. Most difficult *Iyawo* rules by frequency of mention in survey

The Iyawo must keep his/her head covered for the first three months . . .

The Iyawo must be dressed in white during a year and sixteen days both in public and at home. The Iyawo must sleep wearing his/her consecration white plain clothes including (caps; socks, tights, stockings; underwear, pyjamas [*sic*] and nightgown/nightdress). The body must be totally protected by white clothes.

The Iyawo must always be dressed correctly. Clothes must be clean and cannot be ragged in any way.

The Iyawo (if a man) must go out with shoes, socks, underwear undershirt, trousers, handkerchief, long sleeves shirt and must always wear the Igbodun cap under the hat or cap he wears to go out. He must also use a white umbrella. After the third month, the Iyawo can wear short sleeves shirt or pull over [*sic*] . . .

The female Iyawo must go out with shoes, long stockings[,] bloomers, serge skirt, skirt, brassiere (bra), long sleeves blouse, quilla (kind of turban made with white cotton) and a white umbrella. After the first three months, the female Iyawo can wear only a headscarf on her head but the rest of the clothes must be white . . .

The male Iyawo must not wear shorts nor tight clothes. Women are not allowed to wear low necked blouse/dress nor shoulder straps nor tight short skirts nor Lycra shorts/pants of any kind. Whether a woman or a man, the Iyawo should never wear transparent clothes.

Most *iyawos* are expected to dress impeccably in white, modest clothing, including skirts for women and abundant anachronistic underclothing. They must cover most of their body in white. Although accommodations are commonly made for work, *iyawos* are instructed to shield themselves in white clothing even when sleeping. In many *ilés*, rules about covering may be loosened after the first three months. Some do not require *iyawos* to cover their heads after the first three months. Also, most *ilés* seem to permit the wearing of short sleeves after the first three months.

Rules about carrying are also important. It is standard for orthoprax *iyawos* to be required to carry several objects with them wherever they go, especially in the first three months and almost always to religious functions: a white umbrella, a set of special dishes and spoon, a mat to eat upon, and a white bath towel to place over one's thighs while eating seated on the floor. Along with the white "costume," these form the "props" of the *iyawo's* "role" that, according to a dramaturgical sociological analysis (see Goffman [1959] 1990), identify the *iyawo* to others. Finally, there are numerous elaborations on the rules of dress, covering, and carrying—variations that may be specific to houses. For example, *iyawos* may be told not to purchase clothes that have been worn by someone else; in this case, all clothing must be bought new. In another variation—unless I misunderstood one of the survey respondents—some houses may ask that *iyawos* wear only the clothes they purchased for the seven-day *ocha* initiation ceremony.

In their responses to the survey question "What *iyawo* rules did you find most difficult to keep?" thirty-two recalled that *iyawo* rules concerning dress, covering, and carrying were particularly hard to comply with. An additional nineteen respondents referred to these rules as the worst part of the year in white. Iyawo Monette used the survey as an opportunity to vent about what can certainly be a frustrating discipline: "I hate having to wear skirts every day, regardless of the weather. Though I adhere to the rule, it is at times, tremendously difficult. Similarly, I hated all the layers of clothing that have to be worn, even in the summer time. . . . I hate having to carry around my own eating ware. I actually like eating out of my own plates, but hate carrying heavy bags." Eva, who experienced the *yaworaje* as a teen because her mother was warned by the Orisha Elegua that she must do so by the age of fifteen, groaned, "All I wore was white, from the heat wave of 1996, to the blizzards in . . . 1997. [It was] not fun." Although it was foretold when she was sixteen years old that she would be initiated, Maritza waited years before her ordination. She wrote that the worst part of the year in white for her was "the summertime, when we had to wear *bomboches* [pantaloons], slips, stockings, and bobby socks. Not to mention long sleeves. Oh my God!" Wearing white, donning skirts and heaps of old-fashioned undergarments (if a woman), keeping oneself covered, and lugging an extra bag everywhere is not always easy.

Workplaces were a particular source of concern for *iyawos*. Iyawo Alba, who made *ocha* to "fulfill a promise" to her "Baba Chango," worried that "wearing the proper iyawo clothes (skirt, bomboches, pañuelo, etc.) would have stigmatized" her at work, providing a "deterrent for promotions." Luckily, she was granted a relaxation of the rules while on the job. Not all *iyawos* are granted similar flexibility. Sheila, who underwent initiation because of her "deep faith in the Orishas" and health problems, was not given permission to alter *iyawo* garb when practicing her profession. She also found it difficult to monitor her appearance given the taboo on mirrors: "I was going to work with full *iyawo* regalia on, including two head scarves and two layers of cotton. I didn't know how I looked. I didn't know if I properly tied my scarf, and since I lived alone, I had no one to check it out for me." Not only were the prohibitions awkward, but they caused her trouble: "I . . . was reported to my licensing board, launching an emotionally and financially costly investigation into my life and medical practice." Some of those who found that wearing all white to work was problematic persisted despite the obstacles and others adapted by wearing light-colored clothing. The accommodation to mainstream American society of altering the *iyawo* uniform for work has become so standard that it seems to be expected, perhaps as a way of keeping the year in white secret. When I was on the *trono* during the seven-day *ocha* initiation ceremony, I mentioned to an Orisha priest my expectation that I would wear all white to work. He expressed surprise and advised me against doing so.

Iyawos and former *iyawos* found the dress code challenging for a variety of reasons. It marks the wearer as deviant; it is impossible to dress fashionably and avoid "standing out" in a crowd. White clothes aren't slimming; they hide nothing. Whites require a great deal of labor to keep clean. In their first few months *iyawos* must be completely covered even in the heat of summer. They must wear bright whites even during cold winters when white clothes may be more difficult to find. Pilar, who made *ocha* because it was determined through an oracle at her husband's ordination that she would do so, exclaimed, "I could only wear skirts below the knee and long sleeve shirts with nylons and closed shoes. Can you imagine this in Miami?" Iyawo Ronna discovered that it was difficult for her to wear shoes all the time; "I love going barefoot," she said. Harmony wrote, "I hated the all-white stockings in 100-plus [degree] weather. It was the worst." In addition, after a while, white becomes just plain boring. Harmony continued, "The white got very tiring and standing out so much all the time was difficult." Antonio admitted that he became weary of "wearing the same color every day." Also, *iyawo* garb can be tough to obtain. White skirts are simply not fashionable all year round in many parts of the United States and may not be available in stores. Finding completely white shoes can also be a problem, as can finding warmer clothing. Wool socks are rarely made in anything brighter than ivory. Nancy, who underwent the *kariocha* because she believed "it was required for continued life" and "to achieve success and fulfill" her destiny, said, "Living in the mid-west, with the shorter warm season it was hard to find a wardrobe of white clothes. . . . It was hard to find white clothing . . . warm enough to stay warm. Finding white shoes was also a challenge outside of sandals." Isabel, a priest of Obatalá, wrote that she could not find a white coat and instead had to wear several layers to protect her from the cold of winter.

Conventions for *iyawos* regarding dress are gendered. Although both women and men are supposed to cover their heads and wear copious underclothing, in orthodox gendered houses, only *iyawo* men are permitted to wear pants. Unlike men, women must wear several types of underthings and a shawl. Several women survey and interview participants complained about the dress codes for their gender. They found it challenging to wear skirts and nylons, tights, pantyhose, or stockings all the time. Or they resented having to wear extra undergarments and shawls that men are not required to wear. Daniela wrote, "If I had one rule to change I would change the fact that females wear a lot more things than men."

A number of *iyawos* and former *iyawos* recalled that they disliked having to cover their heads all the time, even though many understood the reasons for it. Nevertheless, head covering isn't necessarily easy day after day. Iyawo Peter, who became ordained because "it was marked in odu" and because he believed it would help him to "live in proper alignment," wrote, "Covering my head some-times was a difficult experience." María found it inconvenient: "Having my head covered was okay in the beginning. Then afterwards it became a nuisance." Xavier, who underwent the *kariocha* to further his own potential and because "it was quite natural to do the same year long sacrifice" as his mother and father had done before him, nevertheless found it difficult to wear a hat during the first three months: "I can't stand wearing hats, and I would often rebel and conveniently 'for-get' my hat at home." Iyawo Dana, who made her sacrifices because it was her des-tiny, to improve her health, and because she had a desire to serve, had comparable complaints, "Although I totally understand and would not want to have my head not wrapped while an iyawo, I don't like having to wrap my head every day."

Maintaining a pristine white wardrobe requires quite a bit of effort and can become an obsession for some *iyawos*. Lukumi novices commonly exchange laundering advice, strategies about avoiding stains, and tips on stores that have white skirts, pants, tops, shoes, coats, or umbrellas on sale. Many wrote about the enormous job of keeping their whites spotlessly white. Ernesto, who made *ocha* because it was his "calling," noted simply that "white is difficult to keep clean." Kimberly offered a single-word reason for joining the Lukumi priesthood—"love"—and then gave a similarly terse response to the question on the online survey about the worst thing about the year in white: "stains."

Victor, who dedicated his head to the Orisha Obatalá before undertaking his initiation as a *babalawo,* explained "It is hard watching yourself for every scrape, every speck of dirt and getting changed every time you're messy." Xavier said, "It's surprising how easily all your clothes can have these little stains, and you have no idea how they got there." Shoes are another concern for *iyawos.* Georgia, who lived in the country, wrote of the difficulty of keeping "shoes clean while walking around in the mud." Ángel, who dedicated himself to Orisha out of love, said, "Keeping your clothes immaculate was a great challenge. However in time, I learned to keep them looking new always." Laundering whites is a skill that every *iyawo* learns to perfect with week after week of practice (except those who are fortunate enough to have someone do it for them). In the journal I kept during my *yaworaje* I found numerous mentions of washing clothing. More than once I waxed poetic about the process of sorting, applying various chemicals depending on the type of stain, scrubbing, and folding. Indeed, at times, maintaining my clothes felt to me like a part-time job. Here is an excerpt that I wrote about three-quarters of the way through my year in white:

> Winter is hard on whites. I spent about four hours yesterday just dealing with laundry. And I broke a personal record: 2 bleach sticks in one laundry day! I think I've probably lost another skirt. Somehow that splatter that gets on everything when it's snowy and slushy, stands up to both enzymes and even massive quantities of bleach. Laundry lately feels like I'm slowly losing an unwinnable battle. Eventually all whites lose their whiteness to browns and yellows, right? And the hot washing needed to really rout stains shrinks a good deal of the rest. I'm just trying to make it through four and a half more months without having to spend too much more money on clothes.

Laundry can become a weekly battle when one is wearing only white, no matter what the season or the weather, when s/he has been charged with maintaining those whites spotlessly.

Carrying was also commonly mentioned as a challenge of the *yaworaje.* Iyawos must have umbrellas available wherever they go because they are not supposed to allow their heads to be touched by rain. They must also carry their own plate, bowl, cup, and spoon, along with a mat and towel for eating on the floor. Iyawo Ronna complained about the large bag she had to transport everywhere, "cup, bowl, spoon, umbrella and anything else I might need." Joan noted that "it was difficult to not eat on other people's plates and carry around my own." Luís, who underwent the *kariocha* for health reasons, recalled the trouble of having to remember to bring his plate and spoon wherever he went. Iyawo Rebecca "loved the Orisha and felt called to be their priest," but she became so weary of carrying that she "ended up keeping a spare mat" in the car and an extra cup at work.

Iyawos often felt particularly accountable to follow the rules about white dress, covering, and carrying because of their high visibility. But these rules, simple as they may seem on the surface, required courage, discipline, and labor.

Touch and Exchange. The rules that were next most frequently mentioned in survey responses as difficult to keep during the year in white involved touching and exchanging things with persons who have not been initiated. *Iyawos* are told to avoid physical contact with people who are not initiated Orisha priests, except for children. In addition, they are not to take something directly from people who have not been initiated. Instead, when receiving change from a store clerk during a purchase, for example, *iyawos* are supposed to have cashiers put money on the counter or drop it in a bag. As it was explained to me, the purpose of this rule is spiritual protection. *Iyawos*, who are seen as clean and purified, are believed to be open and vulnerable to the energies of others. However, for the person who works outside the home and the Lukumi religious community and who lacks the luxury of a personal shopper, this rule can be difficult to follow. Cashiers may take offense. Co-workers may be resentful. The breach of norms about social interactions may call unwanted attention to an individual's status as a *iyawo* and raise questions that are not easily answered in brief, casual interactions.

When I was a *iyawo*, my god-aunt in *ocha* advised me about dealing with this restriction. She told me to pretend to be searching for something in my bag when I was at the counter making a purchase. When the cashier would try to hand me the change, I should then hold open my purse and say nonchalantly, "Oh, just throw it in, please." In this way the not-touching was more likely to be interpreted as involving convenience than the potentially offensive issue of cleanliness. This is a useful method, but I found that it did not always work. Sometimes I would forget the pretense until it was too late or I would leave my bag in the car. After experiencing a few hostile reactions in shops, I became worried. It seemed to me that as a *iyawo* I should radiate peace and calmness, not suspicion and negativity. Concerned, I called my godmother and asked her about the rule. The way she thought about it, she said, was that during the *ocha* initiation ceremony I had been cleansed and filled with shiny new light, so much so that I might even attract others. Many of the *iyawo* rules, she explained, were meant to keep me in that spiritual light for as long as possible. Each exchange with strangers risked decreasing my brightness just a little bit.

I was not alone in finding prohibitions against touch and exchange with noninitiates to be especially problematic during the *yaworaje*. Forty-three *iyawos* and former *iyawos* who responded to my survey wrote about difficulties with this taboo. Most commonly they found it troublesome in fleeting interactions to evade physical contact with other people who attempted to greet them. They also had problems avoiding taking things they were handed. Nicolás wrote: "This proscription always made me feel like I was afraid of germs or that I was too 'holy' to touch others." Ruth, a priest of Yemaya, recalled that she "relaxed the rule" for certain friends whose physical contact actually made her feel better after trying *iyawo* days. Kendra found the rule particularly onerous when she was in Latin America, where touch among strangers is customary. Denise wrote that she found the restriction most burdensome when she attended funerals, where she needed to comfort "cousins and others with hugs and kisses." Many *iyawos* and former *iyawos* wrote that this limitation caused social awkwardness and discomfort.

Respondents grumbled particularly about keeping the rules in their workplaces. Businesspeople were expected to greet others with a handshake. Police officers and nurses needed to handle others throughout the workday. Pilar wrote that "it was difficult because I worked in the university and could not shake hands with people I was introduced to." Joan explained, "It was difficult not to shake hands when introduced to the new guy at work, or be able to exchange items in order to avoid exchanging energy. I didn't want to offend anyone while I wanted to protect the Orisha energy newly implanted in me." Iyawo Faith "had to break that rule at work." Paul, who came to *ocha* as a personal calling and after careful research, was unable to avoid touching co-workers. However, he invented ways of dealing with the situation by cleansing himself as soon as possible afterward: "You wipe them off, wash them [spiritually from your hands] ASAP, use *cascarilla* [a chalk-like substance considered to be cleansing], etc." Laura, who listed many reasons for making *ocha,* appeared to have interpreted the rule as only involving people's hands. During her work with vendors, she attempted to shake their wrists instead. For many of the *iyawos* and former *iyawos* who wrote about this question on the survey, avoiding touch and exchange with others was particularly uncomfortable and sometimes impossible, especially in workplaces.

Respondents shared creative ways of complying with the rule. Andy, a priest of Oya, wrote, "My job ... at the time included a lot of handing off of paperwork. I just had to come up with ways to say, 'Oh, just lay it on the desk!' Or I would just step into the office and lay the items on the desk saying, 'I'll just put these here ... Gotta run!'" Joan elaborated: "I had to think fast to find a way to give and get items to someone else without handing it to them directly. Once I had to give my parking ticket to the lot guard by walking a few steps past him to put it on the ledge of the booth window. He reacted by getting mad. At a counter I invented a way to receive change by opening a bag to receive change. That woman was fine dropping the coins into my plastic bag. I noticed [that] how a person responded to my ... assigned taboo was their choice." Despite the ingenuity of *iyawos,* the reactions of strangers varied.

Some *iyawos* reported that their avoidance of touch and exchange elicited negative reactions. Elena wrote that most people felt offended when she did not take money from their hands. Diane explained that "people took me placing the money on the counter and not taking things/change from them directly extremely personally. I had quite a few negative reactions to that. Muslim men were great because they don't want to touch you anyway." Ted recalled, "I got into some strange situations with people cursing at me for not taking money from someone's hands." Georgia, a priest of Obatalá who practiced Wicca before feeling compelled to make *ocha,* said, "Buying items at a cash register became downright stressful. I got good at looking busy fiddling around with my purse when the cashier tried to hand me change. If I asked people to set the money or credit card down before I picked it up, sometimes people got miffed." *Iyawos* found that following a rule that was intended to protect them was sometimes awkward and sometimes caused conflict with others.

Although it may seem more innocuous than many of the other restrictions, the taboo against touching non-initiates and taking objects from the hands of non-initiates presented more widespread and memorable problems than most other rules of the *yaworaje.* Georgia spoke of the human cost of this rule for a single *iyawo* living at a distance from her Ocha community. She might go for months without human touch: "Not touching people was hard. It got so that I craved hugs from the members of my *ilé* who were allowed to touch me." Joyce, a priest of Yemaya who "finally found what" she "was looking for" in Ocha, wrote, "I found the *ewos* [proscriptions] that contradict 'normal society' to be difficult because there is no way to avoid them without looking like a butt-face." The taken-for-grantedness of touch and exchange may be highlighted only when a person is trying to avoid it. Ana recalled that she would often forget about the rule until it was too late: "You forget, and it is not until you are in the middle of touching or exchanging money you go, 'Man I was not supposed to do that!'" Taboos concerning touch and exchange affect *iyawos'* daily interactions with strangers and co-workers at a very basic level, requiring innovative strategies for daily practice.

Curfew and Going Out. The next most frequently mentioned rule as one that was hard to keep during the year in white involved curfews and social restrictions. *Iyawos* are told not to be out at night and not to attend most social gatherings. According to the Web site of the Ilé Osha Oló Obatalá Oshagrinan Adé Yeri Temple (Jane 2007):

The Iyawo must avoid going out before six (6) in the morning and must be back home any time before 6 pm. After the first three months, the Iyawo must go back home before midnight (12). . . .
The Iyawo should not sit in public parks, neither should he/she stand on a corner and he/she must not go to bars/pubs, night clubs, cabarets, market places nor must he/she visit or go to ruined constructions, jails, cemeteries, funeral

parlours, hospitals, burials. The Iyawo should never visit seriously injured or ill people. . . .

The Iyawo should not go to public parties, dancing balls, carnivals, fancy dress balls, (masked balls) or masquerades and should also avoid crowded areas or places. . . .

The Iyawo should avoid dark places like movies (cinemas) and the like. . . .

Although the rules vary from house to house and individual *iyawo* may be given exceptions through divination or through permission from their godparents, when *iyawos* are not at work or attending *ilé* religious events, they must generally be at home. This is especially the case in the darker season of the year, when daylight hours are few. (Some religious houses specify a time when *iyawo* must be home; others tell their *iyawo* to be indoors from dusk until dawn.) Very few social spaces are considered safe for *iyawos*, although in some *ilés*, *iyawos* may be escorted by their godparents or other priests in their religious houses to social spaces that would ordinarily be off limits, such as religious events outside their immediate *ilé*, restaurants, and even movies, though the latter are ordinarily permitted only after the first three months. *Iyawos* who are single and live alone may find this rule isolating, as may *iyawos* who don't work outside the home. *Iyawos* who live at a great distance from their religious house may have fewer social opportunities than those with religious family living nearby.

Because I was single, lived alone, and lived across the country from my *ilé*, I was particularly concerned about the social injunctions of the *yaworaje*. I agonized over the decision to make *ocha*, in part because of general apprehension about the commitment but especially because I worried that the *yaworaje* might deepen my feelings of isolation and depression, some of the same things—because of heartbreak and recovery from cancer—that were driving me toward *ocha*. I worried that given my already poor health, I would sit at home the entire year and watch my butt grow larger, exacerbating my health problems. Given that I did much of my work from home, I envisioned myself going days each week without social contact. Eventually I spoke to my godmother about my concerns. It seemed to me that I would survive the year as long as I maintained two social lifelines: my synagogue and my gym. My godmother agreed that attending synagogue events, even in the evening, should be permissible during my *yaworaje*; it was both religious and a way that I maintained strong connections to my ancestors. When I made the request to attend the gym, I was inspired by my god-aunt, who had attended yoga classes almost every day of her year in white, using the social constraints of the *yaworaje* as an opportunity to improve herself mentally and physically. I believed that such a practice would be perfect during my year in white; I would exercise daily and improve my fitness. I had even figured out how to avoid both mirrors and being seen uncovered at the gym. My godmother agreed to this as well.

It wasn't until a few months into my year in white that I confessed in an online LiveJournal entry that I had accidentally attended the gym seven days in a row. (I had been attempting to go five days a week, ensuring enough rest for healthy progress.) The next time I spoke to my godmother on the phone, I discovered that we had had a misunderstanding. She had no idea I was attending the gym so frequently. It was too much, she insisted. From that point on, she instructed, I was to attend no more than once a week. I thought about my gym routine and its careful (or compulsive) mix of cardio and resistance training. How would once a week be of any use? After months of enduring a hypothyroid state in which I had low energy, gained weight, and was depressed, I was now at a normal metabolic range and finally had a chance to lose some of the pounds I had not been able to shed since my surgery a few years before. In addition, going to the gym served as a sort of social lifeline for me. My exercise routine ensured that I left the house almost every day. What would I do without it? What kind of weird social hermit would I become? I was upset. Why would my godmother take something so important away from me? I considered abandoning my godmother and the *yaworaje*. She didn't seem to understand what was important to my welfare. I did not like being told what I could and could not do. She had changed the rules on me midstream. All of these things whirled through my mind while my heart seemed to beat in my throat. I managed to croak out a request for an explanation: "Why?"

My godmother explained that the gym was a place where people go to "clean themselves," to release pent-up energy and negativity. Isn't that why I went? she asked rhetorically. "But I need to go for my health," I persisted. I heard the beginnings of annoyance in her voice. She had consulted with her elders and they had agreed with her, she told me. The gym was no place for a *iyawo*. If I wanted to go once I week I could. But no more. I would have to come up with another way. There was the sound of finality in her voice. She had made her decision.

Somehow, even though I wasn't thinking rationally, I quashed my rebellious anger and my outrage at being controlled. Yet even as I railed silently at what I perceived as my godmother's misuse of power, I also knew that the real villain of this story was not my *madrina* but my own inner conflict. Looking back, I see that moment as a crossroads. I could have chosen to leave, and I came close to doing so. Instead, I chose to maintain my relationship to my godmother and her house and my commitments to the *yaworaje*. Looking back, I know that my godmother was doing her job. From what I've learned from interviewing *iyawos* and former *iyawos*, my *madrina* was consistently flexible and even indulgent with me, all the while attempting to godparent me in a way that was firmly consistent with her own strict upbringing in the religion. Now I am grateful for my godmother's extraordinary patience in dealing with my sometimes bratty attitude. At the time, I allowed my anger to cool and began shopping online for a stationary bike and making daytime "dates" with friends and colleagues to walk in nearby parks. Although I endured the social restrictions of the year like a defiant teenager, I did manage to endure them.

I was not alone in finding the curfews and social prohibitions of the year in white to be especially difficult. Thirty-four *iyawos* and former *iyawos* noted many specific deprivations of this type. Most listed inessential yet common social situations that *iyawos* longed for because they were accustomed to them. Dozens of Orisha priests recalled finding it difficult to not go out at night. Elena craved the parties she was denied. Phoebe, a priest of Oya, found that not going out to eat in restaurants felt like a big sacrifice. Iyawo Carlos, who had promised to make *ocha* once his wife's serious yet mysterious illness was resolved, longed to dine out again with his healed spouse and have nightly drinks at the bar. Kimberly wished she could go to movies and restaurants. María missed swimming at the beach. Teri, a priest of Oshun who made *ocha* for reasons of health and faith, yearned for "movies, casino[s], parties, [and] dancing in clubs." Frank, a priest of Oshun who came to *ocha* as a "spiritual calling," dreamed of traveling again. Faye, who was dedicated to Orisha for health reasons, felt the absence of "going to social events at night, going out to dinner or coffee with friends, [and] even going to the library or a movie." Although restrictions varied in different houses, *iyawos* were not permitted many of their accustomed social activities, including having dinner out in restaurants, going to the theater, traveling to visit relatives, and having drinks after work at a bar.

Some found curfews and social limitations onerous for practical reasons. For some, the workday did not end before dark. And even when they did, Lukumi novices may not have had time to shop after work before the curfew. Iyawo Viola, who had been told in divination that she urgently needed to undergo the *kariocha,* explained that the curfew during the year in white was difficult: "Not going out at after 6 o'clock. That is when I would do my grocery shopping and errands. I couldn't 'shop' [thoroughly]. It had to be run in and run out." Adriana found it hard to avoid "going out after 6pm." This wasn't because she was "the type to like to go out a lot" but because she would have to plan in advance for her wants and needs: "Sometimes I wanted a snack or something from the store, and it was after 6 pm. It would be a bummer." Faye wrote, "Because of the hours of my shift at my job and because I was a single person who had always been very active, the hardest rule was not being out at night, and staying at home. Since I worked until 7PM or 8PM, I went straight home after work and could not do anything else. It was difficult to buy groceries, take the trash out, etc." Because of practical reasons, generally because of work, several *iyawos* and former *iyawos* admitted that they were not able to fully honor their curfews.

Sometimes what one respondent called "social probation" can be difficult for emotional reasons. Mía explained:

> Although I understand the reason behind nearly every taboo of *yaworaje* it became harder for me to abide by the rules . . . as my depression deepened. I felt isolated and stripped of my normal coping mechanisms so sometimes I desired to break out of that. For example . . . before I was a *iyawo* . . . if I had a stressful day at work, I would go home, get all pretty and have a glass or two of wine and hang out with some friends. As a *iyawo* I would crave that normal social interaction that I would use as a distraction from the anxiety and depression.

Some found that the social taboos affected their mental health. Regina recalled, "I felt very isolated that I couldn't go to a movie or parties." Bella, who made *ocha* "for a better life," believed that although she felt unusually alive during her *yaworaje*, she was not permitted the outlet for her energies that she preferred: "I wanted to go out and dance, but of course I couldn't. I never had the desire before. . . . I felt trapped because I couldn't go out and I really wanted to." With few social outlets, some *iyawo* felt pent up and deprived.

A few described experiencing real sacrifices in personal relations because of the curfews and social restrictions of the *yaworaje*. Sometimes the losses were temporary. Roger, a priest of Obatalá who worked in theater, found it distressing to not support his "friends whose plays" he could not attend. For some, the sacrifices were permanent. Carmen believed her avoidance of social functions for a year "caused a gap with . . . [her] friends that was never again closed." A few *iyawos* and former *iyawos* shared stories of suffering from not being allowed to attend funerals. Elena wrote that the hardest part of her year in white was "not being able to be with my friend when her father died. I was not able to go to the funeral." Identifying her father's death as the worst part thus far of her year in white, Iyawo Viola, who was initiated to Chango, recalled: "I was given permission to be with my mom during this time, but I could not view him, touch him or accompany my mom in the procession. I went to the rosary and sat in the very back, had to be in the church before my dad and I was not allowed to go to the cemetery. I could not be in the gatherings when my cousins were together reminiscing and that was real hard too." Faye was also forbidden to visit her dying father and attend his funeral: "My father died during my year in white, and I was not permitted to attend the funeral. Prior to his death, it had been difficult to visit him because of the restrictions with not being out at nighttime. He always liked me to stop by after work because other people visited him on the weekends. His death was a big shock and it was hard not being able to go to the cemetery to his grave." It is difficult for me to imagine the conflicts between familial and religious duties these *iyawos* experienced. I feel fortunate that I was not put in such a situation during my year.

Iyawos and former *iyawos* shared many difficulties with the curfews and social restrictions of the year in white. They suffered the loss of habitual social activities, found it troublesome to perform necessary functions of working and shopping, endured feelings of deprivation, and/or experienced repercussions in their personal relationships. Although initiates commonly felt that these rules of the year in white taught them important lessons, highlighted negative habits in their former lifestyles, and created space for the solitude that would help them grow, many experienced the social probation of the *yaworaje* as a true sacrifice.

Mirrors, Grooming, and Accessories. Other popular responses to questions about the most difficult rules and the worst parts of the year in white referred to mirrors, grooming and the use of accessories. Twenty-six respondents discussed these themes, describing the hardships of avoiding mirrors; giving up haircuts, hair styling, and nail polish; and wearing cologne and perfumed items, makeup, jewelry and other adornments during the year in white as hardships. *Iyawos* in devout religious houses are instructed to avoid viewing themselves in mirrors during the first three months of the *yaworaje* and sometimes longer. The proscription against using mirrors is another way of protecting *iyawos* from the potentially hostile spiritual realm. Another possible reason for requiring *iyawos* to refrain from using mirrors early in the *yaworaje* is social and psychological. Unable to see themselves, *iyawos* must instead view themselves through the eyes of community members (Brown 2003). The mirror taboo may thus serve to support the transformation and resocialization of *iyawos*. Of course, this prohibition and those against using makeup, perfume, cologne, nail polish, or scented hygiene products; wearing jewelry; and, for women, shaving, plucking, and hairstyling also promote a *yaworaje* free of the burdens and pleasures of vanity and the social pressures of fashion.

Avoiding seeing oneself in a reflective surface is particularly difficult in contemporary U.S. society. As a new *iyawo* first emerging after over a week ensconced in the protective house of Ocha, where all mirrors were covered for my benefit, I felt almost assaulted by ubiquitous shiny panes as my godsister escorted me to the market. It was not just car mirrors but also the glassy surfaces of vehicle and shop windows—all threatened to reveal my image. My godsister calmly suggested that I simply avoid focusing on the many mirror-like objects that surrounded me. The following week, when dressing for work, I would had another problem. How does one prepare for teaching a class of students without seeing herself? How would I know if my head covering was lopsided or if I had grown an unusually large zit?

Some survey respondents admitted that they saw themselves in mirrors by accident; they forgot to look away. Douglas explained, "I would out of habit go right to a mirror or look up while washing my hands." Checking one's appearance when washing hands in public restrooms is generally performed automatically, without thought. Iyawo Monette wrote, "It is hard not to look in the mirror . . .

out in public. Sometimes it is difficult not to look." Iyawo Rebecca explained that while she covered mirrors at home, at work she used the mirror out of necessity, to straighten her wig. Others discussed the practical considerations associated with not using mirrors. Tomás, a priest of Chango, wrote that the worst part of the year was "shaving without a mirror the first three months. It was awful on my face and I had to use the reflection from my laptop to be able to shave." This *iyawo* rule at times brought unexpected hazards. Elsa didn't realize she had a bad case of pinkeye for three months.

Beyond the ban on mirrors, several respondents found other rules related to grooming to be difficult. María, who had "always been into everything beautiful and adornments," was given permission by her *madrina* to "continue to dress and appear at work as I usually did with makeup, jewelry, nail polish, etc., so as not to call too much attention to the fact that I mostly wore white/beige/tan and other pale colors. I toned it down to simple things like plain jewelry, light-colored make up and sheer nail polish. I know these are all big 'no-nos,' but my Madrina assured me that Obatalá would understand and would not punish me for breaking these rules."

María's case seems to be an exception. Vanessa, who had completed her year in white eleven years before she responded to the survey, wrote that as a "typical teenage girl [who loved] . . . to smell pretty, get manicures, etc.," the grooming rules of the *yaworaje* were a sacrifice. Esperanza, a priest of Obatalá who had come to *ocha* through Spiritism and Ifa, felt that the worst part of the year in white was "not using perfume." She "was constantly asking, 'Do I smell?'" Her Madrina "would hug . . . [her] and say 'Ten more months.'" Girls and women were not the only ones who felt frustrated about rules related to appearance, scent, and hygiene. Victor also disliked the protocol concerning grooming. He particularly suffered from "not being allowed a haircut." He wrote: "I am quite vain. I admit that quite freely. I like to look good all the time. I was dating a wonderful guy at the time and I really wanted to ensure that I had good hair. It was alright when my hair first started to grow back, but then it got to an unmanageable length. In our *ilé* there is no haircut for that first year unless your god-parents do it. My god-parents [were] . . . still in Cuba at the time . . . and I couldn't exactly fly to Cuba to get a haircut! Waiting 'til the end of my year [for] . . . a haircut was probably the worst part of that entire year. My boyfriend started to tell me my hair was getting almost as long as a girl's!" Although issues of grooming and appearance may initially seem trivial, the accounts of *iyawos* and former *iyawos* such as Victor and Esperanza demonstrate the importance of such taken-for-granted practices for self-conception.

Miscellaneous. I grouped the next most commonly mentioned aspects of the regimen that *iyawos* found to be burdensome because none were remarked upon frequently enough on their own to treat separately. Twenty-three *iyawos* and former *iyawos* offered responses that I grouped into this broad category. Five mentioned finding the prohibition on dancing memorable. Iyawo Lucy, who is dedicated to Oshun, explained, "When you are getting out of work on a Friday and the weekend is there you are so excited you just want to dance!" Iyawo Faith also wrote about this prohibition: "I love to dance and I missed going to my Afro-Cuban dance/Orisha dance [class] during my first three months." Paola, who committed to Orisha and the year in white because of health reasons and a great interest in the religion, wrote that although her godfather took her to *tambores* (drum ceremonies) during her *iyawo* year, "it wasn't the same . . . [as] dancing salsa or merenge." Other respondents mentioned a variety of other things they enjoyed that were not permitted during the *yaworaje*. Five reported that they missed drinking alcohol. Two brought up the taboo against being wet with the rain. Iyawo Monette thought it was a nuisance to "put up an umbrella for just sprinkles." Sergio recalled impatience with not being able to "work" his new Orishas yet. Brianna, who made *ocha* because she was told by a priest that it was her destiny and because "it was the only . . . belief system that fills . . . [her] soul," found the instruction to keep her head "cool" while at work and while raising teenage boys to be particularly challenging. Others discussed prohibitions against smoking cigarettes, chewing gum, "indulging in cannabis," cursing, travel, and tanning in the sun.

Some referred to restrictions that, in my experience, are not common across *ilés*. These standards were particular to a house or were taboos that a *iyawo*'s individual *itá* (instructions received through divination) required. Tiffany found it difficult to avoid watching television during the first three months of her *yaworaje*. Iyawo Dana, who is dedicated to the Orisha Agayu, was instructed to cover her hands. She found this to be particularly challenging: "Wearing gloves when handling money. I would feel self-conscious or forget my gloves." Camila mentioned a prohibition against eating red foods. Teresa was told not to ride a bike, and s/he paid for her decision to break this rule: "Towards the end of my year, I made a mistake and decided to go out and ride a bike, despite my father's warning. I was so close to completing my year, but I just couldn't wait. Being a young child, it is very difficult for me to be so limited in activity and as a result of my mistake, I broke my ankle." Like other *iyawo* and former *iyawo* who admitted to disregarding the rules of the *yaworaje*, Teresa's was a story of a lesson learned.

Iyawo rules are so numerous and all-encompassing that it is not surprising that the responses were so diverse and that they defied easy categorization. This diversity, which I grouped as "miscellaneous," highlights the all-embracing nature of the year in white, where *iyawo* sacrifice many ordinary habits, practices, and enjoyments that U.S. residents generally take for granted.

Eating. The next themes most frequently discussed in survey questions were protocols concerning eating. During the first three months of the year in white, and sometimes longer, *iyawos* are generally required to eat while sitting on a mat on the floor. A white bath towel is positioned over their thighs, and plates or bowls of food are placed on top of the towel between their spread legs. The plates and bowls, which are connected to the earth from which the sustenance originated, are not to be raised until the initiates have completed their meal. *Iyawos* use only spoons as utensils and they are commonly instructed to avoid talking while eating. When they are at religious functions they are served first and told to wait without rising or speaking until someone has removed the empty dishes and returned them clean. Although these restrictions are lifted for many *iyawos* while they are on the job and after the first three months of the *yaworaje*, *iyawos* are traditionally required to be served and take their meals on the mat during religious events throughout the year in white.

Additionally, *iyawos* are given a set of special dishes at the beginning of their *yaworaje*. They are instructed to eat only from this tableware, which they must carry with them whenever they will be away from home during mealtimes. Using only the designated plate, bowl, cup, and spoon is seen as protection from the energies of others that may permeate plates, bowls and flatware. The avoidance of forks and knives also emphasizes *iyawos'* newborn state. The *estera* (mat) on which initiates eat is seen as a clean, protected space. Some suggest that they are supposed to be silent and separate from others when eating so that the taking in of nourishment becomes a conscious and attentive practice.

Often it isn't until one's routine is shaken up that one can see what is taken for granted in a new light. Although I had become accustomed to the eating routines of the *yaworaje*, it wasn't until I took a trip across the country that I learned that *iyawo* rules about eating can be both comforting and the cause of estrangement. Nearly three months into my *yaworaje* my godmother gave me permission to travel to attend a family gathering. Although orthodox novices are often not permitted to travel or attend such gatherings, my godmother felt that for me, maintaining relationships with my family was important enough that I should be permitted to go. Because I was traveling, I would have to modify my eating routine. I would not always be able to eat on the mat. It would not be easy to take my enameled dishes on the airplane. My godmother suggested that I take the spoon she had given me to all meals, even if I was dining by necessity at a restaurant. The spoon became the security blanket to which I clung during the trip into territory that was unfriendly to a *iyawo*.

The family gathering involved two weddings and a baby shower. I found myself surrounded by people with lots of questions about my weird attire and behavior and constantly having to dodge well-meaning folks with cameras. (*Iyawos* are not supposed to be photographed.) A few days into the trip I lost my spoon. The spoon had become a symbol to me of honoring my *iyawo* status even in situations that weren't very *iyawo*-like. Losing it shook me up in a way that was inexplicable to my perplexed, Jewish family members who were largely unfamiliar with the year in white. I also worried about telling my *madrina* about losing the spoon she had given me. (Of course when I called her she simply told me to buy a new one.)

After the second wedding, there was a small, casual celebratory dinner in my cousin's living room. I was hungry, exhausted, cranky, and upset about losing my special spoon that morning. Because the gathering was small—there were only about eleven of us—and because the meal was being served buffet style, with people sitting both at the table and elsewhere, I decided it would be safe to eat on my mat. It was only after settling with my meal on the floor that I realized I had made a mistake. Positioning myself on the floor felt alienating. I realized that most of the people there hadn't yet seen me eat on my *estera*. They didn't know how to treat me or why I was acting so strangely. I probably should have said something before I sat down but after the long day I wasn't in the right frame of mind to think of that. Eating helped. When I finished my dinner I sat at the table and answered questions from curious family members about the mat and my year. It was then that I discovered that some in the room had assumed that my reason for eating on the mat was to separate myself from them. It had. In the process of attempting to meet both my conflicting obligations to my *yaworaje* and the expectations of my family I ended up shorting them both. I discovered later that I had hurt my sister's feelings. She believed that my behavior had been attention-seeking and self-centered at a party meant to celebrate her new marriage. Although I remain grateful that I was given permission to attend, I now understand more fully some of the reasons for the orthodox restrictions against *iyawo* participating in such gatherings. My attendance at the get-together may have separated me from my family as much as it connected me with them, partly because of my awkward attempts to honor the eating routines of the *yaworaje*.

In response to the survey, seventeen former *iyawos* discussed the trials of eating procedures during the *yaworaje*. They wrote that the most difficult rules to follow were "not sitting at a table," "sitting on a mat on the floor to eat my meals," "having to eat on the floor," and "changing all of my eating patterns." For some, these experiences were the worst part of the year. Some mentioned that observing the rule at work or on the way to work was most troublesome. Douglas explained, "I had problems with the bowl and cup because I work outdoors and often eat on a train." Phoebe recalled, "I . . . would find myself running a lot of errands on my lunch hour, which meant I would be eating lunch at my desk while working. This is not the way to be mindful about eating, but it's what was necessary at the time." Others discussed the discomforts of eating while sitting on the floor with the plate "glued" to the ground, such as having to lean over so as not to spill food. Isabel grew up around the religion but never expected to become initiated. She began to suffer debilitating health problems and her doctors were not encouraging. When she attended a Lukumi drum ceremony, a mounted priest told her she should become ordained to gain the assistance of the Orisha. In her written survey, Isabel told me that she no longer suffered from poor circulation in her legs, but she found that this issue bothered her a lot as a *iyawo*. "Sitting on the mat on the floor" hurt her legs, "but the more I did it the less it hurt." Eva wrote, "Eating on the floor for the first three months, and any Orisha function during and after your three months [was] most difficult because I like my food at table level, and not so far down on the floor where I couldn't even pick up the plate. Now people don't even follow that rule after your 3 months." Alicia, a priest of Oshun who was ordained with her daughter, wrote, "If I were able to bring my plate up to the level of my mouth it would have been easier, but as you know, the plate must stay on the floor." Others focused more on the emotional challenges of the practice. Estevan explained that the most difficult part was "not picking up the plate and serving myself when eating on estera. It drove me crazy. Having to depend on others makes me nuts." Victor mentioned a different aspect of the *iyawo* eating routine: "I found it very difficult to eat on the mat away from my family and friends. This I think was the most difficult of all the rules for me because meal times were always such a social experience growing up. Meal times were about family and community and enjoying each other's company while sharing a meal—breaking bread if you like. . . . I was required to eat on the mat, separated from my family and friends, and eating different foods from others." For Victor, eating on his *estera* seemed like a sacrifice of companionship during mealtimes. Sheila, whose Ocha house was particularly strict, spoke of the inconvenience of this rule: "Having to be on the mat every time I ate, even if it was just a potato chip, was hard." Study participants discussed a variety of the challenges of *iyawo* eating routines. Eating on the mat can be inconvenient and physically hard on backs and hips. It can be difficult to integrate *iyawo* eating practices with work and family expectations. It may make *iyawo* feel separate from those around them. And at a religious event, it means waiting, possibly in uncomfortable positions, to be served by others.

Subordinate Status. Thirteen study participants described another struggle of the year in white that centered on issues of subordinate status.[3] The term "*iyawo*" is a designation of status, specifically gendered and ranked status. Lukumi novices, both male and female, are new wives, and subordinate new wives, to both the Orisha and to other religious community members who have already completed the *yaworaje*. New initiates may be expected to perform "wifely" duties for the community, such as cleaning and cooking, maintaining Orisha shrines, and caring for animals (Clark 2005, 79). In return for this loss of status, novices are ranked over uninitiated members of the religious household.

When a *iyawo* enters a house of Ocha, he or she must greet each Orisha priest who is present (and all who arrive later) with a "salute" that often involves complete prostration. Sometimes this is jokingly called "*iyawo* calisthenics," a reference to the physical effort required to "throw oneself" on the ground (or on a mat on the floor) for each Orisha priest who is present. New initiates may be instructed to be silent when they are among Orisha priests and to avoid arguing or disagreeing with them. In addition, the multiple ways that *iyawos* are treated like children reinforces their subordinate status in the *ilé*.

While I don't recall taking issue with my subordinate status during my *ocha* ceremony, I found myself extremely frustrated at my godsister's *kariocha* the next month. As my godmother's most recently initiated godchild, I was required to attend my godsister on the *trono*. In one case of frustration that made its way to my notes, a young priest who seemed to relish the position of teacher received my silent ire. As he put the plate down before me so I could eat my meal, he instructed cheerfully, "A *iyawo* should never be tired or hungry." "Is he totally nuts?!" I exclaimed in my journal, considering the statement an assault on the validity of my experience. The Sunday morning of my godsister's *ocha*, I awoke early on the *trono.* (I was accustomed to a different time zone.) I believed I was required to accompany her unless I was relieved of the responsibility by another *ilé* member, but I found myself in need of water and allergy/asthma medication hours before anyone came to check on us. While I could hear the "adults" chatting and laughing outside the *trono* room, I was experiencing chest congestion and difficulty breathing. I wasn't in danger, but I was uncomfortable and I felt like I couldn't get my needs met. The more I thought about it, the more upset I became. Yet somehow I had to try to not "leak" my anxiety and anger in a way that would affect my *iyawo* godsister on her big day. By the time someone came to check on us—at what was probably a reasonable hour for them to do so—and give me permission to get my medication, I was nearing an emotional meltdown. Later I railed in my journal, "I'm not allowed to take care of myself and no one is taking care of me!" When I told my *madrina* afterward about this experience she seemed incredulous about the fact that I hadn't simply left the *trono* briefly to tend to myself. Because I had already made *ocha*, the strict rules about not leaving the *trono* area during the *kariocha* were not in effect for me, she explained. But because I had not been in that position before, this was something I did not understand. Whether or not I can be accused of being an obsessive rule-follower, the misunderstanding illustrates the vulnerability of *iyawo* and the complex emotions that can arise when people must cope with dependence and being at the bottom of the totem pole.

Although only thirteen survey respondents discussed issues of subordination as among the most difficult rules or the worst parts of the year, they were an adamant minority. *Iyawos* and former *iyawos* mentioned disliking being treated like children. They found it taxing to "throw themselves" on the floor to nearly everyone present at a large religious gathering. Such vigorous prostration may at times conflict with the expectation that *iyawos* maintain spotless clothing and a pristine appearance. Some complained about having to be escorted to religious events. Iyawo Carlos, a child of Obatalá, wrote that his godmother didn't like to attend drumming ceremonies, which meant that he was unable to attend them during the year. Mía wrote that she particularly disliked "being waited on . . . or more specifically, having to wait for others to provide me with what I needed. I am a very independent individual and I am not shy about taking initiative. It was a challenge for me to have to be seen and not heard or ask for permission to do things and go [to] places. To wait until I was served—Grrrrr!—It was so frustrating!" Along similar lines, Mariposa, who is dedicated to Oshun, wrote, "Not being able to express myself like I usually would because since I was . . . *iyawo,* supposedly I was not to speak when around elders and when I felt they stepped out of line with me, I had to tell my godmother; I wasn't able to handle it on my own. I didn't like that at all!" Iyawo Ashley, who is also made to Oshun, described at length having to confront the issues of autonomy and independence that the subordinate status of being *iyawo raised for her*. As in many accounts of the *yaworaje,* she found the challenges to be both difficult and useful: "Being a iyawo has changed my relationship with my childhood. Being on the trono was like being flashed back to being a baby—which was both fun and terrifying because of how much I had to surrender my autonomy. . . . I no longer think of childhood as an idyllic time. . . . [Instead, I now] have more of an appreciation for the independence and autonomy I have as an adult." This same *iyawo* complained that priests didn't seem to care about what *iyawos* have to say and that when they ask *iyawos* how they are doing, they "project their own experience" instead of really listening. It is only when one occupies subordinate status, she explained, that one can clearly see the operations of power: "Sometimes I feel like everyone has something to say to the iyawo, and there are those priests who just seem to relish the position of authority they have over us. . . . I've noticed these power trips and policing dynamics much more since I have become a iyawo." For some, the line seemed thin between respecting elders and submitting to hazing. Fawn explained, "'Iyawos are seen and not heard.' I love to talk and that was hard—to not add my two cents in a conversation. But it made me humble and taught me [that] sometimes you learn a lot more about people and things if you just listen." Magdalena disliked "doing grunt work for the elders" and being considered disrespectful when she disagreed with them. These few responses are a reminder that being on the bottom is difficult in many ways that are often invisible except to those in a similar position.

Celibacy and Sleep. Several participants mentioned issues related to sex and sleep. In some houses of Ocha, *iyawos* are instructed to refrain from sexual activity for part or all of the *yaworaje*. Although the rules vary among houses of Ocha, new initiates are often not permitted sexual activity for a period of time at the beginning of the year in white that ranges from sixteen days to three months. Following that initial period, *iyawos* may be instructed to engage in sexual behavior only with spouses and/or significant others. Thus, single *iyawos* may be required to be celibate for the year. Godparents may or may not consider significant others, especially cohabitators, to be similar to spouses. In addition, some houses require that *iyawos* sleep on a mat on the floor at the beginning of the *yaworaje*; this requirement is generally removed after three months. In *ilés* that require sexual abstinence and mat sleeping, the two are often merged: the *iyawo* remains celibate as long as s/he is sleeping on the *estera*.

In response to survey questions about the most difficult rules or the worst parts of the year in white, discussions of celibacy and mat sleeping were less frequently mentioned than many of the other rules. These rules are not as common as many of the others during the *yaworaje*. As noted earlier, only 23 percent of respondents admitted to sleeping for three months or more on a mat and only 60 percent said that they had been celibate for the first three months or more of the *yaworaje*.

Nevertheless, eleven participants spoke about these issues, and those who did often indicated that this aspect of the year in white was particularly memorable for them. For Iyawo Ronna, celibacy was a most difficult rule: "In my ilé if you are single prior to get[ting] initiated even after your three months you are not permitted to have sex. This was challenging for me but also good." Douglas wrote that "abstaining and sleeping on the mat was difficult because I was married." Although it was not clear from what he wrote, he seemed to suggest that his abstinence harmed his marriage. Several former *iyawos* complained that they were unable to date during the year or that because they began the year in white single they were required to remain so. One *olorisha* explained that she was unable to observe the rules on sex: "I wasn't celibate for long. It lasted about two weeks and then that was over with. Being on the throno [during the priestly initiation], I felt so tapped into life, the universe and everything, and sex is the stuff of life! I don't feel bad about it. . . . It only happened a few times." Tino had different difficulties with *iyawo* prohibitions concerning sex. He felt that the worst part of the year in white was "having to be monogamous for an entire year when it was pretty obvious I was much more comfortable in a polyamorous or somewhat open relationship." Others discussed sleeping on a mat on the floor as a noteworthy adversity. María stated clearly, "Sleeping on the floor, by far, had to be the worst thing of all during the whole year." Phoebe exclaimed, "I still have a knot in my back from floor-sleeping that has yet to be undone!" Thus, although sexual abstinence and sleeping on the mat were less commonly discussed and practiced, some found them to be a significant sacrifice.

General Rule Complaints. Finally, survey respondents occasionally complained about the restrictions and prescriptions of the year in white more generally. In response to close-ended survey questions, 27 percent of respondents often felt the rules of the *yaworaje* were unfair and 28 percent agreed that the rules frequently didn't make sense. Eight *iyawos* and former *iyawos* offered comments in response to open-ended questions that fell in this category. Some, like Faye, objected to what they perceived to be an irregular application or explanation of *iyawo* protocol: "During my year in white, the rules seemed to change for me every few months without explanation. I would get in trouble because others assumed that I knew more than I did. After my year in white, other iyawos (in the same house) seemed to be permitted to do things that I was not permitted to do." Helen, a priest of Yemaya, felt that the guidelines were inadequately explained: "One of my problems with the rules was that often, particularly in the first couple of months, I only learned about a rule when I had violated it!" Complaints such as these may seem petty until you consider them from the perspective of a person who has devoted themselves to a year of following the rules of the *yaworaje*. It can be demoralizing when a *iyawo* discovers s/he has violated a rule s/he wasn't told about or finds that godsiblings are being held to different interpretations of the rules.

Others objected to observance of *iyawo* rules or to certain aspects of them. For adult *iyawo* who were meeting their grownup commitments during the *yaworaje*, treatment as a child at times seemed unconvincing and unfair. Donna undertook the *kariocha* and the *yaworaje* "to expand . . . [her] spiritual progress and accept responsibility to the Orisa and the priesthood," but she could not easily reconcile the role conflict of being a responsible working parent and being treated as an infant *iyawo*:

> Rules such as eating on a mat on the floor was very difficult for me to comprehend. After fulfilling the responsibility of an administrative position, managing the household budget, shopping, meal preparation, assuring the family had adequate healthy food and for me to then sit on the floor to eat was too much for me. As a *iyawo* being considered a "baby" but being asked to chauffer others from place to place after attending Ocha evening affairs didn't make sense to me as it lacked a "protective" element one exhibits to a baby.

Iyawo Monette described a different frustration with the expectations of the *yaworaje*; she wanted more thorough explanations: "The worst parts are the rules that can't be explained outside of, 'This is how it is done.' For instance, the rules that I listed above [about touch and exchanging items with persons who have not been initiated, avoiding rain, avoiding mirrors, covering, and carrying]—most could not really be explained to me. And though I was able to make some sense of many of them, I have an aversion to rules that don't really make sense and so following them was tremendously difficult." For this Orisha priest, obedience without understanding was disconcerting. Ernesto, an *oluwo*, complained about the fact that rules in the Cuban tradition of the year in white are not found in Africa: "After learning about traditional Yoruba practice (and the fact that in Nigeria, the 'year' of *yaworaje* more or less does not exist), I wondered [about] the point of it all." Ernesto questioned the legitimacy of a tradition that was created in Cuba but is widely attributed to Yorubaland. Grace, who became ordained for health reasons, stated another strong objection: "I think the Iyawo rules are outdated. Like everything, religion must change with the times. Most of the Iyawo rules are antiquated and fit for persons whom [*sic*] do not work outside of the home."

Thus, a small minority had more general complaints about *iyawo* proscriptions and prescriptions. Rules were explained inadequately. They didn't make sense. They seemed to change from *iyawo* to *iyawo*. They were inconsistent with other responsibilities held by adults. Traditions diverged from those on the continent on which Orisha worship was born and do not easily fit in contemporary U.S. society. Nevertheless, those who expressed these concerns usually explained that they had followed the *iyawo* regimen to the best of their ability. Their questioning of tradition or the ways it was implemented or explained became an additional burden of the year in white.

NATIVES, NEWCOMERS, AND RACE/ETHNICITY

Those who answered survey questions and participated in interviews shared many of their experiences with the rules of the year in white. Did cultural newcomers practice and understand their new religious traditions differently from cultural natives? Were those raised in or around the religion more or less likely than those who were not to report following the rules of the *yaworaje*? To have understood the protocol? To have believed the restrictions were fair? Did race and ethnicity matter in this regard?

Although majorities of all respondents believed that their godparents held them strictly to the rules of the year in white, chi square analyses revealed that those who came from a Lukumi background differed in this respect from those who did not have that background. In response to the statement "My godparent/s (Madrina/Padrino) was/were really strict about *iyawo* rules," cultural indigenes (65 percent) were much more likely than newcomers (39 percent) to agree strongly (X^2 = 11.89, df = 3, p = .008; N = 164]). However, whether survey respondents were raised in or among the tradition did not affect their other answers related to *iyawo* rules in statistically significant ways. Regardless of whether or not they had a Lukumi background, participants were almost equally likely to agree that they understood and followed the rules and that they believed them to be fair. Hispanic identity was minimally relevant but, whether or not one identified as Black or white had no significant effect on quantitative reports regarding rules. Fifty-one percent of Hispanics and 37 percent of non-Hispanics strongly agreed that their godparents were really strict about *iyawo* rules (X^2 = 9.36, df = 3, p = .025; N = 151).

CONCLUSION

Iyawos and former *iyawos* discussed a wide variety of rules that they found challenging. The proscriptions and prescriptions of the year in white are widespread and all-encompassing. Most memorable to the *olorishas* who answered my survey were standards concerning dressing, covering, carrying, touch and exchange of objects, being outside the home, mirrors, grooming, accessorizing, eating, sex, sleeping on the mat, and subordinate status. Some felt that none of the rules were difficult. Others complained about the nature and implementation of *iyawo* rules more generally, and some complained about the fact that they were not explained adequately. Although the question "What iyawo rules did you find most difficult to keep?" may have weighted the answers toward the negative, I believe that the responses paint a picture of the intricacies of the *yaworaje* that a mere list of rules would miss. The wording of the question encouraged Orisha devotees to speak honestly of the often demanding and always multifaceted ritual that stretches for just over a year in a culture where many might be reticent to speak to strangers about their secret ways and certainly would not speak negatively. In short, combined with the chapters that describe the *iyawo* experience and *iyawo* relations, I posit that we have here a rare description of the *yaworaje* in its human complexity.

Neither being reared in the Lukumi tradition nor ethnic/racial identity noticeably affected survey respondents' relationships to the rules, with one exception; both cultural natives and Hispanics were more likely to strongly agree that their *madrinas* and *padrinos* held them strictly to *iyawo* protocol. There are several possible explanations for the observed differences. It may be that compared to other groups, cultural natives and Hispanics (and the groups overlap) who answered my survey hold to the protocols of the *yaworaje* more strongly. It may be that they perceive their godparents as being more rigid regimen followers than others. Or it may be that in comparison to cultural newcomers and non-Hispanics, members of both groups are more likely to value strict rule keeping and/or are more concerned than others with presenting a positive view of the religion.

It is important to note that although the *iyawo* regimen is difficult at times, it is designed to protect, teach, and transform. Fully 77 percent agreed somewhat or strongly with the statement "All the hardships I endured as iyawo were worth it. I would do it again." Many attributed their personal and spiritual growth during the year to the rules of the *yaworaje*. Iyawo Faith, whose adversities during the year in white included having to leave her *ilé*, believed that she "gained courage, humility, faith and more through . . . [her] experience." She wrote: "I see this as a life test, one that has made me stronger." Douglas said that being corrected by priests during the year for not following the rules upset him and "that shaking up was what allowed . . . [him] to change." In these ways and many more, following the *iyawo* rules can be considered as both respect for one's godparents, for the Orisha, and for a beautifully complex and challenging culture and as a sacrifice, a gift to the Orisha who are believed to give so much back and to whom *iyawos* have newly dedicated their lives.

One morning, exhausted from too little sleep, I finished packing the car and asked my Warriors for assistance. I refreshed them with cool water and sprayed them with rum. I asked the Orisha Elegua to help me speak well, to guide me in what to say and what not to say so that my words would be well received. I asked Ogun and Ochosi to keep me safe as I traveled, to grant me courage, and to help me find the most direct way through any difficulties. I put my little Elegua figure, a cone-shaped face made of cement with cowrie shells set in it to make eyes, a nose, and a mouth, on a coat on the passenger-side floor of my car. I was headed on a long drive to break up with my godfather, the first priest who performed a divinatory reading in the Ifa tradition for me. I had met the aged Cuban *babalawo* almost two years before, and among other things, he had told me I needed to receive Los Guerreros (the Warriors) from him. I had taken the commitment seriously, as I understood that they would be bound to me in a reciprocal relationship for the rest of my life. After months of consideration, I had decided to proceed with what was an expensive ceremony at the time for me. It wasn't until after I had arranged for the initiation and traveled to receive it, just before the ritual, the he explained that I was now to call him "Padrino" and that I was to become a member of his *ilé*, his house of Ifa. I was surprised. Although I had expected and accepted the attachment to the Orisha, I had not considered an exclusive commitment to him or the other people of his house. A year and a half later, I found myself feeling that given my limited language skills and the geographical distance between my residence and my godfather's house, I had exhausted the social possibilities in the Ifa *ilé*. It also seemed to me that I was being treated more as a consumer than as a participant. I had discovered that there were other possibilities for me in less patriarchal houses, and I found myself making the long journey.

Four and a half hours later I arrived at the home of my godfather. I knocked on the door. No answer. No bell. I called from my cell phone. Padrino answered.

"*Hola? Estoy aqui*" ("Hello? I'm here"), I announced. We had a confusing conversation, but since I had determined that he was indeed home, I walked inside the unlocked front door. "*Hola? Hola?*" I called. Eventually I found a surprised *padrino* upstairs in bed watching TV in his pajamas. I apologized for intruding. He asked if I had called. I told him I had scheduled the meeting with his wife days ago. Hadn't she told him? She must have forgotten. "You want a reading?" he asked. "*No. Quiero hablar*" ("No. I want to talk"), I replied. He asked me to wait downstairs.

I went downstairs and waited. I felt nauseated from nervousness, driving, and not enough sleep. I took deep breaths to collect myself. I realized that I didn't know what to say. But it seemed fortunate that I was to speak alone with Padrino. Although his wife's better English might facilitate our communication, it felt right to speak alone with him. It was through him alone that I was connected to the house. And somehow it seemed proper that I interact in my poor Spanish.

Padrino came downstairs securing his *babalawo* hat to his head, and I greeted him in the traditional way he had taught me, touching the floor and reciting "Iboru, Iboye, Ibocheche." "*Ogbo, ato, asure,*" he replied.[1] "*Que pasa?*" He sat on a chair and gestured for me to sit on the couch. I struggled for a moment with what to say and then several sentences in simple Spanish poured out. I told him that the *ilé* was distant from me. I explained that I wanted to study and work with other Orisha priests. I added that I did not want bad things for him or the *ilé*, that I wasn't talking badly about him or the house, and that I wanted to be a friend to the *ilé*, but I wanted to go elsewhere.

Yes, New Jersey is far, he agreed. But, he countered, he had people who sought out his priestly services from as far as Washington state and Venezuela and Colombia. He asked something about other *olorishas* in Spanish that I didn't quite understand. Guessing, I told him I had spoken with others but I had not yet asked to join another *ilé*. I told him I wanted to speak with him first. Padrino looked almost pleased. He said in English, "You wanted to ask my permission first. I give you permission," he said. I thanked him. I felt so grateful.

He told me that I was welcome back to the *ilé* whenever I had need. "Your Warriors I make with my own hands," he said. Maybe I would visit the *ilé* a couple of times a year, he suggested. He could feed my Warriors. It's not good to keep changing who feeds them, he explained. And I could come to him for the *ikofa* ceremony when I was ready. I nodded but didn't make any promises. Then he told me that he believed I would work with other Lukumi practitioners and would soon return to his house. Maybe you will move closer, he suggested. He said he thought I would make *ocha* the following year, in his house. I tried not to stare or otherwise react to what seemed an absurd statement. Instead, I let it pass.

Then Padrino changed tack. Did I not like the *babalawo* he had assigned to me? I wasn't sure what to say. Padrino had assigned me to another priest, one of his students, to receive divinatory readings. It's true that I felt no sense of connection with the recent initiate. I worried about his abilities (during my only reading with him he had spent more time flipping through a book than he did in speaking with me and shared very little that resonated). Also, I objected to being assigned a godparent, a person who could have such potential influence on my spiritual direction, without being consulted. But all this seemed tangential to the reason I was speaking to Padrino. I had learned a bit in the year and a half since I had first encountered him and his *ilé*, and I now had a better idea of what I wanted from a religious house. I wanted to learn from Orisha priests with whom I could easily communicate. I wanted a spiritual environment where I saw the potential of being a full participant, and I was excited about a *casa de ocha* that practiced greater gender equity than seemed possible in Padrino's *babalawo*-centered *ilé*. I wanted to move on but I wanted to do so cleanly, respectfully.

I struggled for words. Padrino encouraged me to try in English. Instead I told him in Spanish that I felt in my heart that I needed to go. Padrino nodded. Then he told me to go downstairs and speak to Babaluaye and ask for his guidance. I walked down the basement stairs, not knowing what I would see there. I was surprised to find a life-sized, elaborately dressed figure of Saint Lazarus amid a diverse array of many objects.[2] Padrino yelled down the stairs in English that I should kneel and talk out loud to the Orisha. I knelt and whispered for Babaluaye, the earthy Orisha of infectious disease and healing, to help me heal and guide me on my path. Then I tried to take in the majesty of the altar, a huge and varied display of color, shape, and scent laid out before the huge statue—fruit, flowers, saint candles in glass, beaded objects I'd not seen before, pictures, foods, fabrics, bottles—but I was overwhelmed. Soon the cement floor felt hard on my knees. I went back upstairs, told Padrino that Babaluaye was magnificent, thanked him for everything, saluted again, and bolted for my car.

I felt immense relief. The trip was more successful than I had expected. I realized that the exchange could very easily have gone differently. And then, as I drove, exhausted, through rush-hour city traffic I experienced a mental-emotional roller-coaster. First I felt really pleased with myself. I had managed to conduct myself almost entirely in Spanish, despite my poor language skills. I had forged a good outcome. I had shown the respect that allowed Padrino to release me without diminishing his own sense of self. I was not only free of his *ilé* but I was welcome back. Then I felt sad and scared. I wondered if I would ever find groups and relationships in which I might stay. I was now groupless, alone.

Meanwhile, Elegua sat on the floor of the car next to me. He seemed to be laughing at me. I imagined him saying "You idiot! This is what you asked for. Everything doesn't have to be such a tragedy." And I was reminded of how grateful I was to have the Warriors in my life, how much I believed they had helped me already, and how I must honor the man who had made them with his own hands.

SOCIAL STRUCTURES AND THE YEAR IN WHITE

As I discovered while I was an *aleyo* who needed to switch *ilés*, religion may be deeply personal and internally spiritual, but it is also social. Not only does religion provide the socially important function of satisfying the "human craving for meaning," it also serves to maintain social reality (Berger [1967] 1990, 22, 51). The "convert" or religious newcomer who wishes to remain a believer must "engineer his social life in accordance with this purpose." To best maintain faith, one must maximize contact with other believers and minimize associations with nonbelievers (Berger [1967] 1990). Religion is a social endeavor; it is difficult to maintain beliefs, especially minority beliefs, in the absence of a community of believers to validate one's world view. Yet in the contemporary United States, there is a vast multiplicity of meaning producers and most people have many contacts with diverse others. *Iyawos* who have lots of contact with their *ilés*, whose family and community members share common religious beliefs, may have different experiences of the *yaworaje* than those who have less contact with others in the tradition. And this is only one way that one's spiritual house affects the year in white. *Ilé* relations can be friendly and supportive or they can be competitive, unfriendly, or punitive. Elders in the house may give knowledge freely or they may hoard it.

Houses of Ocha are not the only social structures that affect the *yaworaje*. Agents of socialization such as families, places of worship, workplaces, schools, and friends are collectivities that affect our lives as social beings in profound ways. They also provide the settings in which our daily interactions occur. They constitute a large chunk of our social environment. Thus, the story of the year in white is incomplete without a consideration of *iyawos*' relationships. During the year in white, how do *iyawos* deal with their families, friends, and workplaces that are not Orisha-centered? How do new initiates interact within their houses of Ocha? Do *ilés* provide a safe space where novices can be among understanding people who provide extrafamilial support, or are they realms of struggle, misunderstanding, or heavy-handed power wielding? Do families of birth and marriage offer comfort from a sometimes hostile world or are they battlegrounds? Are workplaces accommodating or are they intolerant spaces where *iyawos* must either hide their religious status or fight for their rights? How these questions are answered can significantly shape the *yaworaje*.

In both in-depth interviews and online survey responses, *iyawos* and former *iyawos* spoke and wrote about the support, admiration, hostility, interest, guidance, and indifference they experienced at work, at school, within their *casas de ocha*, and within families of blood, marriage, adoption, and choice. Ursa illustrated the importance of social environment to the *yaworaje* by describing the difference between being *iyawo* in Cuba, where she was initiated, and being home in the states: "I missed being in Cuba, because more people understood what was happening and the religion and the different signs of it." *Iyawos* in the

United States must often perform the year in white within social contexts that are not necessarily knowledgeable or supportive.

In the survey I asked questions about the social relationships in the lives of *iyawos*. Most respondents reported that they maintained good relationships with their godparents during the course of their *yaworaje*. Only 16 percent of those who answered said that they argued a lot with their *godparents* during the year in white. Eighty-seven percent claimed to have spoken to their godparents regularly. Most reported good relationships with members of their house of Ocha more generally; 74 percent said that they developed deep relationships with members of their *ilé* during the year. Fewer (56 percent) claimed that they were pampered in their house of Ocha. Most reported that family (70 percent) and friends (80 percent) accepted their *iyawo* status, although only 49 percent claimed the same of their co-workers. This could mean that co-workers were less tolerant or that they were simply less likely to know about *iyawo* status. Despite this generally rosy picture of the relationships *iyawos* had, it is important to note that plenty of respondents reported that they failed to develop deep relationships within their *ilé* (24 percent) or that they didn't have accepting families (25 percent), co-workers (32 percent), or friends (17 percent). The consequences of poor relations were sometimes weighty: fourteen (8 percent) claimed to have lost jobs because they were *iyawos*. (See Table 4.)

In interviews and in response to open-ended questions on the survey, *iyawos* and former *iyawos* discussed family, friends, the workplace, and *ilé* relations, but the relationships they discussed most frequently, by far, were those with members of their *ilé*.

FRIENDS AND FAMILY

Relatively few respondents mentioned relationships with their friends and family during their year in white. But the information participants shared about these relationships was often significant. Most of the stories about connections with friends in survey responses were told as a way of elaborating about feelings of loneliness experienced during the year in white. Iyawo Carlos lost friendships when people he "knew for years, all of a sudden" thought he was "a nut case" for going through the yearlong rite of passage. Iyawo Rebecca believed that she lost a good friend because the latter needed to make *ocha* herself but couldn't face that truth. Nyesha was told during her *itá* divination that she would break up with the man she was dating. She says that she didn't accept the information at the time but that two months into her year in white the prediction came true. Ivy recalled that her friends didn't know how to interact with her when she was not able to go out to the bar with them during her year in white. Zoe wrote that she found it difficult to explain the restrictions on relationships during the year in white to a person with whom she

TABLE 4.   *Iyawo* Relations with Others

	Disagreed	Agreed	N
During my year in white I argued with my godparents a lot.	82% (136)	16% (26)	167
I spoke to my godparent(s) regularly during my year in white.	11% (19)	87% (146)	168
During my year in white I developed deep relationships with others in my ilé/casa de Ocha/god family.	24% (39)	74% (123)	166
When I was iyawo I was pampered by my god family/ile/house of ocha.	40% (67)	56% (93)	165
My family accepted my being iyawo.	25% (41)	70% (117)	167
My co-workers accepted my being iyawo.	32% (53)	49% (81)	167
I lost my job because I was iyawo.	62% (104)	8% (14)	167
My friends accepted my being iyawo.	17% (29)	80% (133)	166

In reporting scaled responses, I merged "strongly agree" with "somewhat agree" and merged "strongly disagree" with "somewhat disagree." Not every participant responded to every survey item, so I calculated percentages based on the number of responses for each given item. Percentages do not total 100 due to rounding and because some individuals checked N/A.

fell in love, especially since she didn't fully understand the reasons for them. *Iyawos* and former *iyawos* told of friendships that disintegrated because their friends didn't approve of or didn't understand their decision to make *ocha*, because they were not able to continue the activities that had formerly cemented the associations, or because, they believed, it was simply destiny that the friendships should end.

Some survey and interview participants identified relationships with families during the *yaworaje* as the worst part of their year. Iyawo Lola said that the most difficult time during her *iyawo* year was her mother's reaction when she first saw her daughter after her initiation. (She didn't elaborate.) Ana claimed that the worst part of her year in white was "not being able to share it" with her "Jehovah's Witness mother or Grandmother." Iyawo Lucy listed dealing with her family as the most frustrating aspect of the *yaworaje*: "I was brought up in a Catholic Italian family," she wrote. "They didn't understand it and I don't think they ever will." Others described significant family troubles during their *iyawo* year. Iyawo Viola's marriage was strained because her husband didn't "share the same passion" for the religion as she did. Diane attributed discord in her marriage to her previously initiated husband's jealousy about the rules of her year in white, which were less strict for her than they had been for him. Olive, who made *ocha* because of a "deep spiritual longing," reported marital strain because her *babalawo* husband claimed the right to override the rules of her *yaworaje*. (Religious practitioners generally ascribe such authority only to the initiate's godparents.) Hector, who undertook the year in white out of a desire for "completion" and "to be closer to the Orishas," recalled that his "very Catholic" mother gave him a choice between following his religious calling and continuing to live in her roomy house. He chose to strike out on his own.

In contrast, some described supportive friends and/or family. Ursa claimed to have had accommodating associations throughout the year: "My friends were great. We would do air hugs; they understood." Lincoln enjoyed having his friends visit him during his *kariocha* on what is called the festive "middle day." Andre, a priest of Oya, described his interest in Lukumi as difficult for his Baptist mother to accept. Nevertheless, she attended the middle day of his *kariocha* and gave her blessings. Hector's friends offered rides so he wouldn't have to be out after dark. Ines had a rocky road to *ocha*; twelve years after she was introduced to the tradition, she became initiated out of love for Yemaya. She was pleasantly surprised that her boyfriend stayed with her after she was initiated: "I said to him, 'I am going to get initiated and I am not going to have any hair.' And he said, 'I don't care.' And he didn't." In his interview, Iyawo Kenneth reported that his "family was really understanding through the whole thing." Silvia explained that although her Africanist mother and accepting grandmother were surprised about her decision to make *ocha*, they supported her completely. Vincent believed that many of his familial relationships improved significantly during his year in white. Teresa, who received the *kariocha* when she was a child, wrote that she relied on her parents' support when she encountered hostility in the wider community.

Others spoke of the year as being a mixed experience where friends and family were concerned. Faye explained that on the one hand, "many friends questioned . . . my initiation and the reasons for it, and a few broke off all contact." On the other hand, "Some of my . . . friends were very supportive. . . . Several were very nice." They provided transportation so she "could attend holiday events with them." Similarly, Opal, who is dedicated to Yemaya, recalled mixed reactions from family members. Her immediate family and siblings were very supportive, but her mother and her mother's cousin reacted negatively:

During the Christmas holiday . . . I was visiting . . . one of my mother's first cousins. She was just looking at me up and down; she didn't really speak to me. And I had on a really nice white dress and my head was covered, of course. So she calls my mother and says I don't know what she is into, but she had on all white and it is Winter! So of course my mother called and was upset. I said, "Mom, everything I had on, first of all, my dress alone was like 200 dollars." So it wasn't like I was like sloppy or anything like that. . . .

Some reported mixed reactions from a single family member. Lincoln explained that his "wife's cousin kept saying 'Why is he wearing white all the time? He wears white every day! The same thing; everything is white.'" Yet "she was a seamstress" who eventually "hooked him up" with "some nice pants and jackets." Ines initially had trouble with her family regarding the religion, but that changed, she believed, with a little help from her Orisha: "My parents stopped talking to me when I made *ocha*. They thought I was getting into a voodoo religion." Instructed by an *olorisha* in Puerto Rico to give an offering of fruit to the Orisha Oshun, she complied, and this, she believed, transformed the relationships: "By the time I returned . . . [home from traveling], there was a message on my answering machine from my parents, who had not talked to me all those three months." Relationships with family and friends were not static; they often changed over the course of the year.

In interviews, several participants suggested explanations for the negative or ambivalent reactions they experienced from friends and family. Some discussed the importance of perceptions and misconceptions about their new religion. Vincent believed that the hesitance he felt from some of his friends and family members regarding his *ocha* initiation stemmed from derogatory, reductionist stereotypes of Santería as a realm of dark sorcery. He explained (with a touch of sarcasm) that in his Latino community, involvement in the Lukumi religious tradition "is frowned upon . . . except for [in] certain types of 'emergencies,' like a husband cheating on a wife." In such a case it might be deemed acceptable for the wife to seek out an *olorisha* for "a love potion or to break a spell or something like that. But overall, it wasn't something that was totally embraced by my family or a lot of people that I knew, until they saw I was okay and a regular person just like they were." Similarly, Hector, a priest of Obatalá, believed that his relationships were affected by misunderstandings about his religion. He said that he began losing friends once he became involved with Lukumi tradition, even before his *kariocha*. This was mostly due, he suspected, to negative perceptions of Santería and its associations with animal sacrifice. The loss of these friendships surprised him, especially in the case of a romance; his boyfriend insisted that Hector choose between his religion and their relationship. As he had done with his mother, Hector chose the former. Gabriel— who underwent *kariocha* because that was what *odu* prescribed—also lost friends and was estranged from his family. He too, attributed the losses to negative associations of blood sacrifice with the Lukumi tradition and to a general lack of understanding about Lukumi culture. His father, for example, who knew very little about Lukumi, "just thought it was some ridiculous cult I got into." Gabriel, an *olorisha* dedicated to Obatalá, tried to understand the cultural outsider's point of view regarding his religion: "Unless you are in this tradition, it is bizarre." From keeping representations of divinities in soup tureens to shaving initiates' heads, "it is weird," Gabriel pronounced. Yet cultural perceptions of the religion sometimes worked to favor *iyawos*. When Patricia fell on hard times, mostly due to a precarious housing situation, she asked the Orisha Shango, to whom her head had been marked, for assistance, promising to follow through with ordination should he help her get a home. Four months later, she explained, with the help of her family, she "bought a house." Not only were such deals with divinity seen as a normal practice, but Patricia explained that "in the Mexican community," indigenous forms of healing and worship were understood and accepted by members of certain generations:

> Like my grandma understood Santería. She didn't practice and didn't know anything about it, but it is typical in the Mexican culture to have another religion besides church. To go to a *curandero*. So with the older part of my family, they have an intact understanding of alternative religions, if we want to call it that. But with my cousins that are also Chicanos raised here, they understand it less. . . . So it is kind of a mixed bag.

Some *iyawos* and former *iyawos* believed that cultural perceptions of the minority religion affected their relationships with friends and family outside the religion in mostly negative but sometimes positive manners. This is one way that cultural newcomers to the religion, who are likely to rely more heavily on relationships outside the tradition, may experience the *yaworaje* differently from cultural natives.

Some described losing relationships because their initiation changed them. Patricia wasn't sure, but thought her involvement in *la religión* affected some of her friendships. She attributed the distance she began to feel from some of her friends as their surprise at the radical changes she underwent during the year in white. She transformed from an atheist who mostly wore black to a religious person who wore only white: "They respect me and they respect it but it is not for them, so I am not sure if there is a wall or not. . . . I think it was a real shock to them." Lincoln said that he had to drop a number of friendships during his year in white because the lifestyles of his friends weren't consistent with the *yaworaje* and the instructions he received in his *itá* divination: "I couldn't hang around people with drugs, couldn't hang around with drug addicts, couldn't hang around with people who were crazy." Gabriel admitted that his relationships with his friends probably suffered during his year in white because he consistently chose religious affairs over social events that weren't related to Ocha. If he had plans to hang out with friends and got a call at the last minute that there was a drum ceremony, he would "dump" his "friends and go to the tambor." Some *iyawos* shed friendships because of changes in their sense of selfhood, priorities, and/or daily routines. They were no longer the same people who had formed the relationships they were now unable to support or that had ceased to sustain them.

Some interview subjects shared stories of the positive aspects of losing friendships or family connections during the year in white. They believed that bad relationships were purposefully and even systematically being removed from their lives by the power of Orisha. Opal felt that one of the beneficial results of the fact that she had made *ocha* was that harmful relationships were fading away: "All the really dysfunctional people started falling out of my life." In particular, she stopped being close with people who had drug addictions "and things along those lines." Similarly, Ines was told by a priest during her *itá* divination that the Orisha Ogun, "was getting rid of everybody that wasn't good for her." As a result, she explains: "I lost a whole slew of friends." Being "an only child who is not married," she found this particularly difficult, because "your friends are your family." Looking back, she believed she could see the reasons why it was better that her old friends were swept away. At the end of her year in white, an Orisha priest gave Ines an additional explanation for the loneliness of her year. He told her that Yemaya, the Orisha to whom she was particularly dedicated, was sending Ines a message: "Yemaya wanted you to know all you need is her to protect you," the priest said.

WORK

Iyawos are often advised or allowed by their elders in Lukumi to modify the rules of the year in white in order to conform to the needs of their jobs. This means different things for each *iyawo*, depending on the demands of his or her workplace and the extent to which his or her house of Ocha tends toward secrecy. Sometimes it is determined during *itá* divination that particular *iyawos* are to hide their status completely at work. Other times, novices must break or modify specific rules of the *yaworaje*. They may need to wear watches, wigs, or uniforms. They may choose to wear light or pale colors to avoid detection as a *iyawo*. They may not be permitted in their workplaces to wear head coverings. Women may be required by the needs of their jobs to wear pants. They may have to work at night or commute home after dark, especially in the shorter days of winter. Opal, for example, who began a new job during her year in white, felt that she needed to wear normal business attire (in light colors) at her new job.

Iyawos varied in how open they were at work and with specific co-workers about their *iyawo* status. Some, like Patricia "like[d] to keep . . . quiet" at work and not "go into a lot of details" about the year in white and its meaning, even though she thought people at her workplace were curious about her shaved head. Iyawo Ronna wrote that she felt "at times like . . . a secret agent since people" on her job didn't know she was a *iyawo*. Michelle chose not to explain much about her *iyawo* status at work: "At my job, the people that I worked with didn't understand how I was dressed. Especially . . . my head having to be covered with a scarf all the time. They thought that I had cancer. I didn't give them any explanation on why I wore a scarf but I also told them that I was not sick." Camila was instructed via *itá* divination to hide from co-workers that she was a *iyawo* and if she was asked, to deny it. Having made *ocha* for health reasons, Nora said that she "would not deny" her "religion if asked directly," but neither would she "volunteer that information to co-workers." New initiates displayed great variety in their openness at their workplaces, although they tended toward secrecy.

Some felt that their workplaces or their co-workers were especially accommodating about the year in white. Vincent, for example, worked at a hospital where wearing whites was not remarkable. Silvia's job required her to wear white suits and heels at conferences, where she would have to eat in a "banquet" setting. She adapted by bringing her own *iyawo* utensils and dishes. She related a time when her co-workers were true allies, even though they did not necessarily understand the reasons behind her special needs at the table:

> We were at this luncheon . . . and the waiter was coming to take up the plates. And he took my plate. And everybody at the table was like "You took her plate. You took her plate! That's *her* plate." I didn't have to say a word. And most of these people I had never met before the conference. But they knew something was going on; they knew I was going through an initiation and I had to have my own plate. A lot of them said . . . "You look really beautiful." . . . So they looked out for me.

On another occasion, it was the wait staff that was particularly obliging:

> We were at a luncheon . . . at this real high class restaurant where they have five different courses, and every course they come change your plate and all this stuff. So one of the waiters—he was a white waiter but he must have known something about the religion—because I would try to wipe off my plate for the next course, [and] he would say "No you don't have to do that." He would take my plate and spoon and wash it and bring it back. He knew what was going on.

Silvia described especially supportive work relations during her year in white, despite *iyawo* norms of relative secrecy in workplaces. Other *iyawos* and former *iyawos* told stories of difficulties at work. They tired of questions about their unconventional attire and presentation. They found themselves impatient with assumptions that they were sick with cancer. Hector, who, like Vincent, worked at a hospital, also found that wearing whites was not a problem. However, his supervisor harassed him about his head coverings until he was able to locate scrubs that seemed more work-appropriate to her. Elena recalled that she was singled out for abuse at school by an animal-rights activist professor. Ted said that he was discriminated against at work because he was a *iyawo*. Faye believed that she came very close to losing her job. Her absence from work for the *kariocha* was "viewed as proof" that she "was a poor employee," and she was never able to fully mend "relationships with supervisors and management." Wilma, a priest of Chango who underwent *kariocha* because she was instructed to do so in multiple divinatory sessions, recalled being hassled every day at work for an entire year. Chango priest Sheila believed that she was reported to her licensing board because she was inappropriately required by her godparents "to wear full [*iyawo*] regalia to work." Lincoln, a police officer, reported "being called everything at work: the Pillsbury dough boy, this and that." He noticed racial and ethnic differences among his co-workers' reactions: "It was funny because the Latino people . . . were much more receptive than the Black people on the job. The Latinos understood what I was doing. The black people were all 'He is doing that Voodoo thing.' And it was just crazy. The white people were scared—curious, but scared." Ines, who worked as a substitute teacher at an elementary school where head coverings were not permitted, discovered that kids can be cruel:

> I had to buy a wig. . . . When I went to the wig place [before my initiation], they put the wig on and everything was hunky dory. I looked great . . . [But once my head was shaved, the wig] kept riding up on my head. . . . So one time I was working with first grade children. . . . So the first three months [of the year in white] you are not allowed to look in a mirror. So it [the wig] was riding up the back [of my head], and I was bald and they [the children] said, "Look! She has no hair. She is a man!" That went on for three years. I would hear them saying . . . "She's a he!" And . . . they would scream out of the bus, "There she is: the bisexual!" Can you imagine?

Iyawo Kenneth believed he lost his job in an elementary school because of his visibly non-Christian belief and practice: "When I first started there, I was working in the library and people started putting out Jesus books . . . and were treating me a little bit different than other people. Then the principal of the school came in and said you do wonderful work and are great with the children, but we don't think you are a good fit for this school." Carmen was "let go" from her job during her year in white, soon after she was "verbally mistreated" there. Similarly, Peggy—who made *ocha* "to heighten . . . [her] spirituality," said that she had lost her job as a receptionist because of her *kariocha*.

Iyawos and former *iyawos* had a range of experiences with workplace relations during the year in white. Stories of workplace troubles among a minority of respondents may justify the tendency among *iyawos* to keep their *yaworaje* a secret while they are on the job.

ILÉ IYAWO

Years after leaving my first two *ilés* and making *ocha* in another, I have been blessed several times with the opportunity to participate in Lukumi religious ceremony within a particularly efficient, generous, and knowledgeable house of

Ocha in California. Most of the twenty-five to forty people who attend there are related to each other by blood. At the center of the *ilé* are four siblings, their parents of Mexican descent, and the siblings' various children and spouses or significant others, all of whom are Ocha priests or are marked via divination to be initiated to one of the Orisha. Children raised in the house may be given *collares* (colorful beaded necklaces consecrated to the Orisha, also called *elekes*), marked to one of the Orishas (assigned through divination for initiation), and initiated as children. They are raised within the religion, surrounded by adult Ocha priests who are also their parents, grandparents, aunts, uncles, and cousins. They attend regular weekend rituals at which beads and Orishas are "received,"[3] heads are dedicated to specific aspects of divinity, purifications are performed, divinations are assessed, Ocha and ancestors are honored, and life is celebrated with drumming, song, work, food, and dance. Family members and adopted "strays" (as I once heard them referred to in the *ilé)* who enter this house by choosing one of the Orisha priests as godparents and making *ocha* later in life are likely to experience the religion as a place of family, where large groups consisting of several generations frequently eat noisy meals at long tables together, speaking and joking in both Spanish and English.

When I visit the California *ilé*, I am often moved to gratitude. After one trip I wrote in my journal: "Everyone was so welcoming and open with me that I forgot at times that I was an outsider." But then something would happen, like an introduction to someone I hadn't yet met. I'd be introduced by my name and the exclamation "She came all the way from New Jersey!" It was then that I'd wonder how they must see me. Did they think I was crazy for flying across the country just to work an *ocha*? Did they envy my ability to do so? Did they feel sorry for me for not living in such close religious community? And I'd speculate on what they felt about their own religious collective. Did they feel lucky to have such intensive family in their lives? As a single woman living alone whose own *ilé* was geographically dispersed and who longed for family more than anything else, I wondered whether the California house members appreciated what they had, whether they knew the rare value of functional extended family in an increasingly fragmented, alienated social world—if they took it for granted or found it a suffocating nuisance.

Unlike the California *ilé* I sometimes visit, *casas de ocha* are increasingly composed of adults and "strays" who are not necessarily related by blood. These spiritual houses are based on lineage.[4] Lukumi practitioners belong to the *ilé* of the person who initiated them, their godparent. They may also consider themselves to be a part of a larger *ilé* that centers on the original initiator in a particular geographical area. This is the model that Gregory (1999, 41), in his ethnography of Santería in New York City in the 1980s, described as "representative of the major houses of Ocha" in the United States. His research focused on a predominantly

Cuban *ilé* that was multiethnic and included at least three generations of ritual descendants as regular participating members. Such a "well-organized house of Ocha," Gregory wrote, functions "like a corporate family, with various responsibilities" that in the case of large ceremonies "engage dozens of people in intense activity that can continue for a number of days." These autonomous *ilés* often interact with other houses of Ocha, inviting members from nearby religious houses to visit, thus keeping *ilé* members accountable, because "the reputation of a house (and of its *padrino* or *madrina*) rests on how 'correct' its practices are perceived to be by visiting ritual specialists" (Gregory 1999, 41).

One generally becomes a member of a *casa de ocha* by receiving consecrated necklaces (called *collares* or *elekes*) or Warriors (Los Guerreros) from a priest. The priest then becomes the receiver's godparent. These are often considered the first official steps into Orisha worship (Clark 2007), and their recipients are considered to be *aleyo*. Initiatory rituals such as these require two godparents, the primary godparent and a secondary godparent, called the *ayubona*.

Since the beginning of the twentieth century, the ritual houses, or *casas templos* (house temples), that emerged from earlier African ethnic *cabildos de nación* in nineteenth-century Cuba have been modeled on kinship and fictive kinship systems (Brown 2003, 74). A *casa,* or *ilé* "refers not merely to the physical domicile of a priest, but to a ritual 'family' of priests initiated by an elder of Ocha." *Iyawos* are ritually bound to godparents, their *madrina* and/or *padrino*, who are said to have spiritually "birthed" them in the *kariocha*. Likewise, physical representations of Orisha consecrated for *iyawos* during the priestly initiation are said to have been birthed by initiates' godparents and their godparents' Orishas. Other godchildren of the godparent are often considered to be god-siblings to the *iyawo*. House members may also continue ritual kinship references to include god-aunts and god-uncles, god-nieces, god-nephews and god-grandparents. Though a person's place in the hierarchical kinship structure of the *ilé* is determined by seniority (which is determined not by biological age but by the number of years since a person underwent *kariocha*), godparents are generally considered to have the greatest authority over their godchildren, even more than members of an extended Ocha community who are more senior.

Relationships between godparents and their *ahijados* (godchildren) are defined with specific responsibilities on both sides:

> The relationship between the initiate and her primary godparent is the most important human-to-human relationship in the religion. This is followed closely by the relationship between the initiate and . . . yubona. The godparents are responsible for the initiate's spiritual and religious life. The initiate will be expected to salute them first when meeting them at later rituals or other events, and she will be expected to honor them on their own religious birthdays. (Clark 2007, 135)[5]

Godchildren are generally expected to assist, when possible, in the work of *ilé* events. Godparents who survive their *ahijados* are charged with performing funerary rites. Godchildren are expected, as resources permit, to host drum ceremonies for their godparents' Orisha. Godparent-godchild relations sometimes include emotional and material support in addition to ritual support.

While the relationships between a godparent and an *ahijado* may be considered tentative when the godchild is *aleyo*, after the godchild has been initiated as a priest, the bonds are considered to be relatively permanent. One may change his or her godparent until she or he "births" you. After the *kariocha* ceremony, godchildren may (and do) abandon their godparents (and vice versa), but their godparents remain their *madrina* and *padrino* and subsequent relations are seen as adoptive rather than true replacements (Clark 2007). Neil, who made *ocha* for urgent health reasons, told of how difficult it was to make the decision to divorce his initiating godparents and their spiritual house:

> That was probably the hardest thing I've ever done, truly. Nobody wants to leave where they are born. There is a relationship or something that happens inside of you when you are crowned with your crowning godparents. So quite frankly it caused me a great amount of distress to be honest. One of the bigger horror stories in this religion is people leaving a house, finding a new one, and then from that day forward they are always treated like the red-headed step child. That didn't happen to me, but it was probably the hardest decision I ever had to make.

As Neil's case illustrates, although some do leave their initiating godparents, this is considered a weighty decision and is often described as such by those who feel they have reason to do so.

Another model can structure relationships in the religion: that of client to religious practitioner/healer/diviner. This pattern is an old one as well.[6] Today, one only need enter a *botanica*[7] and ask for a consultation from an *olorisha* or *babalawo* as a new client. The priest, guided by the Orisha Elegua or Orula, will read divinatory messages from cowrie shells or palm nuts and prescribe remedies of spiritual baths; prayers; offerings left at railroad tracks, churches, or forests; or sometimes even the initiatory rituals of Lukumi or Ifa. Indeed, one common way that Orisha priests may receive new godchildren is when someone to whom they have provided divinatory *consultas* (consultations) makes the transition from client to godchild.[8] Although relationships between godparents and *ahijados* are supposed to transform from the client-practitioner model to a more familial one, especially by the time the *aleyo* becomes a *iyawo*, the transition is not always easy or complete, and *aleyos* and sometimes even *iyawos* complain that they are treated as clients rather than as practitioners in training. Such occurrences may be magnified for cultural newcomers to Lukumi, especially those who must bridge differences of race, ethnicity, class, language, religious background, and/ or sexual orientation with those with whom they are supposed to be family.

Within the house structure, ideally, *iyawos* have other novices and newly former *iyawos* to provide advice and support. Preferably, they will live near enough to their *babaloshas* and/or *iyaloshas* that they can receive regular guidance and attend religious events in the house every week or every month. These events will help them develop many varied skills of "working" the religion, such as cleaning, taking care of animals, and cooking. If they haven't yet learned them, they may also be taught the foundational skills of prayer (for which spiritual lineage must be memorized), *obi* (coconut) divination, and (sometimes) basic information about the *odu* in the complex divination system. But what of the numerous *iyawos* who come to the religion later in life, who enter from a calling of spirit alone (instead of both spirit and ancestry), and/or who practice in geographical locations far from those of their blood or spiritual relations? Are they treated as kin or client? And which model do *iyawos* prefer?

HAPPY FAMILIES

Iyawos and former *iyawos* who spoke or wrote about their godfamily often described them as sources of support. Star expressed gratitude that her house of Ocha was open and accepting. Maritza liked it that her godfather took her "everywhere" and that her "grandmother in Santo spoiled" her. Laura felt that her year in white went by quickly and without incident because she was "always" at her *padrino*'s house. Isabel reported a smooth year because she had her "godparents around all the time [and] never had anything bad to say about them." Lily believed that she now has a "good foundation" because she lived "in the same state as" her godmother during her year in white. This enabled her "to go to the [religious] functions and get connected and build a relationship" with her "Ocha family." Phoebe felt that her year in white was positive in large part because of her good relationships with her godfamily. Once in a while, she noted, her *iyalosha* even gave her the special treat of escorting her to a restaurant. Iyawo Eduardo raved about his godfather, who he believed to be especially knowledgeable and renowned. He characterized his *ilé* as incredibly "close knit."

Interview and survey participants commonly used kinship metaphors to communicate the feelings of nurturance and connection they experienced during their *yaworaje* in their house of Ocha. Vincent claimed to have an especially close relationship with his godmother: "I actually call her my mom and she calls me her son." Despite frustrating experiences with hostility from coworkers at her workplace, from strangers and acquaintances on the streets, and from friends, Carmen "was always received with love" by her *madrina* "and [was] properly attended to, like her daughter." Iyawo Akeisha portrayed her small *ilé* as warm and "very much like family," a place where she was "welcomed and loved" and fed when she "couldn't afford to eat." She credited her godmother as her primary source of emotional assistance when her biological mother died. For Hector, travel to his godparents' house of Ocha was his favorite aspect of the year in white: "The best part was when I would go to visit [my godparents], the few times I did in that year. I felt that it was more than just a family. I just felt a closeness that I can't explain. It was enough to keep me going until the next time I went. It was very supportive." Sustenance from his godfamily was material as well as emotional; Hector's godmother gave him a battered car when his broke down so he could make the trip home with his Orisha. Iyawo Emma reveled in being the spoiled "only child" of her *madrina*. While she looked forward to having god-brothers and god-sisters one day, she felt that she received a quality and frequency of attention that she wouldn't have had otherwise; she was able to "call her [godmother] on the phone every day." Many described their *ilé* as affirmingly domestic, warm spaces and their relationships with their godparents as caring.

For some, the kinlike attachments within their godfamily were intensified by shared living arrangements during the year in white or parts of it. All *iyawos* are supposed to spend at least a week living with their godparents during the *kariocha*, but some extended the period of cohabitation. Bea described the first three months of her *yaworaje* as "amazing"; this was largely because she lived with her godmother and learned about the tradition during this time. Similarly, following her *kariocha*, Ursa enjoyed living with her godfather for almost a month: "I could be there in that setting that was comfortable. His Orishas and my Orishas [were there]. It felt very cared for and protective and connected." Lincoln practically lived with his godparents:

> I spent my *iyawo* year basically with my godfather. . . . I worked midnights, so I would get off of work in the morning and take the train and go to his house every day. And he would be sleeping, my godfather. He would wake up about 11 o'clock and he would say "What are you doing here, Iyawo?" And my godmother—I think that was before she went to work, before the kids went to school, so she was getting ready my assignment for the day. . . . I slept in his chair downstairs. Or I slept on the floor. Or I would start in the chair and end up on the floor. . . . I had a mat over there, extra everything I had over at his house. Extra plate, spoon, cup, the whole deal. . . . I would do my laundry at his house. I didn't have a washing machine at the time, and he didn't want me to go to a public laundry.

Lincoln described enjoying the familial privileges and responsibilities that he shared with his *madrina* and *padrino*. When Joseph was first told in an Ifa reading by a *babalawo* that he needed to become an Ocha priest, "it scared the crap out of" him, even though "it also felt right." He claimed to have no doubts. Years later, Joseph, who lived next door to his godparents, described a *casa de ocha* that was so much like kin that "they will literally say 'I love you'" whenever he walked out the door. He characterized his godmother as "just like a second mother" and explained that even "the little spats between the godbrothers and godsisters" were just like family. For some *iyawos*, physical proximity to godparents allowed them to experience the belonging and warmth of family during their year or parts of it.

Those who spoke positively about their *ilés* often mentioned the teaching provided there. These *iyawos* were being prepared to be responsible *olorishas* instead of being treated as clients. Shawna described her godmother and her religious household as being particularly focused on careful instruction in the tradition: "She was always very nurturing about educating her godchildren, making sure we learned. It was like on the job training. You got into it and the other godchildren [also] taught a lot." Opal felt that her godfather was especially indulgent about her numerous questions, so much so that she was not bothered when, fed up, he would eventually tell her that "*iyawo* should be seen and not heard." Douglas also described his year in white as an apprenticeship of sorts: "Because my *ilé* lost a lot of people, I did a lot of the work in my *ilé*. I had to be at all rituals and usually was quizzed on the process." *Iyawos* often appreciated intensive learning in their spiritual houses during their year in white.

Iyawos and former *iyawos* also highlighted the companionship and caring they experienced in their houses of Ocha. Opal described a thriving, functional *ilé* that encouraged camaraderie among the several *iyawos* within it. She took pride in the fact that her rapport with her godfather was so strong that he was visibly nervous about the outcome of her *itá* divination. Gabriel recalled enjoying his *iyawo* status in his *casa de ocha*. He liked being served food, as is Lukumi custom, before everyone else, and he enjoyed the company of the other *iyawos* in his extended godfamily. In these ways and more, some religious practitioners described their *ilés* as providing supportive spaces and relationships that eased the seclusion of the *yaworaje*, trained them for future roles as full participants in the religion, and enhanced their emotional, spiritual, and physical well-being.

FAMILY TROUBLES

Not all interview and survey participants felt that their *ilés* were supportive. Some were estranged from their godfamily because of geographical distance, abandonment, or incompatibilities of various sorts. New initiates who were separated from their *ilé* during the year in white commonly indicated that this was the most difficult part of their *yaworaje*. Kendra said that the worst part of her year in white was separation from her godfamily for half a year while she was performing research outside the country. Hector expressed that the geographic distance from his *ilé* negatively affected his *yaworaje*. He often worked on weekends and had to drive several hours to see his family in Ocha. Visiting with godparents required the expense and "hassle" of gas money and car rentals, leading to a lonely year in white during which he "missed all the [religious] parties" and wasn't able to engage in the hands-on learning he longed for. Kelly felt discarded by her godparents. The worst part of the year for her, she wrote, "was not having my godparents by my side." She explained that it was an emotionally difficult time because her "Padrino moved away" and her *ayubona* "did not respond" to her attempts at contact: "I felt alone and in the air," she remembered. Nicole claimed to have been deserted during her *yaworaje* by a godmother who, she believed, "just saw this religion" as a way "to get money." Mark tried to make the best of his situation, but still found the 500 mile distance from his Ocha family to be a hardship: "I felt like I was up in orbit in a space station—away from my family. But thanks to the internet and chat software, I was able to talk (some weeks daily) with my godfamily and godparents . . . so it wasn't unbearable." Ida believed she "was treated very unfairly because of" the *odu* that arose during her *itá* divination. She complained that she was "isolated" and left to navigate the demanding *yaworaje* on her own.

Initiates who were estranged or geographically separated from their godfamily tended to report loneliness during their year in white. Faye, whose godparents were over a seven hour drive away, wrote that she felt "isolated" and frustrated that her godparents infrequently returned her phone calls. Ines shared about the difficulties of a *yaworaje* without godfamily:

> It was very lonely. Not too many people visited me. It was a nightmare. I remember my godfather saying to me—he must have known from my signs [in *itá*]—"If you make it through this year, you'll make it through anything." And I had heard, you know, the iyawo year was hard, but I never knew to what extent. . . . But you know . . . it makes a big difference when you have a house to visit so you are not by yourself. And I lived alone. . . . It was a very rough year.

Sheila also told a story of painful seclusion: "My godparents lived three hours away and none of my godbrothers or sisters were local. I was living far west of the city and many friends would have to commute over an hour to see me. So I was very lonely. I wasn't allowed to [be] associated with others in the religion or go to *botanicas* or local gatherings. . . . I felt controlled." Similarly alienated from his *ilé* during his year in white, Neil, a priest of Oshun, described the time as the most alone he felt in his entire life. Due to the many social restrictions of the *yaworaje*, Lukumi novices rely upon the members of their godfamily as social lifelines. Many reported that when this was not available, they suffered.

Whether or not they were located near their godparents during the year in white, current and former practitioners of the year in white commonly expressed desires for greater guidance or "parenting" from their *madrina* and/or *padrino*. *Iyawos* frequently worried that they weren't learning enough during their year. Such concerns may be due in part to *iyawo* impatience and misunderstanding; in many religious houses, the bulk of the tradition is taught only after a *iyawo* has completed his or her year in white. Sometimes, though, the complaints may point to communication or personality difficulties, or godparents who see their *ahijados* as customers who have already paid for their services, or even as future competition. Having witnessed the daily interactions his godsister had with her godmother when she was a *iyawo*, Vincent, who lived at a greater distance from his *madrina*, "felt sad that" he didn't experience such intensive godmothering. While his godsister's *madrina* would visit unexpectedly to "just check out what she" was wearing, his godmother did not, trusting him to follow the rules on his own. Gabriel also felt he was under-supervised during his *yaworaje*. He complained that he "wasn't learning anything and wasn't being told" what was permitted and forbidden. He admitted to not understanding that he wasn't supposed to drink a beer and to not knowing that he could cease sleeping on a mat on the floor after his first three months. Additionally, he charged that his godmother would rather play dominoes with him than teach him about the religion. Similarly, Mariposa shared that the worst part of her year "was not having any guidance and sort of being nervous about whether" she "was following the rules correctly." Feeling abandoned by her godparents, she also fretted that she "wasn't ever going to learn anything else about the religion as a santera." Ines griped similarly about her *madrina* during the year in white and beyond:

> My godmother never taught me anything. I kept begging her, and she wouldn't teach me anything. So after a while, [the Orisha] Shango said, "Do not argue with her. . . . Walk away." And I did. I didn't see her for years, and I didn't even see her before she died. And that was heart breaking to me. . . . I believe you contribute to the house—expenses, like you contribute to a church. I had no problem with that, and I did it for years of my life. But when you don't teach me, that is your responsibility. It is not something I should pay you for.

Donna felt that she learned little from her *ilé* during her year in white: "My *padrino* was a very compassionate but extremely busy person so learning from him was very limited." In contrast to the many positive stories from interview and survey participants who felt that they were being well trained in the religion, a number of *iyawos* and former *iyawos* spoke of their hunger for knowledge and impatience about learning more about the religion during their year in white; they believed their priestly educations had been neglected.

Heads freshly shorn, considered "babies" in need of special protection following the *kariocha* ceremony, *iyawos* who experienced a lack of support from their godfamily often described feeling vulnerable and forsaken. Nicolás, whose "godmother had a falling out with her godfather and her godchildren," likened his experience during the *yaworaje* to that of "an only child with a 'single parent.'" Yevette explained that her year was "different" from that of other *iyawos* because her godparents "abandoned" her after her first three months. A priest of Yemaya, Carolina wrote that she underwent the *kariocha* as a response "to the call." Without "an elder nearby to guide" her, she considered herself "orphaned" during her year. Deserted by her godparents during her *yaworaje*, Regina described herself as "a babe in the woods left out for the wolves to ravage." Such accounts highlight the emotional need of many *iyawos* for attention and guidance from their godparents.

Occasionally *ilé* problems are greater than distance and neglect. In her novel *How to Greet Strangers*, Joyce Thompson (2013) shares a story of a particularly dysfunctional Ocha family, headed by an elder who abuses power, tightly controls her *ahijados*, sets godchildren against each other, is involved in illegal and exploitative financial dealings, prioritizes monetary gain over spiritual concerns, and greedily doles out religious knowledge and privileges. Sadly, such stories are not limited to the realm of fiction. A number of religious practitioners shared stories that included emotional, financial, or sexual abuse. I have struggled about whether and how to share some of the more extreme stories since I cannot verify any of them. Given that caveat, I feel obliged to acknowledge that too many interviews included such mention; some were of their own experiences, and others made reference to other people's stories. It is thus vital for prospective godchildren to choose godparents and their spiritual house carefully, just as it is important for godparents to choose *ahijados* well.

As in any social group, Lukumi and Ifa *ilé* relations may include abuse. Ines described her first godfather as so controlling that he didn't permit his godchildren to talk with each other. She believed that he had coercive sexual relationships with many of her godsiblings. During her year in white, long after leaving that house, she claimed to have had a sexual relationship with a *babalawo* who, she felt, took advantage of her at a vulnerable time. Gabriel told of Orisha priests he believed to be involved in the "mafia," and shared stories of godparents who took their godchildren's *ocha* money to buy and sell cocaine. Holly underwent a non-Lukumi initiation because she was instructed to do so by a mounted priest and then a diviner; she received Oshun from a *babalawo* ("born from the *odu* of Ifa")—an uncommon initiation in the United States that is likely to limit her participation in Lukumi circles. She likened the behavior of the first Ocha priest she encountered to that of a "conman," who used divination sessions to gauge how much money he could get out of each client/godchild. Jordan, who underwent the *kariocha* before "passing to Ifa"—believed there was "a lot of rape and sexual abuse" in *botanicas*. Moishe's reasons for making *ocha* were multiple; he was told by multiple diviners that he needed to do so, but also he recalled wanting to make *ocha* to relate more closely with Orisha: "I wanted Orishas in my house. I wanted Orishas so I could just pray to them and make offerings to them and honor them." He told a story of receiving fake initiations from a drug-addicted person posing as an *olorisha*. Lani, an *aleyo*, described living and working in a household when she was a teen that was headed by a man claiming to be a *babalawo*. Her participation in the house involved a great deal of cocaine use and an "initiation" by the priest that involved sexual relations. Iyawo Eduardo told of a godparent who was a "coke fiend" and a sexual predator. Most of the personal stories I heard of abuse in *ilés* concerned godparents and a houses of Ocha that the interview participants had left. Obviously when *iyawos* endure such experiences, their year in white is significantly stained.

Relations within *ilés* are shaped by humans with many foibles and are not always ideal. *Iyawos* and former *iyawos* reported a variety of difficulties in their houses of Ocha during their *yaworajes*. They discussed rivalries among godsiblings, inattentive or overattentive godparents, being treated by *ilé* members as "cash cows," conflicts between godparents or between a godparent and themselves, disagreements, accusations, and misunderstandings. Iyawo Jasmine reluctantly left her godmother after a lengthy and complex series of events that she described as involving semi-public arguments on an Orisha community online networking site, scandal, gossip, marital and familial strains. She also said her *madrina* gossiped about her and attempted to control her. Dawn, who dedicated herself to Yemaya because she felt that she "needed the tools" the Orisha would bring her, left the godmother who had initiated her soon after she completed her year in white. The problems, which involved personalities and community politics, began to be apparent immediately after she was initiated, while she was still on the mat during the seven days of the *kariocha* ceremony. Similarly, Robert experienced negativity with his godmother even before his initiation. When he received his first Lukumi reading out of curiosity about his tutelary Orisha, Robert was told he needed "to do *ocha* like yesterday." Although he didn't have the funds for the expensive ceremony and didn't have a godparent, he eventually earned the money through hard work and he met his *madrina* through a series of lucky circumstances. Yet soon after he committed to the *kariocha* the relationship with his godmother soured: "Two weeks before my *ocha* process we went from being best friends to being worst enemies and to this day I can't tell you why." Part of the problem was that "she had been accusing everybody under the sun of trying to steal" him "away from her," though to Robert "it made no sense." Robert had difficult exchanges with his godmother throughout his year in white and separated from her soon after. Robert also confided that his godmother charged him an exorbitant sum for the *kariocha*, at least twice the going rate, and the most expensive I've heard of. When asked how he decided to make *ocha*, Jack, a priest of Oshun, said that he "just did it," that he "totally went in with blind faith, totally and completely let go [of] control." But his godfather disappeared without explanation during his *iyawo* year. Helen told a similar story: "My relationship with my godmother began to deteriorate . . . before my crowning and continued to do so after. She had crowned a set of twins three months before me and we formed a support system for each other but we all felt neglected." Mía endured her *yaworaje* during an explosive time in her Ocha house: "My *ilé* . . . was in the process of dividing; of being split apart by the separation of godparents and godchildren and the result today is two feuding houses that I jokingly call the Montagues and the Capulets."

Some participants wrote about poor godfamily relations that they witnessed in the Ocha community. Lincoln noted what he believed to be a trend of improper and inadequate guidance and teaching in the religion that put older and younger people in conflict: "All parents are not good parents," he said. "A lot of godparents have poor parenting skills." More specifically, he explained that "the younger people in *ocha* . . . they don't salute." They don't know how to respond when called by an elder. There is "a lack of respect." Sofia told a story that is not uncommon. An aunt took her to make *ocha* in Cuba. The aunt became her *ayubona* and a man she met on the island was her *padrino*. When Sofia returned to the states, her aunt moved, leaving Sofia without supervision or community during her *yaworaje*. She warns newcomers to the religion to make sure to choose their godparents well: "I tell people that are first coming into this religion, get to know the people you are getting involved with." Make sure they feel genuine love for the Orisha, she warns, instead of looking to make money from their interactions with you. "Too many people that I come across are wowed because so and so person has a million and one godchildren. And I tell people all the time, 'Are all those children still with this person? . . . Is this person doing stuff correctly or are they short-cutting? Are they doing what they should be doing and not just, what is that phrase, putting up another notch on their belt?' . . . A godparent/ godchild relationship should last until you pass away or he passes away." In contrast to stories of happy Ocha families, a minority discussed difficulties with their godparents and other members of their *ilés* in ways that affected their experience of the year in white.

DIVERSITY DIVISIONS

It is common in Ocha communities for priests in the religion to be reminded that they serve a particular Orisha but they are not that Orisha. Despite identification with an aspect of divinity, Orisha priests are human, with all the weaknesses being human entails. Cultural bias and intolerance of diversity is not unheard of in Ocha communities. I was told stories of sexism, racism, ableism, classism, homophobia, and HIV phobia that strained relationships within *ilés* or within the larger Ocha community. Although most interview and survey participants felt that their own *casa de ocha* was open to diversity, several told stories of intolerance or discrimination they had experienced or witnessed.

Iyawos and former *iyawos* of all ethnic backgrounds spoke about racial and ethnic tensions. Several African American participants spoke of feeling slighted because of their race, especially by Cubans, in ways that are reminiscent of Brandon's (1997) description of racial/ethnic strife between Lukumi practitioners of the two groups in the United States in the 1960s. Shawna, an African American priest of Yemaya, told of her experience with racial discrimination in the larger Ocha community:

> Sometimes if we participate in a ceremony where it is a Cuban based house, the Cubans tend to almost ignore the African Americans. They don't really take us on. They kind of act as if we are there . . . as slaves—to do a lot of work but not give a lot of credence to maybe your years of Ocha or your experience . . . I have even found . . . that if I go to an Ocha that is primarily Cuban, I might assume . . . they are probably older than me in Ocha, so I would salute them. But what I found is that they will let [an] African American salute them even if they are younger than you in Ocha or may not even have Ocha. So I've learned I have to ask and say "Do you have Santo?" And say, "How many years?" And a lot of times they are younger than me. . . . So they'll say "Four years." And I'll say, "I have ten." They don't like to salute African Americans.

Shawna was frustrated by the fact that the custom of saluting one's elders was undermined by what seemed to her to be racial prejudice. More important to her was the lack of respect for her status in the *ocha* ceremonies in ways that seemed to question her legitimate place in the religion.

While some Black Americans have sought an African-derived religion as respite from a white-dominant society, the white Cuban elders many encountered in the religion in the mid-twentieth century United States did not acknowledge the political nature of their religious involvement. Jordan, another African American priest, mentioned this point:

> I have heard many racist things uttered about the original people who practiced the religion: that this is a religion of savages. . . . Some people even deny that this is an African religion. Those people are dying off—basically, the old timers, the Cubans. . . . Now I will tell you the kind of discrimination I have seen is white Cuban elder versus young American Black North American. . . . The White

Latino elders say, "This ain't no political thing.... Don't pull this Malcolm X crap here. This ain't no civil rights movement; this is the Orisha." So they really try to suppress our sense of politics of North American Blacks.

Jordan was one of several participants who noted that while the history of racial discrimination African Americans have endured was what drew many into the religion, they experienced similar discrimination within it.

Some African American Orisha priests promoted racial distinctions. Silvia judged white participants in the religion harshly:

I really don't see why they [whites] are in the religion. Really, I do understand Spirit doesn't have a color and all that other kind of stuff, but we don't have no white people in our house, in our *ilé*. We *would* not have any in our *ilé*. I would really feel some kind of way standing next to a white person calling up our ancestors. "Your ancestors might be the ones who enslaved my ancestors." I personally think that—and it is not personal—they need to find out what their ancestors did. "What did your ancestors worship?" And do that. This is what God sends to *us*. My opinion of the spiritual world: God sends something to every group of people. They all have their word for God in their language; they all have their rituals. . . . It is like for Black people we can't have nothing for ourselves. Everybody . . . wants to be all up in there. And they are changing it around, just like they did to Christianity.

Although Silvia was particularly outspoken, I expect she spoke for other individuals who were not willing to share their true beliefs with a white non-Hispanic researcher.

Some white non-Hispanic priests in the religion claimed to have felt unwelcome in the religion, even at times within their own *ilés*. Ines felt that she was not accepted by her godsiblings in their predominantly African American house: "They were Black nationalists. . . . So I used to cry all the time, because I used to say 'Maybe I don't belong in this [religion], Madrina.' And she would say 'Yes you do. Yes you do.'" Moishe, a priest of Yemaya, began as an *aleyo* in the early 1980s. He felt that white non-Hispanics are more accepted in the religion now than they were twenty years ago, but that problems remain:

It is still bad now. So many white Americans don't think they have any chance of getting into the religion with any kind of legitimate priest. So they'll put up with an amazing amount—things they would never put up with otherwise. They'll put up with homophobia, with racism, sexism. . . . And they'll call it cultural differences or whatever. They'll use whatever excuse they need to, because they are so desperate to be in the tradition and they think there is no other way in. I know it is not near that bad now, but it was that bad then. Because in many cases people wouldn't accept a white American in their house or they would just take them for every penny they had. They figured they had no place in the religion, so they would just rip them off and leave them out in the street.

Implicit in Moishe's account were Lukumi cultural norms both of secrecy and ranking by seniority that created barriers to entry into the religion for newcomers. Difficulties in being accepted into Lukumi communities may have been exacerbated by ethnic, linguistic, and racial differences for both white and Black latecomers into Lukumi.

Subtler racializations of the religion were not uncommon in my interviews. Jordan, who explained that the religion is open to people of all races, also described participating in racial typing:

> There is kind of a belief that this religion is kind of a Black religion. . . . Some people might think that Ifa is for Black people and by Black people and Black people do it better. I think in general Black people *do* do it better and more profoundly, because for us it is a survival mechanism. . . . And I think people when they meet me—they are a little reassured that I am Black. . . . Whereas if I was a white guy with spiky blonde hair or a woman with red hair or Jewish or Korean or Arabic, they might be like "This is a little weird. This is not what I was expecting." This is still a religion of Blacks.

Several of the white non-Hispanic *aleyos*,[9] especially those who were not well integrated in *ilés*, viewed their participation as necessarily on the fringes because of their blood and ancestry. Chris had been involved sporadically and casually for many years in a multiethnic, predominantly Hispanic *ilé*. He confided, "I have been told there are some initiations in this religion that . . . some people are too white to have. If you are not of a certain tribe from Africa, you can't have that initiation." For this participant, as for many others, Orisha worship retained strong associations with Cuban and/or African ancestries.

Yet some white non-Hispanic participants who began with highly racial conceptions of the religion found that their views changed as their involvement grew. Jennifer, an *aleyo* marked to Oshun, was warned that people in the Lukumi community "wouldn't like me because I was white. That they would be mean to me because I couldn't speak Spanish." But she found that this was not the case. When he was introduced to the religion, Alex, who was also an *aleyo* during his interview with me, was respectful but reluctant to participate fully because of his race: "It is not a white people religion, at least initially," he told me. Later, after finding a predominantly white and English-speaking *ilé* within a large multi-ethnic religious community, he became much more involved. He has since undergone initiation into the priesthood.

Some participants provided reasons for the wariness of ethnic newcomers in the religion. Several believed that the history of the religion, bound up with the chains of slavery, granted African Americans an ownership of the religion that whites did not share. Shawna understood the reasons for the reluctance of some African Americans to accept whites in Orisha religions, but she believed the religions should not discriminate on the basis of race:

> I think part of the problem that African Americans have with bringing white people in is several fold. The whole notion that they were the slave owners. "This is ours and this belongs to us. Why can't we have this for ourselves?" "They have no business in this—it is African based." If they have to, then it is, "We don't want to teach them anything." No different than what the Cubans had said about African Americans. . . . I think that we miss the boat when it comes to how we approach people of other cultures with respect to the religion, and we shouldn't. It shouldn't be any different than what we do for ourselves.

Nevertheless, several participants noted sympathy with or sensitivity toward an Afrocentric view of the religion, even as most of those who were willing to participate in interviews with me mentioned a belief that the religion should be open to all. The fact that I am white and non-Hispanic may have shaped their responses.

Some mentioned the concern that white people entering the religion, especially those with a neo-pagan or New Age background, would change the religion in unacceptable or inauthentic ways. This was a concern religious participants of all races voiced. George, who came from a neo-pagan background himself, complained about those who come to Orisha worship from the predominantly white non-Hispanic neo-pagan movement: "I see a lot a Pagans . . . running around yapping about Yemaya and the sea goddess . . . and . . . I think that they have no fucking idea what they're talking about. I see a lot of . . . witchy folks like pull off these ideas from African religions. And it irks me." Amanda, a priest of Obatalá who made *ocha* as a "leap of faith at a time when . . . [she] had no money," was drawn to the initiation after coming to know her husband's new Orisha. She explained that the skepticism in many Orisha communities about white non-Hispanics, especially those from Wiccan, neo-pagan, or New Age backgrounds, is because of the idea that they are cultural "tourists" or casual religion shoppers rather than sincere seekers ready to commit: "Well I think a lot of people—and this is something that makes me cringe—a lot of people who have come to this tradition have tried on a zillion other things that are very New Agey. . . . And you know there is a suspicion with certain kinds of people that this is just the religion du jour rather than a deep life commitment." There was also worry that non-Hispanic whites may feel more entitled than others to modify the religion. Concerned with illegitimate changes to the traditions, Marcos, who said that the decision to make *ocha* "was never a question" for him, offered the example of a group that advocated eliminating animal sacrifice from the religion: "The fear has always been that, 'Oh, we are white, therefore we are better. So whatever changes we make are going to be appropriate because we are white.'" Ironically, the group to which he referred was largely Cuban.

There is also a concern among some participants that white non-Hispanics might use their privilege unfairly in competition with practitioners of other races. Barbara, a priest of Obatalá who was ordained in an African (not Lukumi) line, explained:

> I think part of fear of letting white people in, is that a lot of people of color are afraid that white people are better at business and commodification of things. And that, if you let white people in, they're going to commodify it and sell it, much like people pick on ... [a particular well-known priest who sells Ifa services online. He's] livin' in the light. He's on the internet. You can call him; he answers the phone. Versus, you know, [Black] Baba Shango ... over there in the corner.

Barbara expressed the fear that white practitioners would be more successful economically than practitioners of other racial groups. These fears seemed to her to be confirmed by the success of a published white non-Hispanic priest who is marketing a version of the religion that many practitioners criticize.

Racial-ethnic tensions were not the only issue that affected relations within and between *ilés*. For some, sexuality was another minefield. Some scholars have suggested that the proportion of LGBT people who participate in the Lukumi religion is much higher than their representation in the general population,[10] perhaps "because of its openness to all types of people and the variety of roles open to practitioners," especially in "oriaté-centered communities" (Clark 2005, 148).[11] However, scholars report mixed treatment of sexual minorities in the religion (see Conner 2004; Vidal-Ortiz 2005, 2006, 2011).

A number of *olorishas* and *aleyos* reported sexual discrimination in Ocha and Ifa communities. Andre described having to choose carefully among Orisha venerators to practice with in the late 1970s and 1980s because the homophobia was "off the charts" in some of them. He felt that this was due to the Black nationalism of the time, which viewed homosexuality as "something foreign to Africa, that it was an import by the oppressor and a tool for the subjugation and ultimate destruction of Black people." Dawn discussed a *casa de ocha* that didn't accept her sexuality and told her that she "was lying about" her lesbianism and was "really straight." Jack was upset when he was told that he could not participate in some initiations (in the related Afro-Cuban Palo and Ifa traditions) because of his sexual orientation. Against orthodox rules, he successfully "got scratched" in Palo anyway.[12] Iyawo William, who underwent the *kariocha* as the next step in his search for a religion and a spirituality that was "by, for and about African people," recalled feeling "very perturbed" when he was told he could not become a *babalawo* once it was discovered that he was gay. In the first *ilé* in which he was initiated as a priest, Neil felt that he was treated poorly because of his homosexuality and his HIV-positive status. He left that *casa de ocha* for a gay-positive one. Hector also left a Lukumi house he described as extremely homophobic. As a way of alleviating their discomfort with him, members of his former *ilé* continually made humiliating references to his sexuality in ways he found "emasculating." Moishe also left an initiating *ilé* because of homophobia: "They would constantly remind me of the particular initiations I couldn't receive as a gay person. They would say 'Oh, look, when you salute, don't do it that way, that is something the gays made up.' They would say stupid, stupid things, just typical homophobic things that every homophobe says. . . . Eventually though, I grew my own brain and just walked away from that house."

Although some discussed racial, ethnic, and sexual tensions and discrimination, others described acceptance and harmony. John, an *oluwo*, said, "I think in general the religion tends to be—if you're willing to cross the line in terms of color, language and everything . . . I don't think you should have a problem." A number of accounts referred to spiritual houses that were accepting of people of all colors. Similarly, those who told stories of prejudice against gay people and HIV-positive people were generally discussing an *ilé* they had left, not the house of Ocha in which they now practiced the religion. Moishe even told an emotional tale of reconciliation when he returned to his original initiating *ilé* over a decade after leaving it. This time, he felt acceptance.

NATIVES, NEWCOMERS, AND RACE/ETHNICITY

To what extent did Lukumi and ethnic/racial background affect relationships with family, friends, and godfamily in the *yaworaje*? Were cultural newcomers more or less likely than cultural natives to argue with their godparents during the year? To feel accepted by their friends and family? To have lost jobs during the year? To forge deep connections with godsiblings in their *ilé*? Did relationships differ among Hispanics and non-Hispanics? Or among those who claimed African or European ancestries?

From analyses of survey data on *iyawo* relationships, Lukumi background was statistically significant in two respects. Those who were raised with the traditions were significantly more likely (54 percent) than those who were not (23 percent) to strongly agree that they were pampered by their godfamily during their *yaworaje* (X^2 = 13.43, df = 3, p = .004; N = 159). Either there was a real difference in treatment or perception of treatment or a difference in the desire for reporting positively on this issue. Also, as might be expected, cultural veterans (75 percent) were more likely than newcomers (41 percent) to report that their family accepted their *iyawo* status ($X^2 = 14.90$, df = 3, $p = .002$; N = 157). Given that natives to Lukumi, by definition, are more likely than newcomers to be involved in a religion shared with blood kin, this is no surprise.

Analyses of ethnic background revealed interesting differences concerning relationships at work during the *yaworaje*. Hispanic respondents were less likely than non-Hispanics to report wearing only white to work or school and to remember feeling accepted by their co-workers. Although a majority of those who took the questionnaire reported wearing only white to work or school, the ethnicity of the respondent seems to have mattered: only 52 percent of Hispanics did so, while 73 percent of non-Hispanics did so ($X^2 = 6.33$, df = 1, $p = .012$; N = 142). The finding that only 51 percent of Hispanics recalled their co-workers being accepting of their being *iyawo* ($X^2 = 5.07$, df = 1, $p = .024$; N = 122) is perhaps related; the comparable figure for non-Hispanics was 71 percent. Conversely, those who indicated African ancestry were more likely than those who did not to wear only white to work ($X^2 = 5.50$, df = 1, $p = .019$; N = 159). Seventy-eight percent of those who claimed African descent reported wearing only white at work or school. The comparable figure for those who did not claim African descent was 56 percent.

One explanation for differences in experiences at work is differences in types of workplaces. Although an analysis of various occupations would be difficult in the present study, educational levels differed among Hispanics and non-Hispanics in my survey, as they do in the larger population in the United States. While those who completed surveys reported higher educational attainment than is average in the United States as a whole, 75 percent of non-Hispanic survey participants had completed four years of college, compared to only 50 percent of Hispanics. Jobs that accompany higher levels of education may differ qualitatively from those available to employees with less education, even to the extent of affecting health (Karmakar and Breslin 2008). For example, employment may differ with regard to compensation, autonomy, freedom from surveillance, and security. These factors may offer the average non-Hispanic an advantage in workplace relations during the *yaworaje*. In contrast, in the present sample, those who claimed African ancestry had higher levels of education (16.97 years) than was average in the survey (15.73) and in the U.S. population as a whole, suggesting that they may have enjoyed an easier relationship than most in their workplaces.[13]

An alternative explanation for the ethnic and racial variations in workplace relations looks to historical differences in the relations of various groups to Lukumi. In the early 1960s, when Cuban Americans viewed the religion as something to hide from the scrutiny of outsiders and possible persecution, African Americans saw Lukumi religion as a way of openly expressing pride in their heritage in a country that promises religious freedom (Brandon 1997; see also Falola and Genova 2006; Lefever 2000). Some of these differing attitudes toward Lukumi may persist today, resulting in different levels of comfort with open religious display among outsiders in environments such as the workplace.

CONCLUSION

Social relationships heavily influence the *yaworaje*. Although some research participants discussed their year in white as if they were living in a bubble, most *iyawos* found that they had to continue to participate in social relations, whether they were affirming, supportive, and educational or troubling, frustrating, and heartbreaking. *Iyawos* and former *iyawos* discussed relationships with family and friends, with co-workers, and with members of their Ocha house and community in both positive and negative ways. The difficulties at work that a minority of my study participants reported seems to justify the secrecy concerning the year in white that so many practiced. Survey and interview participants spoke most frequently of relationships in their *ilé*. Most of them mentioned affirming experiences. Participants generally saw their religious houses as spaces of support, family, and training. A smaller number described negative relations in their *ilé*, including arguments; abandonment; racial, ethnic, or sexual prejudice and discrimination; and occasionally other forms of abuse. These more negative responses should be understood in context of the larger number of *iyawos* and former *iyawos* who described speaking to their godparents regularly and developing deep relationships in their religious house throughout the year in white.

Several differences distinguished cultural natives and newcomers. Most notably, the former more frequently reported that they felt pampered in their houses of Ocha and described greater acceptance of their *iyawo* status among family members. Quantitative analyses revealed a tendency toward greater secrecy at work concerning the *yaworaje* among Hispanics and a greater likelihood of displaying the *yaworaje* at work among those who claimed African heritage. In addition, Hispanics reported less acceptance than non-Hispanics of their *iyawo* status among co-workers.

Another important context for any discussion of affiliations during the year in white is the relations *iyawo* have with their Orisha. *Iyawos* and former *iyawos* often saw the growth of such relationships as the main point of their *kariocha* and the discipline of the *yaworaje*. These relations will be discussed in the chapter that follows.

In March 2006, when my second godfather, the late Afolabi, declared that my head was marked to Chango, I was stunned. *"Maferefun Shango!"* he exclaimed. I can't remember if I made celebratory noises or not; I may have tried. But I was confused and embarrassed. I had expected him to have pronounced me a child of Yemaya or maybe a rarer Orisha. I found it difficult to imagine that it was not Yemaya, the maternal divinity of the sea, who would rule my head should I decide to make *ocha*. I felt a very strong connection to her, and most Orisha devotees who played the head-marking game with me guessed she was my spiritual mother, probably because of my ample hair and build and because years before I had taken "Sea" as a spiritual name. (When I did make *ocha* two years later, the *oriaté* pronounced that my spiritual mother was Yemaya. Each priestly initiate is assigned two parental Orisha, a mother and a father, the head Orisha and a secondary "parent" of the other gender in a dichotomously gendered system. But this validation of my sense of connection to Yemaya did not occur until 2008.)

As I came to sit on the low stool before the divination mat to have my head marked, I had proclaimed with a nervous, joking bravado that I was prepared to be marked to "anyone but Chango." My godfather had scolded me, of course. But the consecrated shells fell in a manner that was irrefutably Chango's. After my *padrino* threw the cowries, I watched uneasily as he and my *ayubona* exchanged pointed looks. Then my godfather explained the meaning of the *odu* that had fallen: *Obara Irosun.* He referred to a story of the "King [who] was hanged, yet he 'did not hang'" (Ócha'ni Lele 2003, 260). He told me that Chango was a king who was afraid of being king. "You are afraid to be at the top, to be the best," he exclaimed. He warned me about the power of words as a weapon, especially against myself. He foretold possible problems with my throat. And he said that I could win Chango's protection by hanging green bananas for him until they became black. Chango, the macho, strutting, kingly, womanizing ruler of thunder and the drum had claimed me, and I didn't understand him or how to relate to him. My head was spinning, and even though I had not yet made the commitment to undergo the priestly initiation, I felt as if I were a young bride assigned to marry a man I'd never seen and probably didn't like.

I walked around the next day in a daze. The head marking seemed so permanent. What did it mean about me that I was marked to Chango? What did it say about my future? How could I possibly devote myself—even if I could bear the expense and disruption to my life of *kariocha*—to an aspect of divinity that seemed so very foreign?

I was afraid to discuss my ambivalent feelings concerning my head marking with my godparents. I worried they would see me as childish or disrespectful to Chango. When I found a moment away from them, I called a friend who was a priest of Yemaya. "*Bendicion*, Star. I'm in Detroit at my godfather's. He marked my head to Chango," I informed her without enthusiasm.

"But that's wonderful! Congratulations!" she exclaimed. "*Maferefun Chango! Kabiosile!*"[1]

"I don't understand it," I admitted. "I don't understand Him."

Star described how it takes time to understand the Orisha, especially the ones to whom we are marked. For her, Chango was associated with many positive things: forward motion, action, fire, and confidence. I found that encouraging. Those were all things that I could understand and use, things I believed were lacking in myself. I thought about Karen McCarthy Brown's ([1991] 2011) discussion in *Mama Lola*, her important ethnography on Haitian Vodou, of how she received an initiation to the *Lwa Papa Ogou*, not because she was *like* the Spirit but because he had attributes that she needed, traits she believed he would share with her. Gradually I began to feel more positively about being marked to Chango. I hung bananas for him soon afterward, and my new doctor (miraculously or coincidentally) found a small cancerous nodule in my thyroid that no one else had even considered seeking. Two other doctors marveled they would not have been able to feel the tiny growth by touch as she had.

Almost two years later, I decided to make *ocha*, in large part to gain the blessings of Chango. After my head marking I had undergone what felt like a lot of loss. I lost my thyroid to cancer. I lost a relationship that seemed significant. More important, I lost hope in the future and confidence in myself. I was heartbroken for longer than seemed reasonable, and it occurred to me that I had fallen in love twice in my life, both times to people who embodied the characteristics (for good and ill) of the divine Chango: kingly, confident, and fiery. In both relationships I had found myself first diminished and then dumped. It was time for me to incorporate whatever Chango was willing to share with me into myself instead of relying on others to complete me. It was time for me to become more so that I might have greater success in my relationships and greater joy in living. My relationship with the Orisha Chango moved from a superficial dislike to one of desire, gratitude, acceptance, and pride. Over time, I began to recognize aspects of Chango in my own personality and life.

Beyond the interactions with family, friends, co-workers, godfamily, and strangers are the associations between religious practitioners and the Orisha. "The complex and compelling relationships that slowly emerge between people and divinities form one of the central arenas of oricha religious practice" (Mason 2002, 58). The *kariocha* is meant to initiate change in connections with the unseen world of Ocha, especially with one's tutelary Orisha. Cultural newcomers commonly discuss their increasing dedication to the world of Ocha within the context of deepening affiliations to specific aspects of divinity. Despite the greater likelihood in survey responses that cultural veterans would mention their love of Orisha as reason for making *ocha*, in interviews, newcomers often placed relationships with Orisha at the center of their stories.

Although each individual path differs, religious participation in Lukumi for newcomers generally begins with rituals that require low levels of commitment, investment, and responsibility. Those who progress within the religion increase those levels over time (Clark 2007). For example, a person seeing an Orisha priest for a reading as a client may be prescribed an herbal bath or an offering of fruit to one of the Orisha. She may be required to buy and wear a scarf of a particular color or a perfume. Such activities involve minimal funds, a minimal investment of time, and minimal promises of future participation. The invitation to receive *elekes* (beads consecrated to the Orisha) or Warriors generally requires a *derecho* (fee) of several hundred dollars and transforms the relationship from one of client and priest to one of godchild and godparent and adds the responsibilities that are associated with such a relationship. In addition, the receiving of Warriors or other Orisha involves ceremonies that are considered to begin lifelong relationships to Orisha. Those who undergo priestly initiation must at the very least commit to paying thousands of dollars and submitting to at least a year of restrictions on one's activities.[2] In the *kariocha*, novices begin what is meant to be an irreversible relationship, a mutually reciprocal "marriage" to the Orisha that brings obligations of service.

For cultural newcomers, devoting oneself to the Orisha may require quite a bit of learning, acceptance, and integration of a new world view. Within the accounts of newcomers to the Ocha paths, increasing religious commitments generally grow alongside relationships to Orisha; these affiliations occur within the context of religious socialization processes.

RESOCIALIZATION AND RHETORICAL CHANGE

Sociologists have long understood conversion as taking place within the wider context of socialization, the lifelong project of learning and internalizing the social realities of the groups within one's social spheres (Berger and Luckmann 1967).[3] Socialization is an induction into a social world. Through socialization we learn foundational things such as language, meaning, norms, values, and what constitutes sense and nonsense. Modifications of individuals' beliefs and understandings are taking place constantly; these may be minor or major. Religious conversion, depending on how it is defined and experienced, may involve a near-complete alteration of belief or a minor tweaking of conceptions that are already present. Sociologists Peter Berger and Thomas Luckmann (1967, 157) call the most deep-seated transformations "alternation," such as those that might be considered "world switching." These "radical transformation[s] of subjective reality" are exemplified in some religious, revolutionary political, and military contexts. They are generally accomplished with a special type of secondary socialization, "resocialization," a process that replicates the emotional intensity and identification of the initial social learning one experiences in childhood. Conversion is not something that is solely between a person and their god(s); even the most extreme experiences of religious conversion must be seen as embedded within social interactions.

An important aspect of religious conversion is that it involves a transformation in the ways people speak about, explain, and understand how and why the world works, the reasons people act the way they do, and basic terms and categories for conceptualizing physical, internal, and social worlds. Snow and Machalek (1984, 170) refer to this as a "change in one's universe of discourse." The conversion process often entails an acceptance of the language and understandings present in the new religious community. In other words, it involves the "adoption of a master attribution scheme" (Snow and Machalek 1984).[4] In this central aspect of resocialization, "a number of causal schemes are now interpreted from the standpoint of one pervasive schema. Moreover, matters that were previously inexplicable or ambiguous are now clearly understood" (Snow and Machalek 1984, 173).

The social and the spiritual intersect and intertwine. As in any other religion, involvement in Orisha traditions requires socialization. Among those who come to the year in white, this tends to proceed alongside evolving relationships with Orisha. In what ways did *aleyos, iyawos,* and former *iyawos* describe the process of beginning to see the world in terms of the Orisha during the year in white? And how did they discuss their affiliations with Orisha leading up to and through the year in white?

"A DIFFERENT SET OF EYEGLASSES": THE "ORISHAFICATION" OF EVERYDAY LIFE

For many cultural newcomers, connections to Orisha developed in ways that were both mediated by and unmediated by Ocha priests. Bonding occurred prior to or alongside growing knowledge of Orisha religions through book learning and learning from experience. Jennifer's desire for connection with the Orisha is what fueled her search for knowledge of Orisha tradition. That longing eventually propelled her to the *kariocha* ceremony in which she was dedicated as a priest of Oshun.

> I always felt a very very strong connection with [the Orisha]. I would read things saying you can't know the Orishas unless you are African ancestry. And I couldn't believe that because I always felt that they wouldn't put that much love in my heart for them if I wasn't going to have a connection with them. And so I would just do whatever I could to try to further that and get to know them as best I could on my own. . . . It was really Elegua and Yemaya and Oshun [who] were the ones that called to me early on and . . . I just wanted to learn everything I could about them.

For Jennifer, as for many of the cultural newcomers who interviewed with me, the process began with learning about the Orisha and then starting to see them at work in their lives.

In the interviews I didn't ask specific questions to elicit accounts of change. Nevertheless, in describing their entry into the religion and their growing commitment, several devotees mentioned changes in their perceptions and ways of viewing the world. In Lukumi, each Orisha has numerous correspondences, including colors, numbers, foods, natural forces (e.g., rivers, fire, oceans, volcanoes, wind, thunder), Catholic saints, abilities (e.g., dancing, divination, strength), personality traits (e.g., wisdom, anger, sadness, mischievousness) arenas of human interaction and concern (marriage, sickness and healing, wealth, success, education, sexuality, motherhood, justice, work, technology, the market, cemeteries, opportunity, etc.), and even body types and parts of the body. For example, among others, Elegua is associated with the crossroads, messages, luck, the Christ child of Antocha, San Antonio de Padua, the colors red and black together, Monday, the number 3, and trickery (Olmos and Paravasini-Gebert 2003). The Orisha Oya is linked with Our Lady of Candlemas, St. Teresa of Avila, Little Flower, maroon, nine colors together, the number 9, wind, death, the cemetery, eggplant, chocolate, and a blackfly whisk (Clark 2007, 49). As neophytes learn about the many Orisha and their abundant associations, they may gradually begin to see Ocha in their everyday interactions, in chance occurrences, in their successes and failures, and in weather changes, illnesses, and healings they experience or witness. An interaction with a stranger wearing black and red may be seen as a message from Elegua. The ease with which one finds a parking space may be attributed to the Ogun and how generous one was in giving rum or cigar smoke to one's Warriors that week. Finding an apartment with the number of the Orisha who rules one's head may be seen as auspicious. A windy day may be attributed to the ire or interest of Oya. A string of bad luck may be a message that one owes something to one or more Orisha.

Chris gave a clear description of this process involving the Orishafication of everyday life, in which the aspects of divinity and their correspondences are seen as infusing every aspect of life (and death), a particular brand of the "re-enchantment of the world."[5] After meeting an *olorisha* with whom he eventually shared a romantic relationship, Chris first began to understand the correspondences with Ocha and see their presence in his daily life: "I started just having that sort of mental identification and noticing the world around me in terms of Orisha." He offered a concrete example. Once when he was shopping with his girlfriend, he saw three women "walking down the street" who had the physical attributes he associated with three female Orisha: Oshun, Yemaya and Oya. Although he didn't suggest a particular meaning for this event, he explained that "little things like that" began to occur so that he increasingly had a "mind set of observing the Orisha at work in . . . and alive in . . . [his] world." Star offered a similar account. She began learning about Ocha from the people who were later to become her godparents. Soon, she said, "a lot of stuff started to make sense," especially in terms of the Orisha. Star told of a specific occurrence in which she "picked up a statue for La Diosa Del Mar . . . and . . . had no idea why it seemed important." After she was told via divination that her "guardian angel," the Orisha that "ruled her head," was Yemaya, she understood in a new way her feelings of affinity to the image of a saint associated with the watery Orisha whom she believed had chosen her. The stories Chris and Star told are common ways that newcomers to Lukumi depicted their process of beginning to adopt the Lukumi world view.

Cultural newcomers described different levels of accommodation to the world view of the Orisha. For those such as Gabriel, who was already familiar with the miraculous universe of *los santos*, Africanizing the saints may have been a smaller step than those with other roots: "It wasn't totally new, especially when you come from a Mexican Catholic family." Gabriel explained that his new and old faiths both included "the offerings, the bread, the Day of the Dead, the candles and incense. So it wasn't too drastic of a transition." In contrast, Georgia, who had a neo-pagan background, likened the process to learning an entirely new "symbol set." Distinct from her prior cosmology that was comprised and shaped by the four elements and the cyclic seasons of the year, Georgia began perceiving events as impacted by the complex influences of a dozen or so Orisha.

Georgia described the process: "It is like having a different set of eyeglasses sometimes, when you walk around every day and something happens that sometimes you wouldn't even notice or necessarily think twice about. That, oh, Ogun is talking. Oh, that is Ochun talking." When I pressed her for a specific example, Georgia responded: "Well, sometimes when I inadvertently feel that I am running over more animals than I normally would, that the Ogun of the vehicle needs to be fed. . . . Now when I see a turkey vulture that crosses my path, I think of Ochun, because vultures are sacred to her. . . . So I notice the wildlife more, because certain ones are associated to different Orishas." Similarly, Ines seemed to see her multifaceted personality in terms of various Orisha: "If you look at me, I am very tall. I am like a Yemaya. You know how they depict her as very tall, long hair—that is how I am. I am a large person, not a small person. But really I was this little sensitive flower. And then Oshun, I am like a frou-frou girl. I am always in skirts. I buy so much perfume, you won't believe how much perfume I have. I have a very feminine personality. But I have a wild spirit, a Shango spirit with me." Thus, even aspects of self can be attributed to Orisha. Like Ines and Georgia, several participants spoke of their year in white or the time leading up to it in terms of adoption of a master attribution scheme that centered on the Orisha and their correspondences.

When newcomers began to see the world in terms of Orisha, they often began to develop relationships with these aspects of divinity. Chris described how this happened for him. It began when his girlfriend introduced them to him: "She would talk about this Orisha or that Orisha. And I would be like 'Who is that? What is that? What are you talking about?'" He quickly felt a "very strong attraction, particularly to Elegua and Ogun." Shortly thereafter he believed it was time to solidify his relationship to Elegua: "I went and picked up a little flat stone out of the driveway and got a bottle of white-out out of the kitchen drawer and drew a little Elegua face on it and sat it on my front porch." Soon "there was definitely an Elegua presence that manifested itself through" the rock. Chris spent time regularly with the stone and "began having conversations" with Elegua through it. Eventually his interactions with the Orisha expanded beyond discussions on the front porch and into his self-conceptions:

Orisha give me role models. I can take those archetypal identities and try them on, like different shirts; today I am Ogun, tomorrow Shango. Friday we will argue. Just having role models that I didn't have as a kid is really a big part of it, and another part of it is in all my dealings with Orisha, the one thing I think they all demand from me is integrity, personal integrity. . . . Whether or not I actually spend the time finding out who I am or just get busy with my day and ignore that process, Orisha have made a big difference there.

Although many Orisha priests may not consider Chris's actions to be legitimate,[6] several devotees I interviewed told similar stories of seeding relationships with Orisha in ways that were unmediated by those who have already been initiated. These affiliations were often begun with Elegua—who must be propitiated first in Lukumi ritual—and sometimes involved material representations such as stones or the concrete Elegua heads sold in many *botanicas*.

Alex told a similar story of a gradually progressing yet initially unmediated relationship. Designating an object as Elegua, he developed feelings of great kinship with the trickster spirit: "He is always available to me. Always," Alex said. Although at first it was awkward, Alex communicated consistently with the object he called Elegua: "Every Monday, I would sit down with him and say 'Hey, how's it going?' Or when he would give me things unexpectedly, like a little gift from him, I would say 'Thanks!'" Alex felt that Elegua had brought him many presents, including jobs and money. He would find $20 bills on the ground and often won with scratch lottery tickets. Alex was certain that these were blessings from Elegua: "I know these are not just my imagination and I know I'm not just lucky. I feel like these are gifts." When Alex went to have a divinatory reading in which Elegua was consulted, his feelings were validated: "He responded nicely in my reading. . . . He said, 'You've talked to me a lot. I've never talked back, but I still feel like we've interacted.'" As with Chris, Alex's early relationship with Orisha began with construction of an altar, a space dedicated to Orisha.

Several Orisha devotees spoke of the importance of altars in their growing relationships with Orisha. Priests often instruct *aleyos* to begin their practice in the religion by constructing a place devoted to their ancestors and/or spiritual guides where they will offer prayers and remembrances. Yet many enthusiastic beginners, either on their own or guided by *olorisha*, described constructing sacred space devoted to one or more Orisha in addition to or instead of their ancestors. Cora, who was an *aleyo* when I interviewed her, was so proud of her homemade altar to Elegua that she posted photos of it on the Internet, eliciting negative reactions from some more experienced religious practitioners. Some felt that her sharing was disrespectful, a case of cultural appropriation; others thought it presumed privileges and abilities that were deemed acceptable only for priests in the religion. Only partially socialized in the culture and coming from a neo-pagan background that was less hierarchical, structured, and secretive, Cora was surprised and hurt by the hostility her display of religious enthusiasm had generated: "If the spirits speak to you . . . [even though] you're not initiated, . . . why can't you choose to honor that spirit in a way that speaks to you?" she asked.

Noreen said she filled her home with altars to Orisha, Vodou Lwa (spirits), and ancestors. It's like "living in church," she explained. Another *aleyo*, Lani, also had a house full of spaces dedicated to Orisha. She put particular effort into a shrine for Oya, which included a "horse whip and the many colored skirt, and all of those, you know, bare essentials from Africa." After Lani developed a special affinity for Oya, she made frequent offerings to her at the altar:

> I feel that I cannot do enough for her. She has the biggest spot in my home. . . . I feed her every Wednesday. If there is something especially traumatic or something going on, I feed her special things. One of the ways that would be a special feeding would be to cut up an eggplant into nine pieces, drench it in either honey or red wine. Then I get those little mini colored confetti things from the baking aisle that you put on cakes or cupcakes, and sprinkle the eggplant with that and the colors run. It is beautiful. That is one of the special layings for her.

At other times Lani provided other types of offerings, including "beets . . . plums, dark red grapes, [or] raspberries sometimes. Sometimes I will feed her a portion of the *ebbo* [offering] that I've made for Chango when I've fed Chango for a particularly strenuous battle that I was undergoing. I will use both of them together. They both ate some of each other's food so they could have each other's strength." For many of my interviewees, over time, interaction with Orisha through altars that involved prayer, divination, and gifts—in both traditional and nontraditional ways—produced a growing sense of relationship with them.

SOPERAS, CROWNED HEADS, AND DIVINATION: DEEPENING CONNECTIONS

For those more experienced in Lukumi tradition, consecrated *soperas* (soup tureens and other vessels) commonly served as altars where initiates developed their relationships. When one undergoes the *kariocha*, s/he receives items that have been sacralized to several Orisha. These are traditionally kept in or on ceramic, wooden, or metal receptacles (depending upon the Orisha).[7] Both *aleyos* and *olorishas* may receive Orishas individually in ritual as well. For example, people may receive Warriors to gain a good foundation and a sense of grounding in their lives and for protection. Devotees may be instructed to receive the Orishas Olokun or Asojano for health reasons. In an early divinatory reading, my godfather suggested that I should eventually receive Olokun but there did not seem to be any rush. When a needle biopsy indicated that I probably had cancer, the earlier suggestion to receive Olokun seemed more urgent. Gabriel believed that receiving Orishas improved his health: "I received Olokun with my warriors a couple years ago and after that I had dramatic health changes for the better with my HIV and just with my body. I had a couple of health issues that have totally gone away." After he made *ocha*, his health improved more: "I've been HIV positive for eighteen years. After I made *ocha* I didn't go to the doctor for a long time. I was on my meds still; . . . I just didn't wanna go get poked and have my blood drawn and stuff like that. So the last time I went my test results came out better than they have been in eighteen years!" For many, like Gabriel, a belief in the efficacy of receiving Orisha created emotional connections to them.

Others spoke more specifically of regular interactions with Orisha, often in front of their consecrated containers. Neil, a "young" *olorisha*, explained that honoring his Orisha became a daily practice for him during his *yaworaje* that solidified his relationship to his head Orisha long after the year in white: "Every morning, I definitely throw [prostrate] myself to my Orisha, thank them for another day of challenge and growth and potentially beautiful opportunities for character building and growth, becoming better. . . . I wake up in the morning and I talk to my Orisha; before I go to bed I talk to my Orisha." Similarly, Dawn said that she "sit[s] with Yemaya every single morning. I sit with Egun [ancestral spirits] every morning." Beyond her daily practice she also approached various Ochas when she was in need: "I am always doing some work with one of my Orishas. Right now I am moving, so I am working Oshun a lot. Because Yemaya said 'I already said you could move. Stop bugging me.'" In interacting with aspects of divinity within their sanctified pots, *olorishas* and *aleyos* deepened their connections to otherwise unseen guides and protectors. These relationships are personalized; because they receive "individual shrines for their specific orichas . . . each devotee feels that she has her 'own' oricha with its specific praise names, personality, and taboos" (Mason 2002, 58). Over time, devotees develop personal histories with specific Orisha.

Many of those who interviewed with me believed that Orisha had instructed them or had otherwise assisted them. Star felt that the Orisha guided her about when their pots needed to be cared for. Lani told me Oya communicated more clearly with her than any other divinity ever had. When I asked her what Oya had told her, Lani explained: "It is never just like a clear dialog. It is thoughts that enter my mind. Sometimes I almost hear things on the wind. The 'dialog' is "much clearer when she is properly fed. So I've learned to do that quite regularly." Noreen believed that the Orisha encouraged her "to be a better person." She described relating to the Orisha, especially to Ogun, as spiritual parent(s) who help when she is troubled and are disappointed when she doesn't drive herself: "I was in a very bad relationship and . . . they pushed me very hard to . . . conquer this fear and to heal past this. . . . They want me to succeed, and I feel their frustrations as much as I feel my own frustration when I don't necessarily do as well as I could. They are also understanding at the same time. Very. That's Ogun: very motherly, fatherly. He has that overall in my life." Noreen viewed Orisha as the supportive parents she didn't experience in real life. Similarly, Patricia related to Shango as a protective, providing father: "I asked our dad, our baba Shango, for help for something that was going on. . . . I was getting evicted with my landlord. I had been there ten years. I asked for help with that. We went to court and I won. I asked him to give me a house to live in, and just a few months after that I bought a house at a ridiculously good deal." Like Noreen, Patricia felt that Orisha had brought her many blessings.

Orisha enthusiasts commonly petition Ochas for assistance in specific matters. Each Orisha is believed to like different things, and specific Orisha may develop idiosyncratic tastes: cigar smoke for Elegua, rum for Ogun, anisette for Ochossi, pears for Obatalá, oranges for Oshun, eggplant for Oya, candy for the Ibeji twins, tubers for Orisha Oko, fish for Olokun, seven fruits for Orula, molasses for Yemaya, bananas for Chango, to name only a few. Dawn planned to give an offering to Ochosi to help her in obtaining child support. She also believed that Yemaya had kept her safe and provided for when things were rough: "When my kids were little and I was poor . . . I was never scared. I had my Orisha. . . . I always felt secure. . . . [I would] light a candle for Yemaya and I felt like I would be okay." Sofia believed her rapport with Oshun had begun in childhood when she received a necklace from her father that she now associates with the feminine, watery aspect of divinity. She believes that whenever she asks for something from Oshun, she gets quick results. In these ways and more, many cultural newcomers to the Orisha tradition discussed exchanges with Orisha along their path to the *kariocha* that persisted through the year in white and often beyond.

For most who make the journey from *aleyo* to *iyawo*, relationships with Orisha are intensified through consultations with the oracles of the Orisha through an *olorisha* or a *babalawo*. In Lukumi understanding, divination is performed "to determine not only the fundamental contours of one's destiny, but also the ways in which that destiny is unfolding at the present time and how one might bring out the best possible destiny given their current circumstances" (Clark 2007, 72). Divination is believed to allow recipients to remember the path their *orí* (spiritual head) chose for them before birth so they will be able increase balance and harmony in their lives. In addition, divination is a way of communicating with Orisha, who may agree to help religious practitioners when needed. The process is often a moving experience for the recipient: "In the consulta, the client is objectified and her life is defined and narrated by the oríaté [diviner/ritual specialist], creating an intense sense of self-consciousness" (Mason 2002, 22).

In *diloggun* (divination with cowrie shells) performed by *olorishas* and Ifa readings performed by *babalawos*, various Orisha may offer to assist clients with their problems, sometimes in exchange for contributions or promises. Exchanges with Orisha in times of hardship forge emotional attachments with these invisible beings. Over the course of several *diloggun* readings I have been told that Yemaya loves me and will always love me, that she is my mother and will always take my side. I have been advised that Olokun was "standing up for me," Shango would protect me, Elegua would provide good guidance, Agayu would help me see through others' lies, Ochosi was a father to me (even though he did not "rule my head"), and Oshun would nurse me. At Cora's initial reading, "Shango stepped forward and said 'I got your back for now.'" Shawna was told that Shango would fight for her whenever she stood up for herself. Ines believed that Yemaya had saved her life. She had a "crazy" boyfriend, and the maternal Orisha had told her through divination that he would kill her. Because of what was revealed to her in divinatory consultation, Ines also believed that Shango protected her. Silvia felt that several of the Orisha watched over her: "Shango got my back. Yemaya got my back. Oshun got my back." Jordan, a *babalawo*, was confident that Orunmila always "takes care of his devotees." Patricia noted the accumulative effect of such mediated communication with the Orisha: "It never happens instantaneously, but in time things start revealing themselves to you, one thing on top of another, building blocks of Orula or the Orishas . . . [bringing] to light what they said through the readings." Over time, such messages help worshippers develop emotional and personalized bonds with their spiritual protectors, guides, and parents.

Another important way of communing with Orisha involves interacting with them when they are mounted on possessed priests. Possession or "spirit embodiment" is a common cultural phenomenon (Clark 2005), especially in African-derived religions. One of the main purposes of the *kariocha* ceremony is to prepare the initiate's head to be capable of being inhabited by a particular Ocha. The mounting of priests by Orisha is seen as a highly desirable occurrence at religious events; it transforms the individual phenomenon of trance into a communal event where aspects of divinity may speak and physically interact with their devotees. The possibility and reality of having one's consciousness temporarily replaced by Orisha has great consequence for one's relationship with them: "Just as the priestess possesses her own oricha, that oricha in turn possesses her in trance in ritual contexts, and thus their relationship is mutual. Over time, a powerful and prominent priestess will alter the way that her oricha is understood, as her personality and style will affect the oricha" (Mason 2002, 58). When the Ocha community witnesses the "possession performance" (Brown [1991] 2011) of a particular priest, its members begin to associate that person with the Ocha who rules their head. At the same time, a particular priest's mounted manifestation of an Orisha may shape community conceptions of that Orisha. A common belief is that even when a priest is not fully possessed, bits of the personality and knowledge from his or her tutelary Orisha may shine through the priest in the form of insights, attitude, and behavior.

When Orisha speak and act through the priests they mount, they further their relationships with their human venerators in ways that are often described as particularly memorable and meaningful. Jennifer said that several communications with Oshun through a mounted priest were central to her religious path:

"She wanted to let me know I was her child and that she loved me and it was my heart that brought me to the religion and never to forget that. . . . And it was really beautiful, because she started feeding me her honey and giving me her water to drink and taking care of me and letting me know how much she loved me. It was a really phenomenal experience. She has really been there for me. . . . She has really been there when it counted." When priests become possessed at Ocha events, community members volunteer to act as their attendants. For example, Oshun's attendant carries her preferred refreshments of honey and water. When Oshun fed Jennifer from the sustenance meant for her, Jennifer was moved. The feelings of gratitude and connection Jennifer experienced from her interactions with Oshun through a mounted priest helped her accept the commitment to the *kariocha* ceremony and the *yaworaje*.

Yet relationships to Orisha, like familial human ones, are not always easy. Sometimes they involve anger, guilt, fear, or even indifference. Like parents, at times Orisha are believed to withdraw from or discipline their human children. I once attended a drum celebration in New York after the *asiento* ceremony in which a mounted Oshun stopped the drummers to lecture the gathered participants for about thirty minutes for acting inappropriately toward each other and in service of the Orisha. At another drum ceremony in New York, I was perplexed about why my "father" in Ocha, Chango, nearly ignored me. In California, I saw a priest possessed with Ochosi sternly instructing a mother to watch more carefully over her children. Flaco experienced a mounted Oshun as a scorned friend. Although he spent time with Elegua every Monday, he told me he had gotten into the habit of ignoring Oshun. He rarely burned her candle or spoke to her. He soon came to believe that Oshun had taken offense over his neglect: "The first tambor [drum ceremony] I went to, the two Saints that came down [to possess priests] were Oshun and Elegua. . . . I was next in line to throw myself on the floor [to pay homage] and be blessed by her [Oshun]. She walked past me and ignored me, like I did her." Flaco "felt embarrassed and hurt." At the same event, however, a mounted priest of Elegua gave Flaco a lot of attention. He "blessed me and hugged me like a father would hug his son." The fact that mounted Orisha treated him as he had treated them in their consecrated pots reinforced Flaco's faith in the religion. He now always remembers to acknowledge Oshun. Star described a struggle to relate with the Orisha more generally: "I'm slowly coming to terms with the relationship I have with my Orishas because it's—I don't know—it's like they are a family in the closet that I go visit every once in a while. And on the one hand I'd love to be in the room, every day tending to them, but you know honey, I don't get to the *gym* every day. And so it's a point of willpower; it's a point of trying to figure out what's more important and I still haven't figured that out yet. It's a source of emotional strife." Attachments with Orisha are lifelong, especially for those who have made the commitment to *kariocha*, and like human relationships, they will wax and wane, deepen, diminish, and change over time. Participants commonly viewed their alliances with Orisha as valuable and often discussed them as growing and developing, not unlike marriages or relationships between parents and children.

Undergoing the *kariocha* is an especially intense way of connecting with the Orisha. The priestly initiation is widely believed to be a major growth step that begins an "interdependent relationship between priests and their orichas" (Mason 2002, 57): "After the asiento, practitioners call the new initiate by an oricha's praise name, and the connective relationship between the initiate and the oricha takes on an individual, if public character. The asiento gathers the oricha's presence and transfers it to the initiate. The new santero will represent the oricha in certain situations as well as act as an advocate for that oricha." The rite of passage that begins the *yaworaje* changes the ways initiates are seen by the community and how they see themselves. Alex explained: "You literally get your own gods in your house. That is such a personal thing, such a personal relationship to have a god lifted on your head. . . . Very intimate. . . . You have a personal relationship with the divine every day." Additionally, novices are identified by name with the Orisha who is believed to have chosen them, and they are often considered to have incorporated some of the Orisha's *ashé* into themselves. They become ritual representatives of the Orisha. The *kariocha* is seen as forging an indelible and intimate bond. Metaphors related to marriage and parenting are frequently used to describe it.[8]

Shawna recalled how her relationship with the Orisha deepened once she underwent the *kariocha* ceremony: "I don't think my true relationship with Orisha . . . [began] to happen until I made *ocha* . . . . [It isn't until] then [that] you start to figure out—how do you work with these Orisha? . . . I feel as a non-initiate you have one relationship, and it is not really solidified until you are initiated and then you have more of a road map to deal with the Orisha." For Shawna, as was the case for most who described the *kariocha* to me, the experience vaulted her to a new level with Orisha. For Iyawo Jasmine, the intensification of the ceremony made her Orisha pots almost unnecessary as a conduit for communing with her Ochas: "When I am at a point when I can't go and sit in front of my physical implements for my Orishas, I can say 'Wait, Ogun is inside of me.' Wherever I am—I could be in the park or the grocery store in Walmart— wherever I am if I am confronted with something and I have a problem, it is a matter of reaching deep down inside yourself and the answers are there." Similarly, Dawn said that once one has undergone the *kariocha,* the new, immanent relationship to Orisha is permanent: "No one can take away the fact that I initiated. It doesn't matter—godparents stay, god parents die—but [the initiation] is part of your body now. Not only do you have the tools, but if you believe what we believe, it is part of your body. It can't be taken away." Most initiates see the *kariocha* as a huge step in their relationship with Orisha. Not only do they gain a number of altars in their homes for communing with the *ashé* of Ocha, but a portable sacred space is birthed within their very heads.

Some spoke of connections to Orisha as goals in and of themselves. When I was contemplating the commitment to *kariocha* and the year in white, my godmother told me that perhaps the most important benefit of making *ocha* is that you will never be alone again. (I frequently felt lonely at that time, so this seemed like a great benefit to me.) After *kariocha*, initiates share their homes and heads with aspects of the divine. Moishe said that affiliation with Orisha was his primary reason for practicing the religion. Instead of seeking gain from Ocha, he claimed, he sought relationship: "It is not that I don't feel blessed and I don't feel the Orisha have made great positive changes and have led me in a very positive way in my life. But to me that is sort of a fringe benefit. To me it was all about connecting with the divine." According to Moishe, instead of asking "What can the Orisha do for me?" he asked "How can I bring myself closer to Orisha?" Later, Moishe suggested that his approach was seasoned but that younger devotees often had to first relate with the Ocha as a give-and-take exchange that might mature over time.

Similarly, Iyawo Michael, a dedicant to Oya who underwent initiation because it was "something that was always in . . . [his] heart and . . . mind," spoke of an evolving relationship with Orisha that developed in tandem with his feelings of connection with God. This was an association that he believed changed during the *kariocha*:

> I felt less and less alone and I had proof and an understanding of a power greater than myself being there. Now I talked earlier about seeing God in the trees and the wind and the ocean and everything else, which is absolutely true. But seeing how all of that manifests in my own personal life and the changes that it's brought about, my relationship with the Orisha, my worship of them, my adoration of them, my respect for them, my love for them, is so limited at this point from what it will be. But what I have put into it I have seen direct results in gifts and blessings that they have given to me, which then affect my health, my spiritual attitude, my emotional attitude and my mental state.

For Iyawo Michael, his connection with Orisha seemed to grow over time, and he expected it to continue to do so throughout his life.

Moishe and Iyawo Michael were not alone in viewing feelings of closeness with Orisha as a process. Lani viewed her ties to her "father" Shango as in progress: "He gives me extreme strength. At the times I feel the weakest, I feel his presence the strongest. It is always hot, but at the same time it is always loving. He guides my communication probably more than any of the other Orisha. And it is actually Shango that I turn to when I am having issues of communication with people. I ask him to be guiding me. . . . I am still working on developing my relationship with Shango." Similarly, Jennifer spoke of her consociation with Oshun as evolving: "I started thinking about the anxiety that I felt about making *ocha*, because that is such a huge step. And it is a big transition in your life, so I have always felt a lot of anxiety about it. . . . For years I've had this relationship with Oshun. And Oshun has come to me like every opportunity she gets, and so every time she just always lets me know how much she loves me." For Jennifer, the accumulation of many positive, nurturing experiences with Oshun via divination and communication through mounted priests gradually helped her overcome worries about making the commitment to *kariocha* and the *yaworaje*. Like many of those I interviewed, Jennifer described the Orisha as having agency and using that power to deepen reciprocal relationships to act as recruiters, helpmates, friends, protectors, and parents.

IDENTIFICATION WITH TUTELARY ORISHA

A special extension of the Orishafication of everyday life is the application of the master attribution schema to people, especially to participants in the religion. Perhaps one of the most powerful ways that Orisha devotees relate to Orisha is through identification with—and being identified with—their tutelary Orisha. As *iyawos* are separated from their previous markers of identification—hair, clothing, name, former activities—and are required to adopt new habits, they are encouraged to identify with the Orisha who are said to "own their heads" or to "crown" them. They are given ritual names associated with those Orisha and over time their personal and social identities are believed to merge with the Ocha who rules their head.

There are commonly accepted notions concerning the traits and personalities that an Ocha shares with his or her chosen human children. For example, "Ochún's children are stereotypically considered full of themselves, gregarious, impatient, and fun-loving. Obatalá is thought to be serious—even ponderous, gentle, intelligent, and wise, and extraordinarily confident. His priestesses usually share these characteristics" (Mason 2002, 82). The *iyawos* and former *iyawos* I interviewed shared diverse understandings about the personalities of the Orisha and their human "children." According to Ines, "Yemaya children are always back and forth, back and forth. We are very stubborn people . . . very bossy." Georgia believed that those who are marked to Yemaya tend to be "nurturing and mothering and very emotional." Patricia said, "I don't know if it is for all children of Shango, but we always have something going on in our heads." She also said, "Being a child of Shango, I love to drink and party." Shawna had another vision of Chango "heads": "Children of Shango have a lot of bravado, they always have to be large and in charge." Vincent worried that priests of Oshun tend to "draw a lot of attention" and are frequently underestimated. Iyawo Michael explained that Orisha personality traits can also be seen at the group level: "So in an ilé that's based upon Warriors, right, it's a different energy; Chango has a different energy than Oshun. So Chango's ilé may be run a little bit differently than Oshun's ilé." Ocha houses are often called by the name of the Orisha of the initiating priest at their head, and these decentralized groups are sometimes discussed as having "personality traits" of their own. An *ilé* headed by a priest of Chango or Oya may be characterized as "hot," energetic, and passionate, while one defined by the "cooler" Orisha Obatalá may be seen as more methodical and careful. Those associated with water may be seen as calmer or more nurturing.

At the same time that these attributions occur, cautionary tales are often told of Orisha adherents who attempted to overstep the boundary between being the child of an Orisha and *being* the Orisha. Despite these warnings, devotees identify with Orisha so strongly that their behaviors are often explained in terms of the Orisha with whom they are associated.

Head Marking. For many, identity change begins well in advance of the *kariocha* ceremony. In a classic example of anticipatory socialization, many *aleyos* begin to see themselves in terms of a particular Orisha to whom they have been or expect to be claimed. Tutelary Orisha may be determined in three ways, depending on the particular house of Ocha and the circumstances: through a divinatory reading with the *diloggun* shells by a specially trained *olorisha*, through a divinatory session by priests of Ifa, or (more rarely today) through direct possession by a particular Ocha.[9] The process in which the heads of *aleyos* are "marked" by a diviner must be accomplished in advance of the *kariocha*. Sometimes it is done shortly before the initiation; other times years may pass before a "head is made." Subsequently they are known as a "child of" their tutelary Orisha. *Aleyos* may also be called to service by Orisha speaking through priests in possession trance, though this generally must be validated through divination. Even though *aleyos* understand that they may be marked to a different Orisha (if this has not yet been properly divined) and that head markings are tentative until the *kariocha*, they often begin identifying with an Ocha prior to initiation, sometimes before divination has been performed to identify their tutelary Orisha and sometimes after. An individual may see his or her personality, interests, and past in terms of an Orisha that they anticipate will become their tutelary Orisha, and this may affect their self-expression, such as in their choice of clothing, tattoos, household décor, license plates, online screen names and passwords, and profile pictures, as well as their aspirations and occupations.

Before the head marking ceremony, "there is much theorizing among devotees about the identity of . . . [tutelary Orisha], and many solicit knowledge of 'their' Orisha in anticipation of eventual initiation. Outside of formal divination, one can hypothesize a person's Orisha by correlating the person's personality and the known characteristics of the Orisha" (Clark 2005, 57). Cora's account exemplified the tricky nature of Orisha guessing, in which Ocha attributes are seen as both clear and difficult to apply: "If someone has had their head marked . . . you can almost guess who their Orisha is. Sometimes you can and sometimes you can't. . . . Like if they have a really goofy sense of humor and they are always giggling and laughing, that's an Elegba. . . . Like someone like ['Jessie']; she could only be a Shango. There's no way she can be anything else. I don't know, you can just tell by the personality sometimes." Although Cora was somewhat confident about deducing the Orisha of certain persons, she acknowledged that such conjectures are problematic. Each Ocha has so many correspondences that one might focus on the wrong quality when trying to guess their tutelary Orisha. Along the same lines, attributes of Ocha can overlap (cf. Clark 2005). Both Oshun and Oya may display feminine traits. Chango shares some of Obatalá's wisdom and both are seen as confident. Ogun, Chango, and Agayu are all considered to have the potential for volatility. Yemaya's sometimes turbulent emotional waters can be confused with Oya's stormy nature. Several of the Orisha share the fierceness and discipline of warriors, and many display the discernment, confidence, or imperiousness of royalty. Adding to the complexity, Orisha have many roads (*caminos*), each of which has slightly or sometimes radically different personae. For example, although Obatalá is generally envisioned as a wise, patient, deliberate, and learned elderly man, in some of his aspects he is young and relatively brash or female.

In any case, premature identification with Ocha is risky. What if one identifies with an Orisha and is then marked to another? When I asked her who she thought she would be marked to, Cora was hesitant: "I don't really know for sure. Maybe Obatalá because he seems pretty—I'm trying to be calm and steady and like he's cool. . . . I will be happy whoever it is. . . . I mentioned that Ochosi was kind of, you know, he paid attention to me a little bit. . . . I don't know. . . . I do have a mermaid tattoo." Cora's cautious response underscored her understanding of the hazards of such guessing. Despite her ambivalent reply, she sought evidence in her personality, her past, and interactions with Orisha, such as the concern and healing she received from Ochosi through a possessed priest or the tattoo that might be a clue to an association with Yemaya. Whether before or after initiation, identification with the Orisha who rules one's head is an important way Lukumi practitioners connect with these invisible beings.

I have seen Lukumi priests both encourage and denounce practices of anticipatory identification among *aleyos*. Some participate in Orisha speculation as a form of entertainment—a way to lighten the load of the hard work involved in ceremony and encourage newer members to connect with Orisha. Others disparage such practices as inexact and tentative, presumptuous, and/or "inauthentic" from an Africanist perspective. Raimundo noted that the concept of divining one's ruling Orisha is not a traditional African custom, suggesting that it is therefore a dubious practice.[10] Similarly, having learned of discrepancies between African and Cuban liturgy, Jordan argued that he now understood his affiliation to Oshun in a different cosmological light: "I understand now there is no such thing as a 'guardian angel' Orisha. That is a bunch of bullshit. . . . Santería is very brilliant at converting African concepts into Catholic and Western terms." Some priests I interviewed believed that these types of identification with Orisha were so problematic that they refused to divine the ruling Orisha of *ahijados* (or to allow their godchildren to have this done) until the neophytes were on the verge of undergoing the *kariocha*. (In addition, some who consider the head marking to constitute an obligation to the Orisha to undergo the *kariocha* do not perform this special divination until the devotee is prepared to commit to the ceremony.) Barbara explained that the first priest who marked her head no longer performs head markings very far in advance of the *kariocha*: "When you tell people ahead of time, some folks just kinda go buck wild, you know. They're getting tattoos, and they're buyin' all these yellow and white clothes, and—Yeah, then they're Oshun!—And then you get to the grove and Shango may take your head [instead]. I've seen it happen. And then, the person is in shock. . . . I think he was tryin' to stop us from treating it like a zodiac sign."[11] Some priests in the religion feel that tradition is cheapened when *aleyos* are identified with Orisha prematurely, especially those who have accepted few religious commitments.

Despite variations in the acceptance of the Orisha as personality types, such attributions are very common, even among some who critique the trivialization of tutelary Ochas. Explanations of the behavior of community members are often made with reference to the Orisha who own their heads. Orisha devotees commonly refer to themselves and others with such descriptors as "a Shango kind of person," "Oshun-like," "one of the Yemaya people," or simply as "Agayus," "Oguns," or "Oyas." For example, Lincoln referred to some Lukumi practitioners as "three Oshun men" and later as "a lot of the Oshuns." Georgia said, "I am one of those people that knew that I was Yemaya, up until I got the *itá*. . . . Then I found out I was Obatalá." Ines said, "Yemayas are like that; we are like almost obsessive about stuff." Lani recalled that her godfather approached her "and said you are to be an Oya." Shawna noted that "Yemayas do not receive Oya at the *ochas*." To be fair, most who discuss "Yemayas," "Ochosis," and "Eleguas" to refer to the priests of those Orisha are likely using the terms as shortcuts for "children of Yemaya," "children of Ochosi," and "children of Elegua."

Language often shifts back and forth between using the terms "having," "serving," or "being made to" an Orisha to "being" an Orisha type. This common linguistic pattern highlights the salience of Orisha head marking to social and personal identification among those who serve Orisha.

Many accounts illustrated the seriousness with which participants take their associations with Orisha. Sofia's description of her head marking, which was performed by *babalawos*, illustrates the importance that many assign to this personalized connection to Orisha:

> Up until the day I went to Orula, I thought I was a child of Oshun. I swore that Oshun was my guardian angel. This was so serious I bought a *sopera* for Oshun and carted it for like three years until I was ready to do *santo* [make *ocha*]. And the day I went in . . . [I] was waiting . . . until it was my turn to speak to Orula and the *babalawos* . . . in a botanica in Miami. And I am sitting in the waiting area. I am meditating. I am saying I know who it is but I just want to confirm in my head. And I hear loud and clear. . . . It is a woman's voice and she tells me, "Look in your purse." And I had a cowrie shell necklace . . . She tells me [to] take out the cowrie shell necklace and count the shells. . . . I swear to you on everything Yemaya—because that is the holiest thing next to my children—I swore there were five shells on that necklace. I counted, but it was seven. I counted it three times. I couldn't believe it.

Sofia was so confident that her "mother" in Ocha was Oshun that she had begun preparing for her eventual initiation to the Orisha of sweet waters. She purchased a necklace she believed had Oshun's number of shells and a soup tureen that would hold Oshun's *otanes* after she underwent the *kariocha*. As she awaited her turn to see the *babalawos* who would consult with Orula to determine that she was instead a daughter of Yemaya, Sofia received an internal message that revealed that it was Yemaya's number of shells on her necklace, indicating to her that her true mother in Ocha was the saltwater Orisha. Sofia's anticipatory purchases and her prayers in advance of the divination session indicate the emotional importance of head marking for many in Ocha communities. Sofia saw this as a moment that would change the rest of her life.

Robert, a priest of Elegua, described the head-marking process as he experienced it:

> We went into this room at this little house. There were maybe twenty some odd people there, you know, waiting to pick out their guardian angels. And my friend went in before me and he wanted to be a child of Elegua and when he came out of the room he had this long face. I said "What's wrong?" He said "Oshun took me."

I was like "Cool, but why the face?" He said "That's not what I wanted." I was like okay. So then I went in and it was just like a bunch of old men sitting on the floor. They were like "Okay, take off your shoes" and this and that. I said "Okay," and they proceeded with the process. And then they asked me "Who do you believe owns your head?" And I said "Ogun." They . . . went through and said "No." . . . Then they asked Oshun; Oshun says no. Then they asked Obatalá; Obatalá said no. I was like "Damn! Doesn't anybody want me?" And he [the *babalawo*] said [that] . . . Oshun, Yemaya and Oya were standing up and . . . "They say that this is Elegua's child." . . . Elegua's first words to me [were] "What took you so long getting to me? I was waiting for you."

Robert thought he would be marked to Ogun, the hard-working Orisha of iron and the knife, because he was employed in a kitchen with knives and fire and because he worked all the time. Although he was "crushed" that Ogun had not chosen him, he soon came to love the knowledgeable, playful Elegua. Robert's account, like Sofia's, demonstrates the importance placed on head marking in Lukumi community and conceptualization of it as a deepening relationship.

Many Orisha venerators told stories of dashed expectations or difficult adjustments. Barbara initially rejected her head marking: "First divination, found out I was a child of Obatalá. I'm like, what?! Not! I thought it was Yemaya. [Or] Oshun. I said, I don't feel like Obatalá." For some, difficulties accepting their tutelary Orisha were fueled at least in part by gender issues. Religious participants are chosen to serve Orisha without regard for cultural norms about masculinity and femininity. Men may be chosen by feminine Orisha and masculine Ochas may choose women. Because practitioners identify with tutelary Orisha in ways that are social and personal, including expectations that they will share some of the characteristics of the Orisha who claim them, several described a sense of disorientation when they were assigned to Orisha with genders that differed from their own gender identity. Vincent had a difficult time with his head marking. Before his Orisha was divined he felt a growing relationship with the manly Orisha Chango: "I started reading about Shango and I swore I was Shango. I love music, dance. I love the drum—anything with a drum beat. And my mother had given me a necklace with the pendant that was Santa Barbara. So instantly I started thinking that I was a child of Shango and this was the path." Yet Vincent's journey was not to be so direct. When he had his consultation, it was discovered that a different Orisha ruled his head. "Initially I was not so happy. . . . It was very weird at first to know that I was going to have a female Orisha on my head. And I started thinking 'Why me?' . . . And I just had that initial conflict in that first week. 'People are going to think I'm a girl.' You know, I was younger then. I was just thinking 'Why Oshun? I don't feel nothing Oshun-like.' But soon

I just started to embrace it and let her guide me." Gradually Vincent began to understand Oshun and himself differently, and he looked forward to being initiated as her priest. Similarly, Lincoln had to contend with associations of Oshun with male homosexuality:

> Some men who are straight males—some men had serious problems. . . . I had one person, a first generation . . . guy tell me "Look, you shouldn't be made to a female Orisha. You'll get all faggot." I said, "You know what, I can't even go there." . . . I knew by then . . . three Oshun men who were straight. And I mean he had a valid point about a lot of the Oshun's being gay. But I said "I am not one of them. I don't think I am going to become gay overnight because I have Oshun on my head. I can't worry about that." I said "I doubt—as much as I love women—I doubt if Oshun is making me do that. I don't believe that."

Vincent and Lincoln were confronted with homosexual stereotypes that some assigned to male Orisha enthusiasts marked to feminine Orisha (and especially to the ladylike Oshun).[12] What does it mean for a masculine male who identifies as heterosexual to have his head ruled by a feminine Orisha? How does it affect his sense of self and conceptions of those around him? These are the questions Vincent and Lincoln wrestled with, yet both soon overcame their discomfort.

Women also described struggling with gender identification regarding their tutelary Orisha. When people tried to guess Patricia's Orisha, they often guessed the feminine Oshun, in part because of her "temper." She recalled being "shocked" to discover that she was instead claimed by the masculine Chango, even though the fiery Orisha's personality might include hot-headedness: "I was actually shocked when we did *ikofa* . . . And I was like 'What, I am the child of a male Orisha?!'" Nevertheless, the association soon made sense to Patricia: "I've always been independent and strong willed. . . . I was very different from my friends. At eighteen I was traveling on my own to Mexico or doing things none of my peers were doing. So when I thought about it, it made perfect sense. It did make me appreciate who I am and understand." Similarly, Iyawo Emma began an awkward adjustment when she was marked to a macho Orisha:

C: You knew?

E: Yes.

C: How did you know?

E: I just did. I totally knew, and I did not want to be made to Chango. Sorry, Father.

C: You didn't. Why?

E: I wanted to be made to Oya or Ochosi.

C: Why?

E: 'Cause I love them both so much. And Chango is so manly and I was like, "I'm not manly."

C: Well why did you think Chango then?

E: Well 'cause I have a temper and I have that fiery—like I get really hot and I got really hot one day like a few weeks before and I was like that's gotta be Chango. And I remember sitting there before I went into the room [to get my head marked] and I said, "Madrina I don't know what I'm gonna do if it's Chango."

C: Oh no! What did she say?

E: She was like, "Oh it will be okay." And now I'm so grateful it was him. Like I'm truly grateful.

C: Why?

E: Because he's awesome. Like with my own problems, like he's perfect. You know what I mean? Like if it was anybody else, it wouldn't have been as good. . . . He helps me, you know. Not that the others don't but they help you in different ways and you have that Ocha on your head. . . . So if there was another Ocha that was on my head, that Ocha's energy would have been there on top of my own problems that you walk with, 'cause everybody's got something that they walk with and that might not have helped my problem in the best way, you know.

Iyawo Emma recalled having an affiliation with Chango before her formal head marking, even though she resisted the idea. Her self-concept included some of the attributes associated with the "hot," dynamic, masculine Orisha, but they were parts of herself she did not easily accept. Once she was told that it was Chango who had chosen her, her belief in divination and destiny made it easier for her to accept him as her tutelary Orisha.

Gender identity issues were not the only thing that made the acceptance of head marking difficult for those who wanted to serve Orisha. Georgia described having to adapt her understanding of herself and her relationship to Orisha when she had her head marked. She thought of herself as "nurturing and mothering and very emotional" and as someone who was afraid of the ocean and its power. Thus, she initially believed herself to be a child of Yemaya. Then she was told in ceremony that it was Obatalá who owned her head:

[This] made no sense to me. I didn't understand it. I didn't consider it. And my madrina would say you have to love the Orisha that crowns your head. . . . That is who you are meant to be. And then, then, you start looking at yourself and you start to say "Oh, yeah, this is a thing about myself that is very Obatalá-like." "Oh yeah, there is this other thing about myself that is very Obatalá-like." For me, it was a low alcohol tolerance level, an ease of being an introvert, alone with myself kind of thing. It was an inability to lie effectively. It was because Obatalá is very strict with rules, and I hate breaking rules. I like having rules. . . . I feel very comfortable with established rules, law and order, common courtesy. These are the things that make for a peaceful and productive society, and I feel very comfortable that way and that is a very Obatalá way to be.

Georgia described a period of cognitive dissonance that accompanied her head marking to an Orisha other than the one to whom she had already attached her self-conceptions. Her conflict around the issue was exacerbated by her godmother's admonitions that she had to love the Orisha who ruled her head. Eventually Georgia shifted her mental schema to understand her compatibility with a different Orisha.

Others who were advised to identify with caution or who received the Orisha they anticipated or who expected to replace their Orisha identification with one to the Orisha Orula soon[13] described an easier time. Joseph related a relatively easy experience:

I had originally expected Oya because of the connection I had, but I had [a] santera talk to me and say, "You know what? It may not be. Just prepare yourself for it not being so." I go, "No, it can't be not Oya." But just a few days before, I just realized that "Yeah, it doesn't have to be Oya." Just because you have an affinity for an Orisha doesn't mean that is the one that owns your head. It could be they are just very present in your life. So okay, I just allowed myself to let it go. And when it turned out to be Oya, I was very happy.

Joseph prepared himself to accept whoever claimed him but was pleasantly surprised to be marked to the Orisha he expected. Dawn expected and received Yemaya. Gabriel's affiliation to Obatalá was no surprise to him. A Lukumi *italero*[14] marked Iyawo Kenneth to Yemaya and told him he needed to be initiated as a *babalawo* soon after the *kariocha*. Unlike most who spoke to me about the effect of head marking on their self-conceptions, Iyawo Kenneth claimed that the assignment to Yemaya didn't affect the way he felt about himself. He professed his love for her as his mother in the religion but explained that his subsequent initiation into Ifa, which is dedicated to the Orisha Orula, affected him much more.

Most (but not all) of those I interviewed described identifying with a particular Orisha to whom they were appointed through divination or to whom they expected to be assigned. In addition, once they were promised to an Orisha, others in Ocha communities identified them as being associated with their respective Orisha. The tutelary Orisha of *aleyos* and *olorishas* were seen as significant in defining their personalities. Many described anticipating affiliations to specific aspects of divinity and believing this was salient in how they understood themselves. Some found head marking to an Ocha to begin a difficult period of adjustment. Some, whose gender was different from the gender of their tutelary Orisha, confronted challenges to their identity. Others accepted the associations easily. It is important to note that in Lukumi tradition, religious participants do not choose the Ocha that rule their heads and with whom they become identified; in Lukumi belief, Orisha choose their children. Such lack of choice is inimical to the consumerism of contemporary U.S. culture, in which identity and religion both can be chosen and easily returned and exchanged.

Seeing the Orisha Within. *Iyawos* and former *iyawos* often described shifts in their self-conceptions that took place after they knew the identity of their tutelary Orisha. Several discovered clues in their personality and in their past that explained why particular Orisha chose them. For example, Lani thought her love of the color maroon was probably attributable to the fact that she is a child of Oya. Bea felt that she had a "Shango temper" that softened once she became the spirited Orisha's priest. Sofia believed wholeheartedly that she was a "child of Yemaya" because as a child she was "always into nautical stuff": "I tell my kids when I was eleven or twelve years old, I used to have a t-shirt with an anchor across my chest." Barbara's marking to Oya affirmed her "connection to Egun" and her "sympathy for cemeteries." Neil explained some of the connections he found: "Oshun owns the needle; I am a beader, [a] crocheter. I sew a lot. She owns the blood; I have blood issues. . . . I can see correlations throughout my past, where Oshun has always been there." Silvia asserted that she was not surprised by her head marking because she believed herself to be a "Shango kind of person":

> I am very outspoken. I have always been like that, even since a child. People always describe me as fiery. "She is a rebel." I always stick up for the underdog. Even as a kid. . . . People would try to pick fights with me all the time. . . . I am just a Shango kind of person. I have a lot of courage. People have said to me I am the most courageous person they know; I am not scared of nothing. "If you want to know the truth, ask her. If you don't want to know the truth, don't ask her." And a lot of times I have to watch myself, especially dealing in business, people don't want to hear the truth. So I have to change the way I say things, which sometimes doesn't work.

Gabriel stated, "I am a lot what people would say Obatalá children are." When I asked him to elaborate, he said, "I am always in my head. Pretty mellow and calm. I used to love to drink and party. People would say, 'Obatalás—they always party and are wasted.'"

Iyawos and *olorishas* discussed how their understandings of their tutelary Orisha began with relatively superficial connections but changed or deepened over time. For example, Iyawo Akeisha explained that she was a bit surprised about being marked to Chango because "people say the children of Shango are loud and they fight." Now, she associates Chango with balance and justice and she understands her decision to become an attorney better. In another example, Neil described the change in his understanding of Oshun:

> When they marked my head, I was under the influence, and it was my own thinking, that men were claimed by male Orisha and women were claimed by female Orisha. . . . I didn't know who Oshun was. So when I started doing research on the internet about Oshun, everyone always seemed to talk about her sensuality, her sexuality, love, all those sweet things, money and things like that. And the one thing I have come to find with all the *patakin* [sacred stories] of Oshun, is where there is Oshun, there is always renewals. So for me, Oshun is like renewal in my head. . . . Without Oshun the world doesn't work; nobody wants to be here. She is the one who makes it all worth it.

Although he began with a superficial understanding of the coquettish, sensual Oshun, Neil soon understood this Orisha in terms of the cycle of life and his place within it. Originally Neil had expected to be claimed by Obatalá or Asojano, in part because, as he put it, he was a "walking disease factory." Being marked to Oshun brought deeper realizations about himself:

> It helped a few of the things I didn't understand and didn't necessarily like about myself. Like my vanity. Helped me understand why I have this absolute need to embrace everybody and want everybody to be happy and loving. . . . I kind of understood where my severity comes from. If that makes any sense. It also explained why I am adept at the domestic arts that I do do, as well as cooking. They all belong to Oshun. So in many ways it helped to develop my connection with myself dramatically. It helped to increase that connection, and in that connection, of course, we have a better way of recognizing our divinity.

Neil believed that his affinity with Oshun explained much of his personality, both parts he enjoyed and qualities he had difficulty accepting. Understanding that the traits he did not particularly like about himself were associated with an aspect of divinity made it easier for him to embrace his whole self. In contrast, Gabriel was concerned about the distance his felt from his "father" Orisha:

> I don't know, but of all the Orishas he seems the most distant and mysterious to me. I don't know if that is the father figure, so I have to be—kind of like not relate. But out of all the Orishas he seems the most, like it brought me closer to him but farther from him. I can speak to all the Orisha fine, but when I come to

him, I have to be in penitence to pray to him. I have to stop doing that. My friends tell me to talk to him like he's your buddy: "Hey, Obatalá, what's up? I had a good day." Or "Today sucked."

In contrast to the informal way his friends advised him to take to connect more strongly with the Ocha to whom he was ordained, Gabriel described his approach to Obatalá as in the realm of the ideal only, as "in the white in a meadow with the little dove." Gabriel hoped his feelings of awkwardness would change over time.

Several spoke of how their head marking changed the way they thought of themselves. Moishe said that previously, he thought he was "thick-skinned" and tough. But after he was marked to Yemaya, he let go of that self-delusion and embraced the nurturing, emotional aspects of his personality. Similarly, Ines used to be "always crying and sensitive." She believed that being claimed by Oya changed her: "She made me stronger, made me stand on my own." Jennifer experienced her head marking as an important self-revelation that continued over time:

When I had my head marked and they said I was a child of Oshun, I was shocked. I mean I love Oshun. I had always had this deep admiration for her, but I never would have thought I was her child. I had been working in fields where I was not a very open person. I was not a very sympathetic person when people needed it. I felt completely disconnected from my heart. And I am sitting there in that reading and they are talking about [me] being more emotional and stuff. And I was like what? I don't cry, what are you talking about crying? . . . That is just part of who I am that I never allowed myself to be before.

Jennifer began to see herself differently after the Orisha who ruled her head was revealed. She is a tough businesswoman, but she learned that crying and empathy can be a type of strength.

Everyone around Iyawo Jasmine seemed certain she was "a little Oshun" until the ceremony that revealed that she was "Ogun's girl":

The first thing I did when I got home was get on the Internet and started reading everything. And the more I read about him. . . . My husband and I were sitting side by side at the computer . . . and we were reading about Ogun, and my husband is like "My God, this is a dead ringer. This is just like you." I was like "Who would have thought?!" And for me not knowing anything about Ogun—he is like very industrious, very much for truth and justice . . . loves to cut and that type of thing. Everything I learned about him I was like "Yeah that is me." . . . It did pretty much change the way I saw myself, because once I got to know his energy I came to learn a lot more about myself and why I am the way I am.

Being told the Warrior of iron and the knife owned her head affected the way Iyawo Jasmine felt about herself.

The cultural newcomers to Orisha religion I interviewed commonly described an increasing commitment to the traditions of Lukumi that developed as their connections to the Orisha deepened. They adopted master attribution schemes that centered on the Orisha. They often began dynamic, evolving relationships with these spiritual powers, long before they were initiated into the priesthood. Over time they developed a strong sense of gratitude toward the Orisha and a sense that they were indebted for specific actions they attributed to them. They identified personally with specific Orisha, especially those who "ruled their heads." Their sense of relationship with the Orisha grew as they saw the Orisha at work in their lives, learned about and communicated with the Orisha in ways that were mediated by priests and ways that were not, and eventually, in most cases, identified with one or more Orisha.

CONCLUSION

The connections between *iyawos* and their tutelary Orisha are important in any discussion of *iyawo* relationships during the *yaworaje*. *Iyawos* and former *iyawos* often saw the growth of such affiliations as the main point of their *kariocha* and the discipline of the year in white. For cultural newcomers, increasing commitments are generally formed alongside growing affective bonds with the Orisha. These relationships develop within the context of religious socialization processes. *Aleyos*, *olorishas*, and *iyawos* described increasing connections with Orisha, the Orishafication of everyday life, and the development of a master attribution scheme that centers on perceptions of the agency of the Orisha in the world and in relationship to those who serve them. Initially, many *aleyos* began relating to the Orisha through makeshift or formally sacralized altars. As they progressed in the religion, the focus often shifted to the consecrated objects that are believed to house the *ashé* of particular Orisha. Many created emotional bonds with Orisha when they believed the Orisha had assisted them when they were in need, through advice in divination, healing interactions through mounted priests, and in other ways. A particularly interesting phenomena among Orisha devotees is the tendency to identify with divinities to whom they are (or hope to be) assigned in divination. Many participants told of processes of anticipatory socialization before the official "head marking" to their tutelary Orisha. Devotees are commonly expected to share personalities with the Ocha who have claimed them, and those who shared their stories with me commonly spoke of themselves and other community members in terms of the Orisha who ruled their heads.

CONCLUSION
Two (or More) Worlds

I am walking in the park for exercise with a man who is my colleague and friend. We stroll past trees and greenery along the asphalt paths, occasionally passing other walkers and joggers. I ask him what he thinks of my head covering, a scarf tied behind my head. Does he prefer it or the turban I wore the last time he saw me? I explain that I'm not supposed to look in mirrors at this point in my year in white. He says he prefers what I wore before.

Then he turns to me and says, "They're just rules, you know." I glance at him as he continues. "They're just rules. They're not real."

I consider carefully how to respond. His statement is meant as a gentle confrontation. He's telling me that he worries that I'm taking this religious thing too seriously. He's reminding me that I'm a social scientist who has been trained to think rationally. Of course I've thought about this too. Before I understood the terms "Orisha" or "*olorisha*," I was told by an Ifa diviner both that I needed to make *ocha* and that it was my destiny to doubt the path. Before I had my head made in the *kariocha* ceremony, I realized that my geographic distance from my *ilé* might give me greater liberty about following house rules. Then, during my *itá* divinatory readings, one of the first things Elegua, the Orisha who opens doorways and sees all, communicated to me concerned the importance for me of following the rules during my year in white.

"Are you or aren't you?" the Obá challenged me as she interpreted the shells. "Elegua says you're dressed like a *iyawo*. But are you really? Will you act like one?" This was the beginning of my scolding, designed to drum into me the necessity of strictly enacting the protocol of the *yaworaje*. A serious threat in my *itá* was mentioned, one that could be avoided if only I followed the rules.

But how was it possible to explain all this to my colleague without sounding like a complete nut?

"Jim," I respond, "part of me is a researcher who understands that rules are just cultural rules. But part of me is a believer too. I'm trying to do the best I can. To be the best *iyawo* that I can. Otherwise," I say, gesturing at myself, dressed top to bottom in brilliant white, "what's the point of all of this?"

I think about a sociological concept my colleague will understand, the Thomas theorem (Thomas and Thomas [1928] 1970, 572), which originally stated that "if men define situations as real, they are real in their consequences." Perhaps all divine forces are given their power through human worship of them, human definitions of them as sacred and transcendent. This makes them no less powerful. And isn't this scientific understanding of the spiritual strangely similar to traditional understandings in which Orisha are given life and power through worship? We feed and love them; they assist us. The reciprocal interaction between religious practitioners and divinities is one of the things that most attracted me to the Lukumi path. Our belief, our worship, our practice gives them power, makes them "real."

I remember something my godsister said to me during my *itá*: "Doubt is like a coin. Flip it over to find faith." And then I recall a quote from a brainy, epic early-1990s science fiction television series: "Faith and Reason are the shoes on your feet. You will go much further with both of them together than you ever would with just one of them alone."[1]

Like the double-sided coin, many of those who identify with religious traditions in the contemporary pluralism of the United States can be described as straddling two (or more) realities. I am both Jewish and Lukumi. I am both a social scientist and a religious practitioner. I am an *olorisha* and a member of mainstream secular society. I practice "traditional" ways in the twenty-first century. When I asked the *obá*, the ritual specialist who presided over my *kariocha*, who was a cultural newcomer to Orisha religion herself, how she thought not being a cultural native affected a person's experience of the *kariocha* and the *yaworaje*, she responded sadly that such a person must learn to walk in two different worlds. The pain of this position is highlighted in the traditional *odu Irosun Obara*: "Cats walk on fences; people should not" (Ócha'ni Lele 2003, 195). Despite the difficulties, "fence-walking" appears to be a way of life for increasing numbers in the United States.

The experience of duality and multiplicity is echoed again and again in the stories of *iyawos* and former *iyawos*. Recent Lukumi initiates, regardless of their background, live in at least two worlds. They are more than *aleyos*, less than priests. They must live in the mundane world—shopping, working, going to school—yet they carry visible reminders of the sacred wherever they go. Many are both Lukumi and members of another religion. Whether they are cultural natives or newcomers, white or Black, Hispanic or not, *iyawos* in the United States are enacting a minority religious tradition with a long legacy of social stigma and an accompanying history of secrecy. They must carefully negotiate living in both religious and mainstream domains.

Those who were raised in and around Lukumi religion share an experience of duality with those who were not. Recently at a drum ceremony to celebrate the previous day's *asiento* for a new initiate, I had a conversation with a thirteen-year-old *olorisha*. She told me that when her (non-Lukumi) friends asked her to hang out with them, she excused herself by explaining that she had to attend "church." When one of her peers reminded her that it was Saturday, not Sunday, the young priest was mortified to have been caught stretching the truth. All Lukumi practitioners have their own special relationship with the liminal, carrying their own burdens and crafting their own tools from economic, social, cultural, physical, and symbolic resources.[2] Attending to religious practice among those who traverse multiple borders daily can be instructive to scholars and laypersons interested in understanding contemporary religious identities as they are lived every day.

I interviewed fifty-two cultural newcomers to Orisha traditions in the United States—white, Black, Asian, and mixed, Hispanic and non-Hispanic, priests and *aleyos*—about their entry to and commitments to Ocha and to an *ilé* and about their religious practices and experiences with the Lukumi year in white. I received 197 responses from both cultural newcomers and natives to an online survey about the *yaworaje* that asked about the best and the worst parts of the year and how respondents would characterize the year in white. And I reflected upon my own experience as a *iyawo*. Using these three complementary methodologies, I learned that the people who enjoy and endure the blessings and struggles of the *yaworaje* in the United States are diverse. They come from a variety of ethnic, religious, and personal backgrounds. The participants in my study offered many stories about a special time in their lives. They told me about transformation, healing, and growth; serenity, solitude, and safety; emotional ups and downs; and the challenges of being dressed head to toe in bright whites.

The prescriptions and proscriptions of the year in white are all encompassing and challenging. Most memorable to those who answered my online survey were rules about dressing, covering, and carrying; touch and exchange of objects; being outside the home; mirrors and grooming; eating; sex and sleeping on the mat; and subordinate status. Some felt that none of the practices were difficult. Others complained about the nature, application, or explanation of *iyawo* rules more generally. Despite grumblings about the regimen of the *yaworaje*, a large majority felt that the year had been a positive addition to their lives. Many attributed their personal and spiritual growth during the year to the discipline of the year in white.

Social relationships heavily influence the year in white. *Iyawos* and former *iyawos* discussed connections with family and friends, with co-workers, and with members of their Ocha house and community in both positive and negative ways. They spoke most frequently of relations in their houses of Ocha. Some described negative interactions in their *ilés* that included arguments; abandonment; racial, ethnic, or sexual prejudice and discrimination; and, occasionally, other types of abuse. However, affirming experiences are what I heard about most often. Those who shared stories with me generally characterized their godparents and their religious houses as sources of support, family, and training.

Aleyos, olorishas, and *iyawos* discussed their increasing connections with the Orisha and their socialization into the world view of Orisha, the Orishafication of everyday life. Some Orisha venerators identified with the divinities to whom they were (or hoped to be) assigned in divination. It is assumed within many *ilés* that religious practitioners share some personality traits with the Orisha who have claimed them; initiates often spoke of themselves and other community members in terms of the Ochas who ruled their heads.

While this study of the year in white has described the experiences of a sample of diverse Orisha devotees regarding an extraordinary rite of passage, how does it speak to larger issues of religious identity in contemporary pluralism?

PLURALISM AND LUKUMI

Social scientific theorists suggest that maintaining "religious reality" in the context of multiple world views is of increasing concern to the people in the contemporary United States (see Bruce 2002; Berger 1967). When a variety of religious realities compete for an individual's allegiance, the plausibility of a single religious reality may turn suspect and people may privatize and relativize their religious beliefs and practices. In the face of growing religious pluralism, how do people, particularly members of minority religious groups, maintain beliefs that their singular religious group's explanations are credible? How do religious practitioners such as *iyawos* who are geographically distant from their religious center sustain the religious community that helps them hold on to minority ways of thinking? In an environment in which identification with religion is increasingly achieved rather than ascribed, how do practices and experiences of cultural newcomers differ from those of cultural natives? And how do ethnic and cultural backgrounds affect the experiences, expectations, and motivations of *iyawos* during the Lukumi year in white?

My research suggests that maintaining a religious world view was of great concern to Lukumi novices. *Iyawos* attempted to avoid encountering crises related to the plausibility of their religious beliefs by reducing conflicts with those outside the religious community. They valued spending time with their godparents and others in their houses of Ocha. They made a great effort to maintain community ties when they lived far away from their *ilés*, and they reported that they suffered when they were unable to spend time with members of their godfamily.

Concealment was a common method religious practitioners used to avoid confrontations with potentially hostile outsiders. Secrecy is a time-honored tradition among practitioners of this historically minority religion that has survived slavery in a strict Catholic context (Brandon 1997). Many of the accounts of entry into the religion participants shared with me in interviews emphasized how difficult it was for them to find *ilés* because of secrecy. Although this may be less of an issue today with the proliferation of online networks and Web sites, Reya, an *aleyo* marked to the Orisha Oshun, offered a narrative of the problems she encountered in the 1990s when she was looking for a point of entry into the religion: "I was growing up in New York, but even so, people were very closed off and not willing to share information with anybody. I mean, again, with good reasons; they'd been persecuted for years. . . . I would walk by the botanicas and didn't even know what they were." Although many practitioners in the United States display the religion more openly than in times past, secrecy continues to shape Lukumi religious practice in the United States (Brandon 1997; Canizares 1999; Clark 2007; De La Torre 2004).[3] *Iyawos* are still commonly instructed to avoid disclosing their status at work and are told to modify *iyawo* rules of dress and eating to prevent awkward questions. When contact with cultural outsiders occurs, *iyawos* often reveal little about their status. They may strategize with others in the religion to find the best ways of doing this, for example in situations where money is exchanged or when unfamiliar persons question them directly about their unconventional attire. When I was a *iyawo*, my godaunt suggested to me that I should tell inquiring strangers that I was undergoing a "spiritual cleanse," an answer she believed to be true, even if it was not thorough. When outsiders asked about my strange dress or behavior, I generally offered very little information unless I knew them well. When I was asked if I was a nurse or a chef, I often replied simply "no." Secrecy and withholding information about the year in white were common *iyawo* survival strategies that may be seen as attempts to avoid conflict in a cultural context that includes competing religious views.

In addition, the emotional dependence on relationships with others in their *ilé* that *iyawos* and former *iyawos* described may offer some support for the concept that it is important for Lukumi initiates to have assistance from their religious community in maintaining religious realities. Many emphasized the need to spend time with the members of their godfamily during their year in white. *Iyawos* said that relationships with fictive kin in their *ilés* sustained them through the difficulties of the year. They spoke of wanting to attend Ocha events as often as possible. Those who were separated from their godfamily because of personality conflicts, arguments, abandonment, or geographical distance reported feeling lonely, depressed, and isolated. *Olorishas* who lived far away from their house of Ocha often described the considerable effort they made to travel to see their godparents and participate in events within their religious households, despite the cost of travel.

It does seem that *iyawos* who are surrounded by tight-knit communities of believers tend to have different experiences of the year in white than *iyawos* who are distant geographically or socially from their religious families, though this is only one of many variables that affect experiences of the year in white. Some contemporary *iyawos* in the United States who suffer from geographic mobility and dislocations used modern communication technologies to stay connected to their godfamily and the larger Lukumi community. *Iyawos* who are separated from local communities can call, text, Skype, e-mail, and join groups of Lukumi practitioners on online communities and social networking sites.

As religious worship diversifies and more people choose religious practices and identities outside their ethnic group, questions of within-group differences come to the fore. In the Lukumi religion, the reasons of cultural natives and newcomers for making *ocha* did not differ, at least in terms of broad categories. For the most part this was also true of Hispanics and non-Hispanics, those who claim African descent and those who did not, and those who identify as European or white and those who do not. The difference I found was that those who identify as Hispanic were more likely than those who do not to mention love of the Orisha or desire for connection to the divine as a reason for making *ocha*. However, qualitative analyses revealed that gradually evolving relationships with Orisha were central in the narrative of most cultural newcomers, whether they were Hispanic or not.

Similarly, the answers of cultural natives and cultural newcomers about experiences during the year in white overlapped in most respects. The same was true when I compared the responses of members of different ethnic groups. However, those who were not raised in or around Lukumi traditions either recalled the year as difficult in a handful of specific ways, such as not missing the year after it was over, feeling vulnerable during the year in white, and looking forward to the year ending, or they were more comfortable discussing negative aspects of their experiences in an online survey than those who were raised in or around Lukumi practice. Cultural natives were more likely to characterize themselves as being pampered in their house of Ocha, despite their greater likelihood of claiming that their godparents were especially strict about the rules for the year. They were also more likely to report that their families accepted their *iyawo* status.

For the most part, quantitative findings on race and ethnicity were a mixed bag. Whites were more likely to report feeling vulnerable. Blacks were less likely to recall gaining weight. Hispanics more often claimed that their *madrina* and *padrino* were strict about the rules of the year. Those who claimed Hispanic status were less likely than those who did not—and especially less likely than African Americans—to report wearing only white to work. Those who identified as Hispanic were also less likely to report that co-workers accepted their *iyawo* status. While the differences found were modest, that there *were* differences suggests that cultural background in heterogeneous religious groups is a topic worthy of scholarly attention. Instruments specifically designed to tease out differences between cultural newcomers and natives might yield even greater results. Some of the distinctions that I found point to inequalities in access to resources that may affect individuals' experiences of the year in white (and their experiences of identifying as a Lukumi practitioner more generally), such as job security, families who share one's religious preference, and the ability to gather the funds required for religious initiation.

Religious pluralism is both a challenge to traditional faith as well as its rallying cry. Religion dissolves in places and becomes stronger in others, strengthening especially in cases of cultural defense (from outside persecution, for example) and cultural change (Bruce 2002; Stark and Roberts 1982). In U.S. contemporary pluralism, cultural transition is a permanent presence that pushes traditional groups to fight for survival and spurs back-to-the-books religious reactions. Lukumi religion offers an example of this: many previously uninvolved Cubans engaged with Lukumi *after* they emigrated as a way of mitigating the stress of adapting to a new culture (Brandon 1997). And African Americans have found in the religion a means of affirming membership in a group that claims African heritage (e.g., Brandon 1997; Brown 2003; Lefever 2000).[4]

Despite the individualizing of religious identification for Lukumi in the Unites States (Sandoval 2006), Lukumi practitioners of all ethnic, racial, and religious backgrounds join the religion because they are seeking communal ties. In a social environment where strong bonds are increasingly being replaced by loose connections (Wuthnow 2002), more and more people seek a sense of belonging. However, because Lukumi is historically grounded in Cuba and Africa, it has special relevance for those who identify as Black and Hispanic. Practicing Lukumi can be a powerful way for Cubans and other Hispanics to assert and sustain their identities as Cubans or Latin American people (Gregory 1999). African Americans have identified Lukumi religion as a means of connecting with their African roots, honoring their ancestors, and resisting identification with and distinguishing themselves culturally from the U.S. cultural mainstream (Gregory 1999; Lefever 2000).

Olorishas mentioned the importance of ethnic and racial identity in shaping their experience with Orisha traditions and the year in white. Most interview and survey participants felt their own *ilés* were open to diversity, but some had stories to tell of intolerance or discrimination they had experienced or witnessed in the religious community. Occasionally, *iyawos* and former *iyawos* described feeling isolated because their ethnic or racial status was different from the predominant group in their religious household. Although many Ocha houses are now diverse, some many remain ethnically or racially segregated.

PERSONAL ANSWERS AND COMMITMENTS

In response to an invitation to a party to honor the fifth anniversary of my initiation to the priesthood, a work colleague told me that she looked forward to attending the annual celebration again. She mentioned her surprise that five years later, I was still keeping the obligation I had accepted in the *kariocha*. A scholar of social movements, she explained that few social groups are able to enjoy such commitment over time, especially since I did not have a local Ocha community to assist with preparation for the event or to attend it and because the celebration required so much work on my part. Although her statement made sense from a certain sociological perspective, it did not seem surprising to me that years after my initiation to the Orisha Chango I was continuing to honor my religious responsibilities. Of course I was frustrated about the great amount of labor involved, work that is often made lighter by local members of a godfamily. And I fantasized about scaling down the effort in subsequent years. But at the same time it is common for priests to celebrate their *ocha* birthday annually for decades. Although I have heard of people getting rid of their Ochas, discarding the consecrated rocks, *soperas*, and other items, religious commitment within Lukumi remains high, at least in part because of the great investments—of money, time, and identification—it requires.[5] And many *olorishas* persist in religious commitment, regardless of whether their godfamily is nearby or not. The year in white can thus be seen as an investment in the religion that serves to protect those who have enjoyed and endured its pleasures and hardships from some of the vicissitudes of religious identification in the contemporary United States.

In the narratives of my interview and survey participants, I sought answers to my own questions: What attracted me so strongly to these practices and ideas that were so foreign to ones in which I was raised? I cannot say that I emerged with definitive answers. I originally committed to Orisha in large part to fill an emptiness within, to heal, to strengthen myself in order to improve my relationships, and to find family and community. I love my *ilé* and many of their members passionately; we have experienced intensity and magic together. Because I live thousands of miles from most of them, I have found some local venues where I can celebrate and "work" the religion with others. I hold these opportunities, rare as they are, as precious. Still, I often feel that I continue, as I have always been, on my own. Years after the *kariocha*, faith and doubt are both my constant companions. I continue to honor the Orisha. I continue to teach and think and write as a social scientist. I use analytical skills and social scientific methodology, but when I am confronted with the unknown, I often reach for the comforting assistance of Ocha.

LESSONS FROM LIVING THE YEAR IN WHITE

The year in white in the Lukumi religious tradition is a cultural phenomenon practiced by a growing number of people of all ethnicities and races in the United States. Once a rare honor attained by a minority of Orisha devotees, it has become an expectation for most members of these communities in the United States. The *yaworaje* is many things to many people. It is a year of sacrifice and devotion to the Orisha and one's Ocha community, a lengthy period of religious testing, an opportunity to transform one's habits and identity, an exercise in visibly living on the margins, a yearlong experiment in deviance from social norms, and a time of integration following the *kariocha*.

The year in white offers an intriguing site for the study of everyday coping strategies and the privileges and problems involved in traversing cultural, religious, and ethnic boundaries. *Iyawos* in the United States inhabit two (or more) worlds, the borderlands between cultural realities (see Anzaldua 1987). *Iyawos* use a variety of methods to deal with visible deviance and sidestep potential religious "plausibility crises," including secrecy and withholding information from strangers, maintaining connections with spiritual kinship networks and with aspects of divinity, and adhering strictly to scores of prohibitions and detailed instructions concerning presentation, eating, sleeping, movement, socializing, and more. Lukumi novices and *olorishas* discussed many of the joys and struggles they enjoyed and endured during their special year, including apparently miraculous and painful mental, physical, emotional, and spiritual transformations; sensations of special protection and vulnerability, blissful quietude and distressing isolation; and feeling nurtured and railing against subordinate status. Many who exemplified the multi-ethnic and multiracial worship that is still so rare in the United States mentioned racial/ethnic discrimination, segregation, and misunderstanding.[6] This study of the *yaworaje* highlights both the attractions of and obstacles involved in attempting to enact "traditional" ways within contemporary pluralism in the United States.

The year in white is an exceptional example of "everyday" religion. Those who undergo it go about their daily lives in mainstream, secular society while covering freshly shaven heads, wearing bright white clothing offset only by silver and brass bracelets and several strands of consecrated multicolored beads, while avoiding their reflections in mirrors. They give up being away from home after dark, appearing in photos, dancing, going to movies, eating in restaurants, and many other ordinary social situations. In contrast to work that focuses on the seven-day *kariocha*, this investigation of the yearlong ritual that follows privileges the ordinary over the spectacular and emphasizes the sociological and religious import of this transformative religious practice in which the extraordinary and the ordinary merge. Like practitioners of the year in white who are believed to carry the sacred wherever they go, adherents of religions in contemporary society expand the religious realm to include not only churches, synagogues, and mosques but also private homes, groceries, subways, laundromats, libraries, sidewalks, and workplaces. The year in white is a lesson in lived religion.

Studying the *yaworaje* shows that religious practice often straddles and blurs the boundaries of the sacred and the profane, bringing the unseen world of the Orisha into the mundane activities of eating, sleeping, dressing, grooming, working, and socializing. And as much as some would like to dream of a year in white with no stains—as a bubble that would keep them safe from the ordinary world of car troubles, family dramas, work woes, housecleaning, curious or hostile strangers, child care, grocery shopping, and lots and lots of laundry—*iyawos* and former *iyawos* explain that the realities of daily life are an inseparable part of the extended religious rite of passage. When the sacred and the profane collide, *iyawos* must learn to carry and nurture serenity within.

In the context of expanding cultural and religious pluralism in the United States, the year in white reminds us that understanding religious pluralism involves more than adding a few more groups to the accepted categories of Jewish, Catholic, and Protestant.[7] Although Yoruba-derived religions have 10–25 million practitioners in West Africa alone (Prothero 2010) and possibly up to 5 million in the United States (Ontario Consultants on Religious Tolerance 2005), they are often neglected or dismissed because scholars are unable categorize them within the canonical East/West divide (Prothero 2010). Complicating matters, followers of Yoruba religions may also be practicing Christians, Jews, or Muslims. Of the 147 *iyawos* and former *iyawos* who indicated on my survey that they were raised in a religion other than Lukumi, Ifa, or Yoruba religions, fifty-eight (39 percent) reported that they continued to practice the religion in which they were reared (most often Catholicism), whether occasionally or more often. In response to the question "Do you still practice the religion in which you were raised?" Otto, who undertook the *kariocha* in order to, in his words, "be who I am!" said that he believed that "all santeros have masses said and attend." Although he greatly overstated the case, he does bring up the fact that many Cuban Lukumi have historically merged (and continue to merge) Catholic and Lukumi practices. Abrahamic and exclusivist definitions of religion risk dismissing large swathes of religious experience by those who practice religion in non-Christian, non-Judaic, and non-Muslim contexts and/or those who practice their religion in additive ways

Indeed, contemporary religious practitioners—both in and out of congregations—may draw upon elements from a variety of cultures and traditions. They may exchange former beliefs for new ones or they may incorporate new elements into their religious practice. They may draw on Abrahamic traditions, Eastern faiths, African or African-derived practices, or upon the "occulture" (Partridge 2004). This is the true religious diversity—religion as it is lived and practiced in a pluralist society today.

Spiritual "seekers," who are frequently dismissed as religious transients, *do* at times commit. Many of the cultural newcomers in my study who once resembled the religious itinerants Roof (2001) describe as "seekers," Wuthnow (2005) characterized as "spiritual shoppers," and "Madrina Julia" spoke of as "people who think they're just passing through the religion" eventually underwent the *kariocha* and the *yaworaje* and spent thousands of dollars, submitted to a year of many restrictions, and began what is generally expected to be a lifetime of service to the Orisha. Seekers should not be dismissed wholesale as those who are unable to commit; some simply may not have yet found their niche.

This project provides an example of how autoethnography may be fruitfully applied to a mixed-methods approach, particularly to studies that use multiple methods to study the sociology of religion. Although autoethnography is increasingly being used in sociological research, its legitimacy remains contested (Ruiz-Junco and Vidal-Ortiz 2011) and it has not been much used in the sociology of religion.[8] I believe that the method is particularly well suited for research in the sociology of religion because of its utility in exploring our understanding (*verstehen*) of embodied phenomena (Spry 2001), its efficacy in interrogating insider-outsider issues, and its capacity for including the "emotions as part of the rational analysis of the social, inviting readers to a form of knowledge that does not exclude their own feelings" (Ruiz-Junco and Vidal-Ortiz 2011, 195). As one part of a mixed methodology, I believe that autoethnography can really shine.

Finally, this study of the year in white expands conceptions of conversion, possibly even transcending the usefulness of the term itself. Many *iyawos* and former *iyawos* displayed the adoption of the master attribution scheme that sociological literature about religious conversion describes as they come to view the Orisha as agents who influence their lives. Their accounts included examples of beginning to see the world in terms of the actions and influences of a variety of Orisha, exchanges with aspects of divinity through consecrated and unconsecrated altars, and interactions with Ocha via divination and possessed priests. They described identifying with the Orisha to whom their head was marked and undergoing the *kariocha* in which tutelary Orisha were ritually seated in their heads. Instead of describing religious conversion as a sudden, radical alteration of faith that involves jettisoning previous religious beliefs and practices, participants described a variety of paths, including a gradual (and sometimes additive) process of seeing invisible beings at work in their lives as their relationships with those beings grew and they began to identify with them.

Although the year in white is extraordinary in itself, viewing it from the perspectives of cultural newcomers to Lukumi traditions highlights the religion as it is lived by increasing numbers of practitioners today. It is my belief that more stories of the *yaworaje* should be told by both cultural natives and newcomers in Cuba, Puerto Rico, the United States, and elsewhere. In the contemporary pluralist environment of flux and flow, consumption, fragmentation, and diversification, borders multiply, as do the meaning systems they mark. Individual choices for identification—whether on the basis of religion, ethnicity, sex, gender, or occupation—expand. Increasingly in the West we are multinational, multicultural, multi-ethnic, multireligious people who are engaged in the project of self-creation. How cultural newcomers and natives to the *yaworaje* navigate the racial and ethnic categories that have traditionally demarcated religious identities; how they deal with issues of insider and outsider status; how they resolve the disparate beliefs, values, and obligations that flow between a minority religious world view and mainstream Christian-dominated secular society; how they bridge religious differences within their families of birth; and how they reconcile their religious expectations with the needs of their workplace are issues of importance to scholars of religious identification and practice. And these are the issues that were discussed in the rich narratives of cultural newcomers and natives to the Lukumi year in white in the United States.

APPENDIX A
RESEARCH METHODS

I used a mixed-methods approach in this study,[1] in accord with a "reflexive sociology" that takes "itself for its object" and "uses its own weapons to understand and check itself," thereby "increasing the chances of attaining truth." In so doing, I do not seek "absolute truth"; instead, I acknowledge the impossibility of doing so and attempt to exercise "epistemological vigilance" (Bourdieu 2004, 89). In such a view of the sociological enterprise, "social scientists, themselves," must also be "objects under study" because we are "shaped by and participating in the reality of society that is the object of" study (Fries 2009, 328). For much (if not all) of social science, no objective stance can take a researcher outside the social fields he or she studies. Thus, social scientists must be honest about their own standpoints. A mixed-methods approach is one way of attempting to counterbalance inevitable bias.

In this study, I used two qualitative methods and one that is both qualitative and quantitative. I believe that each of the three methods work to enhance the others. Each offers distinct strengths to the project, although each has its limitations. The fifty-two interviews offer a depth of qualitative experience. The 197 survey responses bring breadth and opportunities for some limited quantitative analyses. And the autoethnographic fieldwork provides perspective, situating the researcher within the research. I used data from all three methodologies to explore the Lukumi year in white as it is experienced mostly (but not exclusively) by cultural newcomers to the traditions.

All three methods rely heavily (though not completely) on retrospective self-reports of former *iyawo*. The survey and the interviews include both *iyawo* and *olorisha*, although the latter predominate in both. The autoethnographic accounts were also heavily dependent upon memory. While depending on reported memories has limitations, especially regarding the validity of retrospective accounts, it has some advantages as well. Those who describe the *yaworaje* as something that happened to them in the past may have the benefit of distance and the ability to reflect on the importance of various aspects of their experience. Former *iyawo* have greater freedom from the actual or perceived control and scrutiny of godparents and Ocha communities that often accompanies the year in white. Nevertheless, retrospective accounts must be judged as influenced by many factors, including the explanatory discourses in social circulation (such as the "Orishafication of the world" within Ocha communities and scientism in the larger community) and the desire of respondents to provide coherent narratives and/or positive renderings, in this case, of religious practices that have a history of stigma and persecution.

IN-DEPTH INTERVIEWS

Beginning with several contacts in the United States whom I knew to be involved in Orisha devotion, I began conducting confidential interviews in person and over the phone in 2006–2007. In snowball fashion, I asked participants to refer other potential interviewees; the initial result was forty in-depth interviews. Some participants shared the project's letter of solicitation with the e-mail list of their religious house. One priest invited me to post the letter on online networking sites where Orisha venerators congregated. In addition, as I met more practitioners of the religion I invited them to take part in the interviews. Later, in 2009, after I decided to focus my research on the Lukumi year in white, I conducted twelve additional interviews with participants who had participated in an online survey of *iyawo* and former *iyawo* and who had indicated a willingness to be interviewed.

To narrow the scope of the project and comply with Institutional Review Board regulations,[2] I required interview participants to be at least eighteen years old, be involved in Orisha worship in the United States, and be a resident of the United States (or have substantial ties to the religion in the United States). To highlight the experience of cultural newcomers I limited interviewees to fluent English speakers who had not been raised in Orisha-worshipping families. I asked interested participants to complete a brief questionnaire related to demographic information and their level and type of involvement in Orisha traditions and I invited them to participate in confidential, audio-recorded interviews. The interviews ranged from thirty minutes to just under three hours. Most lasted about one hour and twenty minutes.

In the interviews, I asked *aleyos*, *iyawos*, and *olorishas* open-ended questions about their experiences with Orisha traditions (e.g., "What most attracted you to Orisha devotion?") and their identification with regard to the Lukumi and other Orisha religions (e.g., "Has Orisha worship changed you? How?" and "What kinds of religious things do you do on a regular basis?"). As suggested by Spradley's (1979) ethnographic method, I attempted to approach interviews with the attitude that I was learning from informant experts. I often attempted to take the "conscious attitude of almost complete ignorance" (Spradley 1979, 4) and encouraged participants to lead the interview where they might. I informed interview participants that I was seeking "their story" and I attempted to allow conversations to take shape naturally, exploring each participant's unique journey.

The fifty-two interview participants resided in nineteen U.S. states or territories. According to U.S. Census Bureau divisions, twenty were located in the western United States, four in the Midwest, thirteen in the Northeast, and fourteen in the South. Twenty-six participants identified as white, non-Hispanic; thirteen as Black or of African descent; eleven as Latina/o or Hispanic; and two as multiracial. Participants ranged in age from twenty-seven to sixty-two with a mean of forty-one.

Although my initial interviews were of "Orisha worshippers," my initial contacts and networks were primarily with those engaged in Lukumi and Ifa traditions, and thus most research participants were from those traditions. Thirty-seven participants had undergone priestly initiations as *olorisha* (Lukumi priests) and/or *babalawos* (priests of Ifa), and seven were still *iyawo*. The others were *aleyos*, those who had not undergone priestly initiation but who had experienced less-intensive ceremonies such as "receiving" Warriors or *elekes*. A large majority identified their religious practice as Lukumi or Santería. Several listed Ifa or Yoruba as their primary religious association, alone or in addition to Lucumi/Santería. One participant identified her religious practice only as Vodou (though she incorporated substantial Orisha reverence in her practice). Many participants also listed their involvement in other religious or spiritual traditions, including Spiritism, Catholicism, Wicca, Judaism, Palo, Vodou, and Abakua.

THE SURVEY

To complement the interviews and incorporate some comparison with cultural natives to the religion,[3] I constructed an anonymous online survey of English-speaking *iyawo* and former *iyawo* regarding the *yaworaje*. The instructions stated that the survey was for people who were at least eighteen years old and were not residing in correctional facilities (to comply with Institutional Review Board requirements) and who experienced their *iyawo* year (or at least parts of it) in the United States. The survey included a range of open-ended, scaled, and multiple-choice queries about demographics (age, gender, race/ethnicity, religion of birth, current religious identification, geographical location, language), religious status (year and level of initiation within the religion, the types of religious communities with which they were involved), and experiences with the year in white (e.g., How did you decide to become initiated? What was the most difficult part of the *yaworaje*?).[4] I promoted the survey on a variety of online networking sites devoted to Orisha religious traditions and collected 197 survey responses from January to May 2009.

Participants received their initiations in Cuba, Nigeria, Puerto Rico, Panama, Mexico, Brazil and in several U.S. states, including New York; California; Florida; Texas; Illinois; New Jersey; Michigan; Virginia; Washington; Washington, D.C.; and Colorado. Survey respondents ranged in age from eighteen to sixty-one; the average age was thirty-eight (N = 152). They were 29 percent male and 71 percent female. Twenty-four percent (36) of those who answered the question on race and ethnicity reported African, Black, or African American ancestry; 28 percent (43) reported that they were white or Caucasian or had European heritage; 52 percent (79) said that they were Hispanic, Latina/o, Cuban, Mexican, or Puerto Rican; and 3 percent (4) said their ethnicity was Asian. The sample was well educated; the average years of education for the group was just under sixteen.

Twenty-two percent (44) said that they were *iyawo*; 63 percent (123) reported that they were *olorisha* (Orisha priests); 31 percent (61) said they were *iyalosha, babalosha, madrinas,* or *padrinos* (Orisha priests with godchildren in the religion); and 5 percent (10) identified themselves as *oluwo* (Orisha priests who were also priests in the related Ifa religion). I suspect that some people who were *iyalosha/babalosha* did not identify themselves as *olorisha*, even though respondents were asked to check all that applied. The "*ocha* age" (years since becoming initiated) of respondents ranged from less than one (i.e., *iyawo*) to forty-seven; the average age was just under ten years. Approximately 74 percent (146) spent most of their *iyawo* year in the United States. Twelve percent (24) were raised in Orisha-worshipping households, 9 percent (18) were raised in Orisha-worshipping communities or neighborhoods, 5 percent (9) had been initiated as priests when they were children, and 64 percent (125) "began worshipping Orisha/Ocha/Saint" when they were adults. (See Figure 4.)

Seventy-three percent (106) identified as heterosexual or straight; 20 percent (29) as gay, lesbian, or homosexual; and 6 percent (9) as bisexual or queer. Respondents identified a variety of religions in which they had been raised, and many reported more than one religion. Sixty-three percent (97) had been raised Catholic; 32 percent (49) indicated Protestantism or general Christianity; 11 percent (17) had been raised in Yoruba, Lukumi, Santería, or Ifa; 5 percent (7) noted other religions, including Buddhism and Islam; 3 percent (4) claimed Espiritismo or Spiritism; and 2 percent (3) noted that they were not raised with religion. The level of education of the group ranged widely. Eleven percent (17) had completed high school and/or technical/vocational training only, 23 percent (35) had some college, 6 percent (9) had associate's degrees, 77 percent (40) had bachelor's degrees or had completed college, 23 percent (35) had master's degrees or some graduate education, and 8 percent (12) had doctoral degrees. The occupations of respondents included: pastry chef, *babalawo*, graduate student, nail stylist, nurse, manager in a retail store, lawyer, accountant,

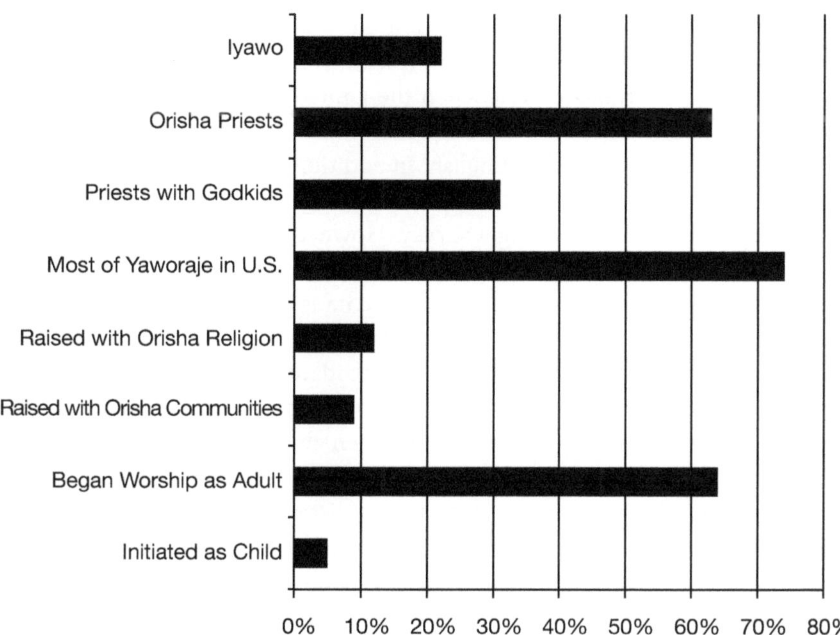

FIGURE 4. Survey respondents' status in Orisha religion

social worker, counselor, construction worker, teacher, business owner, police officer, artist, librarian, bartender, legal secretary, interior designer, psychiatrist, and medical assistant. Many respondents did not answer questions on income; some even questioned why I would ask. Of the 122 who replied, 17 percent (21) reported an income of $29,000 a year or less, 43 percent (53) earned $30,000–69,000, and 19 percent (23) reported an income of $70,000 and above.

How much information respondents provided varied. Some answered only part of the survey. Many were extremely generous with their words; they answered the open-ended questions in much greater detail than I had hoped.

The great strength of the survey method is its ability to gather information from larger samples than would otherwise be possible (Babbie 2007). Its weakness, however, results from the standardization that makes larger samples possible. To reduce the inflexibility caused by standardization, I left a great many questions open-ended, even demographic questions. This allowed me to increase the possibility that each question would be relevant to diverse respondents' experiences, but it reduced the utility of the survey data for quantitative analysis. Another weakness is that any survey relies on respondents to answer truthfully in an anonymous environment. Any type of self-reported data has this problem, but the survey respondent who doesn't even have to look a person in the eye when answering a question may provide answers that are less reliable.

Given its small size, the language I used, and the electronic platform I employed, my online survey is not a representative sample of the *iyawo* experience or even of the *iyawo* experience in the United States. It is skewed toward those who have Internet access, frequent online Orisha-related networking sites, and communicate well in English. In addition, a clear research focus that allows the researcher to tailor the instrument to answer specific questions is the best method of constructing a survey. However, I conducted this research project using a grounded theory approach (Strauss and Corbin 1990), in which the research focus emerges gradually as the data is gathered. Had I known the specific research foci when I first launched the survey, I would have asked some questions differently. For example, if I had standardized questions of ethnicity and race and offered a separate question about Hispanic status instead of the open-ended question I used, I would have been able to place more confidence in ethnic analyses of the data. If I were to craft the survey again, I would ask more questions that were clearly designed to distinguish cultural natives from newcomers, and I might ask more about reasons for making *ocha*. However, in response to open-ended questions a surprising number of survey respondents shared detailed stories, widening the study as a whole and allowing me to make some comparisons between cultural newcomers and natives.

AUTOETHNOGRAPHIC FIELDWORK

In autoethnography, also called reflexive, postmodern or narrative ethnography, researchers use their own experiences within a culture "to look more deeply at self-other interactions." In addition to situating the researcher as an important part of the study, autoethnography also highlights "the researcher's personal experience . . . [as] important for how it illuminates the culture under study" (Ellis 2004, 47). Autoethnographic methodology problematizes the notion of objective social research by acknowledging the salience of the researcher's standpoint on the information obtained. Such "self-reflexive critique upon one's positionality as researcher inspires readers to reflect critically upon their own life experience, their constructions of self, and their interactions with others within sociohistorical contexts" (Spry 2001, 711). In short, autoethnography can be seen as "a text based on the self-as-social" (Ruiz-Junco and Vidal-Ortiz 2011, 194). In addition, autoethnographic data may offer glimpses of a phenomenological account, a detailed examination of, in this case, religious experience at the level of consciousness from the perspective of one of the experiencers.

Autoethnography is perfectly suited for an exploratory cultural study of religious identity and practice such as this one, because as the researcher, my presence influenced the information received and its interpretation. For example, my status as a white, Jewish, non-Hispanic professor affected who spoke to me and what they were willing to share. My insider credentials also influenced my participants. Many potential interviewees asked about my status within the religion before agreeing to speak with me regarding a religion with a long history of secrecy. They asked if I was initiated as a priest in the religion. They wanted me to identify the Orisha to whom I am ordained. And they required that I locate myself by naming my *madrina* in this lineage-based tradition. As my status changed from *aleyo* to *iyawo* to *olorisha*, the knowledge and experience others disclosed with me changed too. In one particular example, a high-status priest refused to interview with me until after I underwent the *ocha* initiation ceremony. When I asked what had changed, she joked, "Now you're a member of the club!" Once I had undergone the *kariocha*, she saw me as having a recognizable investment in the religion that I did not have before.

Autoethnography is increasingly used in sociological research, though its legitimacy is contested (Ruiz-Junco and Vidal-Ortiz 2011). Most recently, it has been used especially in studies of embodiment (Spry 2001)—for example, to study issues related to sexual and gender identification (e.g., Etorre 2010; Wagner 2009), trauma and assault (e.g., Chubin 2014; Reilly 2013), racial and ethnic identification (e.g., Gatson 2003; Vidal-Ortiz 2004), sports (e.g., Drummond 2010; McMahon and Thompson 2011), and health (e.g., Etorre 2006). Although it has not been used much in the sociology of religion, I believe the method is particularly well suited for this type of research because of its embodiedness, its ability to interrogate insider-outsider issues, and because autoethnography allows for the use of the "emotions as part of the rational analysis of the social, inviting readers to a form of knowledge that does not exclude their own feelings" (Ruiz-Junco and Vidal-Ortiz 2011, 195).

I began my autoethnographic fieldwork informally after I happened upon a moving Ifa ritual to honor the ancestors in the summer of 2005. Within a year I experienced a *consulta* with the Ifa priest who had led the ritual, received minor initiations in the religion,[5] and sought an additional divinatory consultation. In subsequent years, due to circumstances both in my control and outside of it, I consulted with priests as a member of two Lukumi houses before settling with my current Lukumi godmother and undergoing the *ocha* ceremony in 2008. I documented in written form my experiences within the religion. I began this documentation in earnest in the six months before my priestly initiation and continued through my *iyawo* year and beyond. In particular, I wrote about how the religious experiences and daily life as *iyawo* affected my sense of self; the interactions I had as *iyawo* with others in my family, my synagogue, my apartment building, and my workplace; and the difficulties and joys of the year in white. While I cannot generalize my particular experience to those of others, I believe my in-depth documentation and reflection helps contextualize and humanize my research and its presentation.

Many of my autoethnographic entries are edited creations from extensive field notes that I began as soon as I could write them. Although note-taking is mostly not permitted during religious ceremonies, at least in my religious house, I often wrote as soon as I could find time to do so, using "emotional recall" and "systematic sociological introspection" (Ellis 2004). The process is "similar to . . . 'method acting'" in which one imagines "being back at the scene emotionally and physically. Revisiting the scene emotionally leads to remembering other details" (Ellis 2004, 118). For example, the story of my interaction with Madrina Julia in Chapter 1 was first written in a hotel room to which I escaped immediately following a tambor ceremony in California. Writing and rewriting the entry multiple times, I remembered additional details with every pass—what was said, what I felt, what was going on around me—until I felt confident that I was able to reconstruct the entire conversation and my reactions to it. I did the same for other entries that begin chapters. Some autoethnographic excerpts drew upon an online LiveJournal that I kept before, during, and after my *yaworaje* and electronic and paper journals that I kept at various times.

The ability to audio- or video-record the interaction with Madrina Julia or any of the others I include in this book would have maximized the accuracy of the reporting, as all memory is suspect. Sadly, this was not possible. Yet autoethnography calls for a different type of validity and reliability than other social scientific research methods. Although "memory is fallible," exact recall of events is impossible, and different people "often tell different stories about what happened," in autoethnography, questions of "reliability" concern not whether another researcher in a similar situation would have experienced it in the same way but instead whether or not the researcher's account is "credible": "Could the narrator have had the experiences described, given available 'factual evidence'? Does the narrator believe that this is actually what happened to her or him?" (Ellis, Adams, and Bochner 2011). Similarly, in autoethnography, validity is not based on whether the researcher's narratives are efficacious outside their laboratory context; there *is* no laboratory that is separate from the messiness of real life. Instead, it "means that a work seeks verisimilitude; it evokes in readers a feeling that the experience described is lifelike, believable, and possible, a feeling that what has been represented could be true" (Ellis, Adams, and Bochner 2011). The purpose of autoethnography is not scientific "objectivity" but the use of engaging text and experience to promote a cultural understanding of the relationship between self and others (Chang 2008). Autoethnography is thus "part art and part science" (Ellis 2004, 37).

Of course autoethnography has potential problems, including "excessive focus on self in isolation from others, . . . overemphasis on narration rather than analysis and cultural interpretation, . . . exclusive reliance on personal memory and recalling as a data source, . . . [and] negligence of ethical standards regarding others in self-narratives" (Chang 2008, 54). I have done my best to avoid these pitfalls. However, an important limitation of the autoethnography in this particular project is that the experiences that I share risk being seen as universal or even as representative. They are not. My experiences were mine alone, and no *iyawo* will experience the year in white in exactly the same way as I did. A minority of *iyawos* (though a large and growing one) are cultural newcomers, and an even smaller number of them are (like me) white, non-Hispanic, Jewish professors whose intellectual interests include sexual and gender identification, social justice, power and agency, and a social-theoretical leaning toward a middle-of-the-road social constructionism.

The autoethnographic aspects of the study demonstrate the importance of the researcher's perspective in collecting ethnographic data. They acknowledge the partiality and situatedness of all knowledge about people and their cultures and relationships. When the subjects of social scientific study involve culture, religion, relationship, emotion, and belonging—thick description and in-depth understanding best grasped through cultural immersion—a fully etic, traditional distancing from the subject no longer seems productive or even possible. When social scientists attempt to engage with "extraordinary experiences"—the mystical and spiritual realms of dreams, visions, possessions, and altered states of consciousness—so frequently described in numerous religious cultures, an "experiential rather than a rationalist approach" (Young and Goulet 1994, 8), a movement beyond "participant-observation" to the embrace of "participant-comprehension" (Young and Goulet 1994) may reduce ethnocentric bias and promote deeper understanding. Especially when sociocultural issues get sticky, it seems most honest to acknowledge the perspectives, complicities, and clear or complex allegiances of the researchers. Denying they exist will not make them disappear. In the postmodern ethnographic tradition, I go beyond merely acknowledging my position. While I honor the rich and varied experiences respondents shared with me, I also embrace my own story as one that can be instructive sociologically and one that affects and is influenced by the other stories shared in this book.

APPENDIX B
THE SURVEY

Bendicion and Alafia!

My name is C. Lynn Carr (Iyawo Chango Dina). I am an associate professor in the department of sociology and anthropology at Seton Hall University. I am also a member of a Lukumi house/ile in the Pimienta line. I am seeking to survey people about the iyawo year in the Lukumi/Santería/Regla de Ocha traditions as they are practiced in the U.S.

Purpose of Study: I am interested in how people experience the iyawo year in the U.S., and in how people from different backgrounds experience the year differently. I will use this information to write scholarly chapters and articles. To attempt to give back, I will share aggregate information from quantitative items of the survey in online location(s) that service members of Lukumi/Santeria/Regla de Ocha communities.

Duration: Answering the survey will take about 15 minutes to over an hour, depending on how much the participant wants to contribute.

Procedure and Instruments: I ask for basic information about survey participants' lives, information about participants' relationship to Ocha, and information about survey participants' iyawo experience. The survey participant may skip questions or return to the survey at a later time.

Voluntary, Anonymous, and Confidential: Participating in the survey is completely voluntary and anonymous. Survey participants' names will not be attached to their surveys. As the researcher, I will not know survey participants' email addresses unless survey participants choose to share them. When I write about the survey information, I will modify information (such as names) that I believe might disclose survey participants' identities.

At the end of the survey, participants will be asked if they are interested in participating in the interview portion of the project. Participants who are interested in participating in in-person or phone interviews will be asked to provide contact information or to contact the researcher on their own.

Risks and Benefits: There are no known risks or benefits associated with the survey. The information I obtain from the survey will add to the general knowledge about the iyawo year, and the social-scientific study of religion.

Compensation and Alternative Procedures: There will be no compensation for participation in the study. There are no alternative procedures.

Contact Information: For questions about the research, please contact C. Lynn Carr, Department of Sociology and Anthropology, Seton Hall University, South Orange, NJ 07079. Answering questions in the survey indicates consent to participate.

INSTRUCTIONS

In the questions below, "iyawo" means only the year-long status of a new priest in the Lukumi, Santeria, and Regla de Ocha traditions.

This survey is for people who are 18 years old or older and not residing in correctional facilities, who experienced parts of their iyawo year in the U.S.

Please answer as completely as you can. Please use comment boxes to best reflect your experiences. If needed, you may save your responses and complete the survey later. However, the survey will close on May 31. While there is information I need from all participants, I am much more interested in getting to know you and your story than putting you into boxes.

1. Please check all that apply:
   I am Iyawo.
   I am Olorisha/Santera/o (Please list years in comment box below)
   I am Iyalocha, Babalocha, Madrina, or Padrino.
   I am Oluwo.
   I made Ocha/Saint in the U.S.
   I made Ocha/Saint in Cuba.
   I made Ocha/Saint elsewhere. (Please explain in comment box below.)
   I spent most of my iyawo year in the U.S.
   I was raised in a family that worshipped Orisha/Ocha.
   I grew up in a community or neighborhood that worshipped Orisha/Ocha.
   I made Ocha/Saint when I was a child.
   I began worshipping Orisha/Ocha/Saint when I was an adult.
   Age in Santo/Ocha? Where you made Saint/Ocha? _______________

2. Why did you make Ocha/Saint? _______________________________
3. Please answer the following questions about your iyawo experience.
   | *Strongly disagree* | *Somewhat disagree* | |
   | *Somewhat agree* | *Strongly agree* | *N/A* |

I love/d being iyawo!

I was so young when I was iyawo that I don't remember much.

During my year in white my health improved.

I worried a lot about money during my year in white.

During my year in white I usually felt protected and safe.

I wished I had been given more information about the year in white before my initiation.

My year in white changed me for the better.

I wore only white to work during my iyawo year.

My year in white helped me to deal with emotional issues from my past.

During my year in white I often felt deep feelings of gratitude.

I often felt the iyawo rules were unfair.

After my year in white I missed being iyawo.

During my iyawo year I was often depressed.

I slept on a mat on the floor for 3 months (or more) during my year in white.

My year in white helped me to fix what was wrong in my life.

I gained weight during my year in white.

I followed iyawo rules completely.

During my year in white I often felt vulnerable.

I changed a lot during my iyawo year.

Many of the iyawo rules didn't make sense to me.

I can/could barely wait for my year in white to be over.

During my year in white I felt lonely a lot.

All the hardships I endured as iyawo were worth it. I would do it again.

Other (please specify) _______________________________

4. Please answer the following questions about your experiences with others when you were iyawo.

Strongly disagree	*Somewhat disagree*	
Somewhat agree	*Strongly agree*	*N/A*

During my year in white I argued with my godparents a lot.

I spoke to my godparent(s) regularly during my year in white.

During my year in white I developed deep relationships with others in my ilé/case de Ocha/god family.

When I was iyawo I was pampered by my god family/ile/house of ocha.

My godparent/s (Madrina/Padrino) was/were really strict about iyawo rules.

My family accepted my being iyawo.

My coworkers accepted my being iyawo.

I lost my job because I was iyawo.

My friends accepted my being iyawo.

During my year in white most people I interacted with didn't know I was iyawo.

5. How would you describe your year in white? What was the year like for you?
6. What iyawo rules did you find most difficult to keep? Please explain.
7. What were the best parts about your year in white? Please explain.
8. What were the worst parts about your year in white? Please explain.
9. Demographic Information/Info about You:

This information will allow the researcher to make sense of your responses. Please answer as completely as you can.
Your city and state
Where you lived during your Iyawo year
Age
Sex
Race/Ethnicity
Language(s) you speak well?
Religion(s) you were raised
Do you still practice the religion in which you were raised?
Highest level of education completed
Current job or career
Approximate yearly income
Current religion(s) and/or spiritual tradition(s)?
Current gender and sexual identity? (gay, straight, bi, etc.)
Are you currently a member of an Orisha worshipping house/community?
What is the primary language spoken in your Orisha house?
Thank you!

Thank you for participating in my survey on the iyawo experience in the U.S. Please direct any questions or comments to C. Lynn Carr (Iyawo Chango Dina).

If you are interested in being interviewed about your iyawo experience—in person or over the phone—please include your contact information below or contact C. Lynn Carr (Iyawo Chango Dina) by phone or email with your contact information.

If you add your contact information here, the survey will no longer be anonymous, but it will be kept confidential. There may be a time delay before you are contacted for an interview. As I am only able to interview a certain number of people, I may not be able to contact everyone interested in an interview.

Comments? Want more information about being interviewed? Please include your email address and/or phone number below—or contact the researcher.

APPENDIX C
INTERVIEW AND SURVEY PARTICIPANTS

Although it is not usual to name and list research participants when large numbers are used, it is also not common for researchers to rely so heavily on qualitative narratives from so many. The alternative is to leave the great many survey participants "unnamed," referring to them, for example as "a 29-year-old African American *olorisha* from Texas" or "a 48-year-old white, non-Hispanic Orisha priest from New Jersey." After soliciting advice from reviewers and colleagues, I decided instead to provide a lengthy table in the hope that it would help humanize the narratives.

Although I gathered more demographic information on participants, such as occupation, income, and gender/sexual identity, I share only a few details because of space concerns and the need to protect the privacy of participants. Because of the requirement of anonymity and the confidential nature of my data, some religious practitioners may be included twice, in both surveys and interviews. Missing demographic information is more likely to indicate survey participants' decisions to protect their privacy than the researcher's decision. I have listed here all of the interview participants, but I have listed only the survey respondents whom I quoted. In addition to the 162 participants listed here, data from 87 others were included in aggregate information throughout the book.

Demographic Information about Research Participants

Pseudonym	Place of Residence	Sex	Age	Race/ Ethnicity	Religious Background	Years Initiated	Interview or Survey
Adriana	New York	F	30	Hispanic	Catholic	3	S
Akeisha	Pennsylvania	F	30	African American	Catholic/ Baptist	<1	I
Alba	California	F	36	Chicana	Catholic	<1	S

(continued)

Demographic Information about Research Participants

Pseudonym	Place of Residence	Sex	Age	Race/Ethnicity	Religious Background	Years Initiated	Interview or Survey
Alex	California	T	27	White	Catholic		I
Alicia	Florida	F	46	White/Hispanic	Santeria and Catholic	7	S
Allison	Florida	F	44	White Hispanic	Catholic	<1	S
Amanda	California	F	59	White	Episcopal	4.5	I
Ana	New York	F	28	Black Puerto Rican, Italian	Jehovah's Witness	1.5	S
Andre	New York	M	46	African American	Baptist	24	I
Andy	District of Columbia	M	39	White	United Baptist	4	S
Ángel	Illinois	M	43	Puerto Rican	Pentecostal	13	S
Antonio	New York	M	30	Puerto Rican, Filipino	Catholic	7	S
Ashley	California	F	28	Latina/Asian	Buddhist	<1	S
Barbara	Washington	F	42	African American	Christian	4	I
Basil	Washington	M	46	White	Episcopal		I
Bea	Nevada	F	37	African American	Christian	8	I
Beatriz	Florida	F	36	Cuban, American	Catholic	12	S
Bella	California	F	29	Italian, Spanish	Catholic	27	S
Bianca	California	F	45	Black	Jehovah's Witness	9	S

Demographic Information about Research Participants

Pseudonym	Place of Residence	Sex	Age	Race/ Ethnicity	Religious Background	Years Initiated	Interview or Survey
Brianna	New York	F	50	Puerto Rican	Catholic	5	S
Camila	Florida	F	39	White Cuban	Catholic	1	S
Cantrice	Georgia	F	47	African American	Baptist	20	S
Carlos	New York	M	25	Hispanic	Lucumi	<1	S
Carmen	Florida	F	50	White Cuban	Catholic	32	S
Carolina	New York	F	46	Latina	Pentecostal	7	S
Chris	Maryland	M	39	White	Protestant		I
Cora	Oregon	F	46	White	Christian		I
Cristal	New York	F	29	African American	Baptist	<1	S
Dana	California	F	40	African American	Catholic, Methodist	<1	S
Daniela	New York	F		Puerto Rican	Catholic	28	S
Dawn	California	F	42	Black	Metaphysical	4.5	I
Denise	Pennsylvania	F	35	African American	Catholic	<1	S
Diane	New Jersey	F	39	Black	Episcopalian	5	S
Donna	—	F	70	African American	Roman Catholic	10	S
Douglas	Illinois	F	34	African-American	Catholic	3	S
Eduardo	Virginia	M	61	Hispanic	Catholic	<1	I, S
Elena	California	F	29	Hispanic	Santeria/	1	S

(continued)

Demographic Information about Research Participants

Pseudonym	Place of Residence	Sex	Age	Race/ Ethnicity	Religious Background	Years Initiated	Interview or Survey
Elsa	New York	F	30	African American	Church of England	2	S
Emma	California	F	28	Caucasian	Catholic	<1	I
Ernesto	District of Columbia	M	39	Latino	Santeria, Catholic	10	S
Esperanza	New York	F	51	Hispanic	Catholic, Afro- Cuban	5	S
Estevan	New York	M	35	Puerto Rican, German	Spiritualist	4	S
Eugene	New York	M	57	African American	Christian	17	S
Eva	Florida	M	27	Hispanic	Catholic/ Lukumi	12	S
Faith	Florida	F	42	White	Protestant Christian	<1	S
Fawn	Illinois	F	43	African American	Catholic	10	S
Faye	Ohio	F	57	White	Christian and Animist	4	S
Fiona	Oregon	F	31	White	Methodist		I
Flaco	Texas	M	40	Mexican	Catholic		I
Frank	New Jersey	M	39	African American	Christian	11	S
Gabriel	California	M	39	Mexican	Catholic	12	I
Gavin	Florida	M	43	White	—	6	S
George	North Carolina	M	33	Caucasian	Protestant		I
Georgia	Pennsylvania	F	36	White	Lutheran	4	I, S
Gillian	Oregon	F	33	White	Methodist	2	S

Demographic Information about Research Participants

Pseudonym	Place of Residence	Sex	Age	Race/ Ethnicity	Religious Background	Years Initiated	Interview or Survey
Gloria	Florida	F	32	White	Catholic	32	S
Grace	Florida	F	26	Hispanic	Catholic, Spiritualism	1.5	S
Halie	Colorado	F	34	Black	Catholic/ Baptist	<1	S
Harmony	Pennsylvania	F	32	African American	Christian	2	S
Hector	California	M	48	Mexican	Catholic	2	I
Helen	Arizona	F	59	White	Catholic	13	S
Henry	New Jersey	M			—	4	S
Holly	Ohio	F	53	White	Protestant	10	I
Hugo	Arizona	M	36	Puerto Rican	Seventh Day Adventist	1	I
Hunter	Arkansas	M	49	Caucasian	Catholic	1	S
Ida	California	F	38	Hispanic	Catholic	8	S
Ines	Illinois	F	58	Caucasian	Catholic	12	I
Isabel	Florida	F	39	Hispanic	Catholic	18	S
Ivy	Michigan	F	40	White	None	8	S
Jack	Arizona	M	54	Caucasian	Baptist	7	I
Jasmine	Texas	F	36	Mixed	Muslim	<1	I
Jennifer	Oregon	F	30	Caucasian	Southern Baptist		I
Joan	Maryland	F	42	Mixed European	Roman Catholic	10	S
John	New York	M	62	African American	Protestant	18	I
Jordan	California	M	39	African American	Catholic/ Buddhist	9	I

(continued)

Demographic Information about Research Participants

Pseudonym	Place of Residence	Sex	Age	Race/ Ethnicity	Religious Background	Years Initiated	Interview or Survey
Jorge	Florida	M	38	Cuban	Catholic	26	S
Joseph	District of Columbia	M	37	White	Baptist	3	I
Joyce	Michigan	F	34	Caucasian	Catholic	3	S
Karen	Washington	F	31	White, Native American	Southern Baptist		I
Kelly	Florida	F	41	White	Catholic	2	S
Kendra	California	F	29	Black	Christian and Jehovah's Witness	3	S
Kenneth	Colorado	M	32	European American	Presbyterian	<1	I
Kimberly	New York	F	56	African Descent	Baptist	13	S
Kirstin	California	F	55	Caucasian	Christianity	4	S
Lani	Texas	F	37	Caucasian	Methodist		I
Laura	California	F	30	Latina	Catholic and Lukumi	2.5	S
Leon	California	M	48	Latino	Catholic	2	S
Leslie	California	F	27	White	Roman Catholic	2	S
Lily	New York	F	43	Asian	Buddhism	3	S
Lincoln	New York	M	57	African American	Christian	18	I
Lola	Maryland	F	38	Cuban	Catholic	<1	S
Lucy	New Jersey	F	28	Italian	Catholic	<1	S
Luís	Georgia	M	42	Latino	Lucumi	22	S

Demographic Information about Research Participants

Pseudonym	Place of Residence	Sex	Age	Race/ Ethnicity	Religious Background	Years Initiated	Interview or Survey
Magda-lena	California	F	33	Mexican American	Catholic	2	S
Marcos	Texas	M	34	Mexican	Catholic	9	I
Margot	Oregon	F	30	Caucasian	Unitarian/ Mixed		I
María	Florida	F	38	Cuban	Catholic	1	S
Mariana	North Carolina	F	40	Latina	Protestant	2	S
Mariposa	Florida	F	24	Cuban, Colombian	Catholic	2	S
Maritza	New Jersey	F		Hispanic	Catholic	4	S
Mark	Pennsylvania	M	35	White	Roman Catholic	3.5	S
Matías	California	M	18	Puerto Rican	Catholic/Ifa	<1	S
Mía	New Jersey	F	30	Puerto Rican	Catholic	2	S
Michael	California	M	38	Hispanic White	Catholic	<1	I
Michelle	California	F		Puerto Rican, Filipino	Catholic	7	S
Moishe	Michigan	M	38	Hebrew	—	16	I
Monette	New York	F	28	African American	Christian	<1	S
Nancy	District of Columbia	F	36	African American	Christian	8	S
Neil	Washington	M	41	Caucasian	Christian	1.5	I
Nicolás	California	M	39	Mexican American	Catholic	12	S

(continued)

Demographic Information about Research Participants

Pseudonym	Place of Residence	Sex	Age	Race/ Ethnicity	Religious Background	Years Initiated	Interview or Survey
Nicole	New Jersey	F	33	Puerto Rican	Catholic	14	S
Nora	California	F	55	Hispanic	Catholic	22	S
Noreen	Maryland	F	41	Caucasian	Catholic		I
Nyesha	New York	F	40	African American	Baptist	29	S
Olive	Virginia	F	56	Caucasian	Catholic	2	S
Opal	Georgia	F	47	African American	Baptist	18	I
Otto	Connecticut	M	60	African American, West Indian	Catholic	30	S
Paola	Florida	F	49	Hispanic	Catholic	28	S
Patricia	California	F	36	Chicana	Catholic	<1	I
Paul	Texas	M	46	White	Catholic	4	S
Peggy	New York	F	61	Caucasian	Catholic	44	S
Peter	Colorado	M	31	European American	None	<1	S
Phoebe	Oregon	F	32	Caucasian	Slightly Protestant	1	S
Pilar	Florida	F	54	Hispanic	Catholic	29	S
Raimundo	California	M	30	Hispanic	Catholic	1.5	I
Rebecca	Oregon	F	32	Caucasian	Southern Baptist	<1	S
Regina	Illinois	F	57	Caucasian	Roman Catholic	12	S
Reya	New York	F	37	Multiracial	Mixed/ Agnostic	0	I

Demographic Information about Research Participants

Pseudonym	Place of Residence	Sex	Age	Race/ Ethnicity	Religious Background	Years Initiated	Interview or Survey
Robert	New York	M	38	Afro American	Baptist	7	I
Roger	New York	M	28	Caucasian Mexican	Catholic	2	S
Ronna	Florida	F	33	African American	Baptist	<1	S
Rosa	California	F	30	Hispanic, Latina	Catholic and Lukumi	28	S
Ruth	District of Columbia	F	41	Caucasian	Episcopalian	5	S
Samuel	Pennsylvania	M	49	White	Protestant		I
Santiago	New Jersey	M	27	Cuban	Catholic	3	S
Serena	California	F	41	African American	Baptist/ Catholic	5	S
Sergio	Florida	M	48	Cuban	Catholic, Espiritismo	38	S
Shawna	New Jersey	F	54	African American	Episcopal	10	I
Sheila	Oregon	F	38	White, Hispanic	None	2	S
Silvia	Pennsylvania	F	55	African	Methodist	8	I
Sofia	New York	F	46	Puerto Rican	Pentecostal	8	I
Star	District of Columbia	F	39	Caucasian	Christian	3	I
Tamara	Pennsylvania	F	39	White	Catholic		I
Ted	New York	M	33	Latino	Catholic	8	S
Teresa	California	F	26	Cuban, European	Santeria, Ifa	16	S

(continued)

Demographic Information about Research Participants

Pseudonym	Place of Residence	Sex	Age	Race/ Ethnicity	Religious Background	Years Initiated	Interview or Survey
Teri	California	F	46	Mexican	Catholic	4.5	S
Tiffany	North Carolina	F	37	African American	Church of God in Christ	2	S
Tino	Michigan	M	37	European	Christian	3.5	S
Tomás	New Jersey	M	36	Hispanic	Catholic/ Born Again	1.5	S
Ursa	Maryland	F	42	White	Catholic	11	I
Valentina	Florida	F		Hispanic	Yoruba	2	S
Vanessa	New Jersey	F	28	Puerto Rican	Pentecostal and Catholic	12	S
Victor	—	M	30	Cuban, European	Santeria and Catholicism	15	S
Vienna	Texas	F	33	White	Catholic		I
Vincent	New York	M	32	Latino, Mixed	Catholic	9	I
Viola	Nevada	F	40	Latino	Catholic	<1	S
William	—	M	37	Black	Christian	<1	I, S
Wilma	Tennessee	F	49	African American	Catholic	9	S
Xavier	California	M	23	White Cuban	Lukumi/Ifa	3	S
Yevette	New York	F	59	African American	Catholic	4	S
Zelda	New York	F	34	Black	Episcopal	2	S
Zoe	Florida	F	33	Cuban American	Catholic, Espiritismo	1	S

The information about residence that participants provided is not necessarily where participants experienced the year in white; it indicates where they lived when I interviewed them. In cases where informants lived outside the United States, I have not included their residence in order to protect their identity. It should be noted, however, that research participants lived in the Virgin Islands, New Zealand, Brazil, and Canada as well as in the United States.

Answers related to "race/ethnicity" or "religion raised" are not consistent because I mostly used the language interview participants provided on written questionnaires that preceded the interviews or in open-ended questions in the survey. Where necessary I have edited these and other answers for length, grammar, and spelling.

When it was clear to me that participants listed the number of years they had been involved in the religion rather than the number of years since their *kariocha* initiation, I reported the latter. Those with less than a year listed were *iyawo* when I interviewed them. Those without a number listed under years since *kariocha* were *aleyo* when I interviewed them, though many have since undergone the *kariocha* and the year in white.

NOTES

INTRODUCTION

1. Despite the fact that much Cuban and other New World participation in Lukumi religion involves—and has historically involved—socially white persons, and despite the fact that much of what we know as Lukumi practice today is largely of twentieth-century Cuban creation (Brown 2003; Palmié 2013), "Afro-Cuban" is a commonly recognized term among scholars and religious practitioners for Lukumi and other traditions that trace ritual lineage, devotions, and/or divinities, even in part, from involuntary African migrants to the island and/or to borrowings from religious practice in West Africa. Palmié (2013, 27) problematizes the term "Afro-Cuban" as misleading because: 1) it harbors assumptions about the racial composition of its practitioners—"'Africanity' and 'blackness' often do not, and simply *need not* coincide"; and 2) it presumes a "cultural survival" directly from Africa to the New World, an overly simplistic understanding of origins. Although the terms Lukumi, Lucumí, Santería, and Regla de Ocha are sometimes used interchangeably, they carry different connotations (Clark 2007). Because many practitioners find the term "Santería" offensive (see Falola and Genova 2006; Clark 2007), I will use Lukumi where possible.

2. *Iyawo* is pronounced by some as a three syllable word and by others with two syllables, dropping the first. The year in white is also referred to as *iyaworaje* and *iyawoage*. Clark (2005, 157) explains that the term "is a mixed Yoruba-Spanish word referring to the extended initiation period that begins with the initiation itself and concludes with the dismantling of the first birthday altar a year later. It is only after the completion of the iyawoage and his reintegration into the secular community that the new priest is considered 'fully crowned.'"

3. Orisha, also pronounced Oricha (Spanish), are divinities or aspects of divinity in Lukumi religion. They are seen as "specialized forms of the one Supreme God." Also referred to as *santos* (saints) and Ochas, they are "specific parts or forces within God which govern different parts of the universe" (Edwards and Mason 1985, 1). Orisha "in popular etymology" literally means *orí* (head) and *sha* (select), or "select head" (Mason 1992, 5), with the understanding that "head" means both "first in rank and head in status" and "the very essence of personality." Clark (2005, 13) explains that the Orisha are the "knowable aspects of *Olodumare*, the great god behind the gods." Unlike the less accessible chief deity, the Orisha "represent a level of power that is approachable through ritual action." Although there are dozens of known Orisha and many of them have multiple aspects or "roads," some of the most common Orisha in the Lukumi system are the three warriors Elegua, Ogun, and Ochosi; the dignified, intellectual father and judge Obatalá; the long-suffering, watery, feminine Oshun; the ruler of markets, cemeteries, and winds Oya; the diviner Orunmila or Orula, to whom the all-male *babalawo* priests are specially devoted in Lukumi's sister religion of Ifa; Babaluaye or Asojano, who is associated with healing and infectious disease; the maternal, oceanic Yemaya; the miraculous Ibeji twins; the volcanic Agayu; Olokun, the mystery at the bottom of the ocean; and Chango, the thundering, dancing, carousing king (see Clark 2005; Murphy 1988; Edwards and Mason 1985).

4. Yoruba culture is commonly accepted by religious practitioners and scholars as the origin of Lukumi religious tradition and the basis for a growing identity group characterized by ritual and belief that honors the Orisha in various ways around the globe (Falola and Genova

2006). Nevertheless, "Yoruba" was a label Christian missionaries mistakenly applied in the mid-nineteenth century. The term "held little meaning" before that time and was not much used by religious practitioners until the mid-twentieth century (Palmié 2013, 45). Prior to this time, those we call "Yoruba" today were from "ethnically and culturally diverse West African kingdoms" who worshipped different divinities (Brown 2003, 115) and did not identify as a single group with each other. To acknowledge the history of the term is to accept the dynamic and socially constructed nature of traditions that are commonly discussed as being of ancient African origin. In short, Lukumi religion is a New World creation made of elements from disparate parts of Africa; it was not passed in toto from one continent to another (see Brown 2003; Palmié 2013).

5. Anthropologist Sandra T. Barnes (1989) estimates the number of Orisha worshippers around the globe at 70 million. Historians Toyin Falola and Ann Genova (2006, 4) reckon that the number is closer to 75 million, although they admit that "there is no scientific basis to arrive at any number." Prothero (2010) cites an estimate of 100 million Yoruba-derived religious practitioners worldwide. Management scholar Donald McCormick (2013, 718) mentions "Santería" as one of "two of the fastest growing religions in the USA," although he provides no support for this claim.

6. Brown (2003, 129) dates the earliest references to the 1930s. However, historian and Obá Miguel "Willie" Ramos asserts that he found the term being used to refer to Lukumi practitioners two decades before that in Cuban newspapers (personal correspondence).

7. African studies scholars Falola and Genova (2006, 10) do so by distancing Yoruba religion from the similarly stigmatized "voodoo" of Dahomey. Theology professor Joseph M. Murphy (1988, 2) calls the "images of sensuality and evil" associated with the religion "little more than our society's cultural projections of repression, insecurity, and racial prejudice." Anthropologist Steven Gregory (1999, 11) argues that sensationalist depictions of African religious beliefs have long been used as evidence of racial inferiority: "Fantastic stereotypes of witch doctors, cannibals, and zombies served to provide moral and political justification for the oppression and exploitation of African peoples as slaves and later as second-class citizens of racially and class-stratified societies."

8. In *Church of the Lukumi-Babaluaye, Inc. v. City of Hialeah* (1993), 508 U.S. 520, the U.S. Supreme Court ruled that the city of Hialeah, Florida, had violated First Amendment rights to freedom of religion when it prohibited the Lukumi church from practicing animal sacrifice. In a more recent case, *Merced v. Kasson* (2009), 577 F. 3d 578, the U.S. Court of Appeals, 5th Circuit, found similarly that the ordinances of the city of Euless, Texas, prohibiting animal sacrifice created a substantial burden on "free exercise of religion without advancing a compelling governmental interest using the least restrictive means."

9. Mason (2002, 9) notes the dramatic growth of this "Cuban-planted religion" among non-Cuban "Latinos and increasing numbers of African Americans and Euro-Americans." Curry (1997, ix) observes the quick diversification of the religion within its decentralized "house" structure: "At the time of my first writing, there were Cuban Houses, Puerto Rican Houses, Black Houses, and Multi-ethnic Houses. Now, depending upon the part of the country one considers, there are [also] Polish Houses, Mexican Houses, and Houses of other ethnic groups." (Although I am aware of predominantly white non-Hispanic houses, I cannot verify that specifically Polish houses exist or have ever existed in the United States.) Asserting that the growing diversity within Lukumi has granted it the maturity (and troubles) of a full-blown world religion, Canizares (1999, 25) paints this shift as a "transformation from a basically localized primal religion, dependent on Cuban soil, to an essentially universal religion expression (albeit with an obvious African flavor) that encompasses all who will enter."

10. Obá is a Yoruba title meaning "ruler" or "chief." It is given to the *oriaté*, the "ruler of the [divination] mat . . . and ritual specialist who presides over the initiation of Santería priests and other rituals" (Clark 2007, 163).

11. A major ritual focus in Lukumi tradition is placing the spiritual essence of Orisha within rocks (*otanes*) that are thereafter considered sacred.

12. *Babalawo*—"fathers of mystery"—are priestly initiates of Ifa, the cult of the Orisha Orula/Orunmila (Clark 2007, 25). Lukumi and Ifa are different religions that share aspects of divinatory systems and Orisha veneration. Houses of Orisha devotees vary in the extent to which they are interconnected with the other religious system. Some are very connected, others mostly separate. Brown (2003) divides the community into the (all-male and supposedly heterosexual) *babalawo*-centered and the *oriaté*-centered groups, which are more diverse in terms of gender and sexuality. In my experience, there is more of a continuum than a complete division of types. At issue is the relative power of each type of priest in the practicing communities. Clark (2005) provides an in-depth discussion of this topic, especially where gender is concerned. Palmié (2013, 185) notes that "the tendency of anthropologists to gravitate toward babalaos . . . led to a proliferation of 'ifa-centered' scholarly accounts," in which, for example, initiated devotees of Orula were discussed as the "high priests" of the religion, a status not universally recognized among Lukumi practitioners, especially among those enjoying *oriaté*-centered practice.

13. Spiritism (or *Espiritismo*) is a European practice of communing with spirits and the dead that became increasingly grafted into Cuban and Puerto Rican Lukumi practice beginning in the mid-nineteenth century (Olmos and Paravasini-Gebert 2003).

14. Brandon (2002) explains that instead of the church/congregation structure common in Christian organizations, Lukumi practice in the United States today is organized through a lineage-based, decentralized structure of "houses," also referred to with the Yoruba term *ilé* and the Spanish phrase *casa de ocha*. Members of the religion belong to the *ilé* or *casa de ocha* of the person who initiated them, referred to as their godparent, their *madrina* or *padrino*, or their *iyalosha* or *babalosha*. They may also consider themselves to be a part of a larger *ilé* composed of the original initiator in a particular geographical area. See also Curry (1997, chapter 3).

15. *Aleyo* or *alejo* refers to a Lukumi practitioner who is not initiated as a priest in the Lukumi or Ifa religions. Curry (1997, 170) explains that the term means "stranger-resident-in-the House." The *aleyo* perspective on a ceremony is distinct from a priestly perspective, as much of the ceremony occurs out of sight (behind a sheet).

16. See Appendix A for a detailed discussion of my methods.

17. In 1985, prolific pioneering science fiction author Robert A. Heinlein published *The Cat Who Walks through Walls: A Comedy of Manners*. In the novel is a feline who manages to follow the protagonist everywhere, walking through walls when necessary. The title refers to the physics thought experiment about Schrödinger's cat.

18. Not surprisingly, in a study of forty countries, Barro, Hwang, and McCleary (2010, 20) found that religious conversion—defined as "movements across major religious groups"— was positively related to degree of religious pluralism.

19. In contrast to this trend, a growing group of scholars attend to African American participation in the religion. For example, Curry (1997) provides a case study of an African American *ilé*. Lefever (2000) and Hucks (2012) examine the combination of Black nationalism with Orisha worship in the founding of Olotunji Village in South Carolina. See also the many selections in Falola and Genova's (2006) anthology devoted to this topic.

20. Central to sociologist Harold Garfinkel's (1967) "ethnomethodology," breaching experiments involved observations of people's reactions to norm violations in order to highlight the taken-for-grantedness of social interaction. For example, Garfinkel examined the gender-passing practices of male-to-female transgendered "Agnes" to derive a list of cultural gender norms that most members of that culture assume to be "natural."

21. In other examples, sociologist Richard Travisano (1970, 598) separates conversion from the more reversible and less comprehensive "alternation." David Gordon (1974) recognizes conversion ("a radical discontinuity in a person's life") as distinct from "consolidation" (a combination of world views) (Snow and Machalek 1984, 169).

22. The image from Phillips and Kellner was originally used to describe religious "switching." I believe it is an apt metaphor for religious identification and practice more generally.

23. One exception is Kleinmann (2012, 279), who examined the effects of conversion status on Islamic radicalism. He found a "difference in the factors that lead to radicalization in convert and non-convert homegrown [U.S.] Sunni militants."

CHAPTER 1

1. Sandoval (2006, 65, 91, 76) suggests that "the fashion of initiating so many people started in the 1950s" in Cuba. Before this time, there were many "Santos parados (standing saints) . . . uninitiated individuals who performed as priests." This was preceded by a trend in turn-of-the-twentieth-century Cuba that emphasized "that rituals were only efficacious when they were performed by knowledgeable, professional priests." Such ritual "inflation" also affected subsequent ceremonies. The *pinaldo* ceremony was originally created to confirm as "priests" those with *santos parados* who did not have the Orisha "seated" on their heads in the *kariocha* (see Brown 2003). It was thus an alternative path to the priesthood. Today the *pinaldo* is commonly required of priests in certain circumstances and is seen by some as "the completion of their Ocha . . . initiation," allowing them to initiate godchildren without their godparents' assistance (Orishanet n.d.).

2. A more complete discussion of *iyawo* rules can be found in Chapter 3.

3. *Orí* is the "head," an essential aspect of one's spirit, and a driving force of the personality. Obatalá is the Orisha known as the King of the White Cloth who owns *orí*, "where spirit dwells"; thought; and dreams (Matibag 1996, 60). *Orí* also houses a person's destiny (Murphy 1988).

4. For example, Curry (1997, 101) provides a day-by-day description of the seven-day initiation ceremony from the perspective of the *aleyo*, but of the year that follows, she says only that "the Iyawo occupies a special liminal status—not yet a priest but no longer an alejo." Gregory (1999, 91) mentions the *yaworaje* only in his discussion of the economic cost of the religion: "The initiate or yaguó must wear all white for a period of one year and sixteen days. Consequently an entirely new wardrobe must be purchased and specially laundered."

5. *Ashé* (or *aché*) is a Yoruba term meaning "power, energy, blessings; energy of the universe; ritual power; also name of empowered material" (Clark 2007, 160).

6. Many Orisha are associated with royalty and warriors. For example, Obatalá, Chango, and Oshun are viewed as royalty. Elegua, Ogun, and Ochosi are depicted as warriors.

7. Interestingly, the term *iyawo* is used to refer to new Orisha priests "on both sides of the Atlantic" (Clark 2005, 43). The *iyawo* is a new bride to the Orisha to whom she or he is assigned, regardless of the gender of the initiate and the gender of the Orisha.

8. Along these lines, McGuire (2008) proposes that many sociological conceptions of religion were influenced by the Christianity of the long reformation in ways as foundational as

specifying the relationship between the sacred and profane, the nature of divine power, the nature of individual religious expression, and what constitutes authentic religious tradition and identity.

9. As Smith et al. (2013, 918) urge, "Until sociology expands its focus to incorporate a greater variety of religions from all regions of the world, it will not only remain parochial in its substantive focus, but will be hindered in its ability to imagine new theories and paradigms for making sense of religion in the world as it is unfolding."

10. These can be considered what some have called "conversion narratives." As such they can be seen as windows into the "ongoing process of identity formation and reality constitution" through which religious practitioners construct their identities (Sremac 2010, 22; see also Stromberg 1993; Snow and Machalek 1984).

11. Throughout the text, when I first introduce research participants (and when possible), I will attempt to offer a bit about what each has shared with me about their reasons for undergoing the *kariocha* ceremony and the year in white.

12. See Chapter 5 for a more in-depth discussion of divination and its relationship to conversion in Lukumi.

13. I have changed participants' names throughout to ensure confidentiality. Please see Appendix A for selected demographic information for named research participants.

14. *Maferefun* means "thanks be to" (Murphy 1988, 179).

15. *Ikofa*, also called "hand of Orula" or *awofaka* (for men), is a ritual initiation performed by a *babalawo* in the Ifa religion, a tradition related to Lukumi. The purpose of the ritual is to gain protection over untimely death and knowledge of one's destiny (Clark 2007). Mason (2002, 28) describes this ceremony, in which one is said to "receive Warriors," as "the beginning of a person's 'road in the saint.'" It is often the first initiatory ceremony for newcomers to *ilés* that rely heavily on *babalawo* priests. During the ritual, initiates receive objects specifically made for them that are said to contain the *ashé* (power, life energy) of the Warrior Orisha Elegua, Ogun, Ochosi, and Osun. I was told that *Los Guerreros* would protect and ground me, and give me strength. The ceremony also serves to connect recipients to a specific godparent and their *ilé* or religious house. See Clark (2005), Mason (2002), and Murphy (1988) for more detailed descriptions of the ceremony of receiving Warriors.

16. A *bembe* is a "drum and dance festival for the orishas" (Murphy 1988, 176).

17. In the Lukumi divinatory system of *diloggun*, sixteen cowrie shells are thrown. It is believed that Orisha speak through the patterns of the shells. Cowries can fall in open or closed positions. The resulting 256 patterns of the shells are called *odu*. Each *odu* is associated with specific memorized verses and stories, situations, advice, rituals, and liturgies (see Bascom [1980] 1993; Ócha'ni Lele 2003).

18. Oyo and Ilé Ife were city-states in precolonial Yorubaland (Clark 2007). Ilé Ife was a "sacred city of the Yoruba"; it is believed that it was the first city (Sandoval 2006, 6).

19. Unle Meji, also called Ogbe Meji, is the name of a particular *odu* in Lukumi divination. I was told that the situations it described were separation, the rule of the intellect over the heart, and the "head seeking a crown." Ócha'ni Lele (2003, 375) explains that the *odu* speaks of a person who must become an Orisha priest or "he will wander through life unfulfilled." It also foretells broken relationships and warns against attempts to grow and learn too quickly.

20. The *asiento* takes place in an area designated as *igbodu*, which, literally translated is "sacred grove" (Olmos and Paravasini-Gebert 2003).

21. Personal communication, 2014.

22. Each observation should be independent. In addition, when expected and observed values are compared, "no more than 20% of the expected counts are less than five and all

individual expected counts are 1 or greater" (Yates, Moore, and McCabe 1999, 734; see Bolboacă et al. 2011). In this book I report as significant only findings for 2 x 2 tables (those with degrees of freedom of 1) where all cells had expected counts of 5 or above and for 2 x 4 tables (those with degrees of freedom of 3) where no more than 1 cell had an expected count below 5.

23. There are important limitations in my survey data in this respect. My survey question for race/ethnicity was open ended. I could not tell in many cases if respondents had Cuban or Puerto Rican ethnic backgrounds when they answered simply "Hispanic," "Latino," "Latina," "White," or "Caucasian," which many did. A better test of possible differences would have asked more specific questions about ethnicity and included separate questions for race and Hispanic status.

CHAPTER 2

1. *Itá* is "diloggun divination performed as part of asiento initiation"; it "tells the initiate's past, present, and future" (Clark 2007, 161).

2. *Babalosha* and *iyalosha* mean "father" and "mother" of Orisha; both are contractions from the Yoruba. Although some discuss these terms as synonyms for *olorisha* ("owner of Orisha") (see Clark 2005; Olmos and Paravasini-Gebert 2003), in my experience the term is reserved for Orisha priests who have initiated godchildren in the religion via the *kariocha*.

3. Not all survey respondents answered all of the open-ended questions; the total number of responses for each survey question ranged from 144 to 152. I used the larger number when computing percentages.

4. *Abokú* is a temporary status the initiate holds at the beginning of the seven days of *kariocha*. Brown (2003) explains that the initiate becomes *abokú* at the river ceremony a day before the *asiento* and passes to *iyawo* status during the *asiento*. *Abokú* status, which is associated with death, is even more liminal than *iyawo* status.

5. When priests are "possessed" by their tutelary Orisha so these aspects of divinity can communicate and interact with their devotees, they are often referred to as being "mounted" by the Orisha who rule their heads. For more discussion on spirit embodiment, see Chapter 5.

6. Ordinal variables are those whose answers are categorized in a ranked fashion and can thus be assigned numbers, though the intervals between the assigned numbers do not have real value (such as might be the case in a question asking about income). Ordinal variables are derived from questions in the survey such as "I love/d being iyawo!" and "My friends accepted my being iyawo" with survey answers: "strongly agree," "somewhat, agree," "somewhat disagree," and "strongly disagree." There were thirty-four ordinal variables, but I also created and ran chi-square analyses for "dummy" variables for each of the thirty-four questions, collapsing "strongly agree" with "somewhat agree" and "strongly disagree" with "somewhat disagree." In this chapter I report on only those variables concerning *iyawo* experience generally; those concerning the rules of the year or relationships will be reported in subsequent chapters. For a complete list of survey questions, from which the variables were derived, please see Appendix B.

7. This finding was also statistically significant in a 2 x 4 table, i.e. before I collapsed somewhat and strongly agree and somewhat and strongly disagree: ($X^2 = 9.14$, df = 3, $p = .028$; N = 168). Another variable was found to be statistically significant that I have chosen not to report as such. In response to the statement "My year in white helped me to deal with emotional issues from my past," 50 percent of non-Hispanics strongly agreed that that the year in white helped heal their emotional issues (compared to 30 percent of non-Hispanics), but only 24 percent of non-Hispanics and 49 percent of Hispanics somewhat agreed with the same measure. Given that a nearly equal percentage of Hispanics and non-Hispanics responded positively to this measure, the findings are difficult to interpret in a relevant manner. The result of the chi-square test was $X^2 = 16.30$, df = 3, $p = .001$; N = 135.

CHAPTER 3

1. An *oluwo* is an Orisha priest who is also a *babalawo*.
2. Note that percentages do not add up to 100 due to rounding and because many respondents answered with more than one category.
3. I categorized serious power issues in houses of Ocha as "*ilé* relations," a topic I discuss in the next chapter. This may have produced an undercounting of the number of respondents who had difficulties with subordinate status.

CHAPTER 4

1. This is the phrase as it was initially taught to me. From the Yoruba, the greeting is: "*Àbọrú bọyè, bọ ṣíṣẹ́*" which means "May your sacrifices be blessed and accepted." The full response, which is often truncated in practice, is "*Ogbó, atọ́, àsúre, Ìwòrìwofún*" which can be translated as "May you live long and be of good health, blessings of Ìwòrìwofún." (Abimbola and Miller 1997, 146). The latter is the name of an *odu*, one of 256 patterns in the Ifa and Lukumi divinatory systems that is associated with specific memorized verses and stories, situations, advice, rituals, and liturgies, as well as being personified in sacred stories.
2. The altar was a temporary one, created for the annual celebration of the Saint Lazarus Day feast that had occurred a few days before I visited. In retrospect, the fact that my godfather had enjoyed such a celebration without my awareness, disallowing me from assisting or paying my respects, was good evidence of my peripheral status in his *ilé*.
3. When a person has a ritual performed on their behalf in Lukumi tradition, it is commonly described as "receiving." A person "receives" Warriors or Olokun or Oya, for example. In these rituals the initiate (or receiver) obtains objects specifically made for her or him that are said to contain the *ashé* (power, life energy) of the Orisha in question. The ceremony of *elekes* is also discussed in similar language since the initiate receives consecrated beaded necklaces at the end of the cleansing ritual.
4. See Brandon (2002) for a detailed discussion of Lukumi house structure. See also Clark (2007). And see Palmié (2013) for a discussion of the move from blood to spiritual kinship.
5. The *ayubona* or *oyubona* is "the 'second' god-parent to whom the *iyawó* becomes linked in ritual kinship and who tends to the *iyawó* most intimately during the initiation" (Brown 2003, 369).
6. Bastide ([1960] 2007) wrote about how in Brazil, both slave owners and their families and freed men and women of various ethnicities came to the knowledgeable practitioners of the "African" religions to purchase medicine and spell work when they needed spiritual assistance with issues of health, wealth, children, or love. Bristol (2007) wrote similarly of curandera/os in seventeenth-century Mexico who faced the Inquisition when disgruntled patrons turned on the healers in whom they had once placed their hopes. Of course these relationships have very different contexts from contemporary *consultas*.
7. *Botanicas* are religious supply stores that sometimes carry items used by Orisha devotees and occasionally employ *olorishas* and *babalawos* who offer divinatory consultations. For in-depth descriptions of *botanicas*, see Murphy (1988 and 2015).

8. See Mason (2002) for a detailed description of the interactions and relationships involved in priestly consultations.

9. In this chapter and the next I draw on interviews more heavily than in prior chapters. Some of the people I interviewed were *aleyos* who had not yet undergone *kariocha*.

10. Clark (2005, 148) estimates "that between 30 percent and 50 percent of all santeros are gay men and lesbians," although she offers no details on how this was measured. Vidal-Ortiz (2011, 907–8) claims to have witnessed a "high presence of self-identified gay men, sometimes between 30 to 50 percent of all men," but suggests "lesser estimates . . . for lesbian women." In my online survey—which is in no way statistically representative of *olorisha* in the United States—38 of the 153 who answered the question on "current gender and sexual identity" (25 percent) indicated that they were gay, lesbian, bisexual, queer, or transgendered. The latter number is higher than in the general population but lower than estimates by other scholars. I have attended some *ocha* events that seemed to be populated mostly by LGBT persons and others at which sexual minorities were nearly invisible.

11. Oriaté is the "ruler of the [divination] mat . . . and ritual specialist who presides over the initiation of Santería priests and other rituals" (Clark 2007, 163). Brown (2003) discusses the distinctions in the *ocha* community between *babalawo*-centered and *oriaté*-centered groups.

12. Practitioners commonly refer to initiations in Regla de Palo as getting or being "scratched." This is because the initiates' bodies are marked with cuts. See Olmos and Paravisini-Gebert (2003).

13. According to U.S. census data, 29.9 percent of U.S. residents 25 years old and over completed a four-year college degree or more in 2010. The same was true for only 13.9 percent of Hispanics. It should be noted that education levels among my survey respondents as a whole, including Hispanics, were higher than is generally seen in the U.S. population. This is explained in part by the online method of the survey and by the fact that the language of the survey was English. Hispanic-identified questionnaire takers averaged 14.88 years of education; non-Hispanics averaged 16.45 years of education. In my sample, 78 percent of those who claimed African heritage had completed a four-year college degree, compared to 19.8 percent of African Americans in the United States in 2010. For the census data, see Table 229. Educational Attainment by Race and Hispanic Origin: 1970 to 2010, http://www.census.gov/compendia/statab/2012/tables/12s0229.pdf, retrieved July 28, 2014.

CHAPTER 5

1. *Kabiosile* is a traditional praise for Chango. Murphy (1988, 179) defines it as "'Welcome home.' Ritual greeting to Shango." About this phrase, Bascom ([1972] 1990, 3, 21) writes, "when thunder rolls, his worshipers shout 'Welcome, we prostrate ourselves before you' (Kawo, kabiye sile)." However, he explains that the related "Kabiyesi is sometimes translated as 'Long live the King' or 'Your Royal Highness.'"

2. Mason (2002, 60) discusses the high level of financial commitment of those who undergo the *kariocha*: "The ceremony dedicates the remainder of . . . [the initiate's] life to orichas, and it routinely costs between $5,000 and $15,000 in the United States." One priest I interviewed told me his godmother charged him $25,000 for initiation to Elegua in 1999 or 2000. Although ordination to one of the warrior Orishas is generally at the more expensive end of the range, this cost seems to have been out of the ordinary.

3. Sociologists Theodore Long and Jeffrey Hadden (1983) suggest a modification of understandings of socialization such as Berger and Luckmann's by analytically separating the social learning that is characteristic of groups from individuals' internalization of that group's

beliefs, values, and norms. A person who learns the norms, values, and beliefs of a group does not necessarily have to incorporate those aspects of culture into her own practice and belief. This would encourage scholars to focus on the methods groups use to teach new members. It is also useful to neither deny the agency of "converts" by analyzing them as easily brainwashed dupes nor lose sight of the power of social groups to influence individuals. I will discuss both social training and internalization of beliefs, values, and norms, as each has great implications for *iyawos'* and former *iyawos'* identification with Orisha. Many who shared their stories with me implicitly and explicitly spoke to both social learning and internalization.

4. In their research on the Nichiren Shoshu Buddhist movement, sociologists Snow and Machalek (1984, 173) identified "four rhetorical properties" of converts: "biographical reconstruction, adoption of a master attribution scheme, suspension of analogical reasoning, and embracement of the convert role." In other words, converts reviewed their past in light of the new religion, they considered reality through the lens of their new belief system, they understood their new mindset as unique and different from all others, and they called themselves changed persons. Three of these four patterns are present to varying degrees in the accounts of cultural newcomers to Orisha traditions in the United States. (Suspension of analogical reasoning is better applicable where an individual "converts" to an exclusivist religion.) In this chapter, I am most interested in "adoption of a master attribution scheme," as it seems to be at the heart of the resocialization process and often includes both reexamining the past through a new lens and seeing oneself as a changed person.

5. In contrast to theories about the secularization of religion that were once in vogue, many contemporary scholars argue that conditions of postmodernity may spur a religious resurgence and that religions as they are currently practiced may take new shapes (see Giddens 1991; Lyon 2000; Partridge 2004). For example, Partridge (2004, 66) describes a "religiocultural shift" of religious "re-enchantment," involving what he calls the "occulture" or "cultic milieu" comprised of a "complex mixture of diffuse spirituality, amorphous networks, and structured groups and organizations." These are found, Partridge claims, not only in New Age and neo-pagan movements but also within much of popular culture. They include claims that one is spiritual rather than religious, an interest in alternative religious paths, and the inclusion of Eastern spiritual beliefs and practices in everyday life, such as alternative healing methodologies and yoga.

6. In Lukumi practice in the United States, Elegua figures, which generally are made of stone or concrete, are considered to hold the *ashé* of the Orisha only when they have been empowered through ritual by trained priests.

7. For example, in the typical *kariocha* made to Obatalá, the initiate receives Elegua, Oya, Oshun, Yemaya, Chango, and Obatalá. An initiate to Chango generally receives Elegua, Obatalá, Oshun, Ibeji, Agayu, Yemaya, and Chango. See Mason (2002) and Olmos and Paravasini-Gebert (2003) for a detailed discussion of the initiation ceremony.

8. See Clark (2005) for a discussion of both types of metaphors used in Ocha communities.

9. I thank my adoptive *ayubona* Okandekun for this explanation.

10. Brown (2003, 114) describes the shift at the turn of the twentieth century from the traditional West African practice of receiving only one or two Orisha in the priestly initiation to the present-day practice of including a larger slice of the "panteón Lucumí" (Lukumi pantheon) as one of the "great innovations" in Cuba. This is now a standard Lukumi practice.

11. The *asiento* takes place (generally in private homes) in an area designated as *igbodu*, which, literally translated is "sacred grove" (Olmos and Paravasini-Gebert 2003).

12. See Conner (2004) for a discussion of gender and sexual complexity among divinities and their devotees within the African diaspora.

13. This occurs in the case of *oluwo*, those who begin as Orisha priests but then "pass to Ifa." That is, they become *babalawos* after undergoing a special ceremony.

14. An *italero* is a specialist in divination. Brown (2003) discusses the evolution of this role in Lukumi ritual.

CONCLUSION

1. The quote is from the final episode of season four of *Babylon 5*, "The Deconstruction of Falling Stars," which aired on October 27, 1997.

2. According to social theorist Pierre Bourdieu (1986), each of us has a varied set of cultural resources that we have "absorbed from the social structure in the course of socialization" and internalized in an embodied way (Fries 2009, 330) that we bring to various "fields," social spheres with their own structures of power, rules, understandings of reality. Beyond economic power, these cultural resources include various types of "capital," including cultural, social, physical, and symbolic.

3. According to professor of ethics and Latino/a studies Miguel A. De La Torre (2004, 207), despite a history of secrecy, practice of the religion has become more open in the United States "since the 1992 U.S. Supreme Court decision protecting the constitutional right of the believers to offer sacrifices." Raul Canizares (1993, 26) similarly believes the "attitude of secrecy is changing, especially in multiethnic ilés." Anthropologist George Brandon (1997, 156–157) notes that secrecy in the religion does more than merely protect worshippers from "persecution or disapproval, [and] for the protection of the things [of worship] themselves"; it also flows from African traditions in which esoteric power is guarded in mystery: "The stones, blood, and herbs remain hidden, concealed in the place where the strong powers reside, more powerful and more truthful because they are hidden."

4. It is possible that religious minority group status may create a "siege mentality" of sorts within its members, strengthening individuals' commitments to their groups. Theoretically such processes may assist in mitigating the privatizing and relativizing tendencies of pluralism and its plausibility crises discussed above. My data does not refute or support this possibility.

5. Social psychological research has long linked high costs of group entry to perceived value of the group and thus to commitment (Aronson and Mills 1959). I thank Dimitris Xygalatas for this insight.

6. As with most voluntary associations, religious organizations tend toward homogeneity with regard to race, class, and culture and occasionally with regard to gender and age (Chaves 2004). Drawing on the National Congregations Study of 1998 (Chaves 1998), Emerson and Kim (2003, 217) estimate that "nearly 90 percent of American congregations are at least 90 percent one racial group, and nearly 80 percent of congregations are at least 95 percent one racial group." Christerson, Edwards, and Emerson (2005) cite religious organizations as both the largest volunteer groups in the United States and the most racially segregated.

7. Much of the sociology of religion in the United States remains focused on Christianity or on the "tripartite settlement" of Protestants, Catholics, and Jews, while minority religious practice has historically been relegated to the ghetto of "new religious movements," despite the longevity of some of these religious forms. In *America and the Challenges of Religious Diversity*, sociologist Robert Wuthnow (2007) asserts that contemporary religious diversity is moving beyond the bounds of varieties of Christianity and Judaism to include growing numbers of Muslims, Hindus, and Buddhists. Wuthnow describes three approaches to dealing with religious pluralism in the United States: "spiritual shopping," "inclusive Christianity," and "exclusive Christianity." The approaches and most of Wuthnow's survey questions refer to

Christianity. Although 11–20 percent of Wuthnow's sample said they were not Christians, he does not elaborate on their approaches or their accounts.

8. As recently as July 2014, the Sociological Abstracts database included no autoethnographic items written by scholars in sociology departments whose research focused on religion or religious identification.

APPENDIX A

1. For a recent discussion of the place and state of mixed methods in sociology today, see Pearce (2012).

2. All research in U.S. university settings that use human subjects must undergo review by the Institutional Review Boards (IRB) to ensure ethical treatment.

3. As comparisons of cultural newcomers and natives were limited to English speakers, I expected them to be instructive rather than representative.

4. See Appendix B for a copy of the survey questions.

5. I first underwent the ceremony of receiving Warriors (Los Guerreros). I then received what I've come to understand is less common (though it was somewhat expensive): a sacralized *egun* (ancestor) stick.

GLOSSARY

aboku: A temporary status of the initiate at the beginning of the seven days of *kariocha;* associated with death.

aché (or ashe): Yoruba term meaning "power, energy, blessings; energy of the universe; ritual power; also name of empowered material" (Clark 2007, 160).

Agayu: An Orisha associated with volcanoes and chasms.

ahijado: Spanish for godchild.

aleyo (or alejo): Those in the religious household who have not undergone priestly initiation.

asiento: From the Spanish word for chair or seat; refers the part of the *kariocha* initiation in which the tutelary Orisha is said to be "seated" on the initiate's spiritual head.

Asojano: (also known as Babaluaye) An Orisha of infectious disease and healing.

ayubona: A secondary godparent responsible for caring for the initiate's needs during the *kariocha.* The *kariocha* begins what is supposed to be a lifelong relationship between the godchild and the *ayubona.*

babalawo: A priestly initiate of Ifa, the cult of the Orisha Orula/Orunmila, the diviner.

babalosha: A male *olorisha* who has one or more godchildren.

Babaluaye: See Asojano.

casa de ocha: Spanish for "house of Ocha." May refer to a physical space (generally the home of the initiating godparent) but primarily refers to one of the decentralized and sometimes overlapping groups of Lukumi practitioners that consist of a godparent and his or her godchildren. It may also refer to multigenerational groups of smaller *casas de ocha* headed by a senior initiating godparent, for example a godparent and his or her godchildren and their godchildren. Used synonymously with the Yoruba *ilé,* meaning "house." Some may consider themselves in certain respects to be a member of multiple *ilés* the *ilé* of their initiating Lukumi godparent, the *ilé* of their *ayubona,* the *ilé* of their godparent's godparent, and the *ilé* of their *babalawo.*

Chango (or Shango): The kingly, masculine Orisha of thunder, drumming, and dance who rules the tongue.

collares: Spanish for necklaces. Refers here to colorful beaded necklaces ceremonially consecrated to the Orisha. Also called *elekes.* Each Orisha is associated with specific colors and bead patterns, and some Orishas have multiple "roads" (personalities) with varying patterns associated with each one. Receiving *elekes* is considered by many to be a minor initiation that formally enters one into the religion because it connects the initiate to a godparent and his or her Orishas.

consultas: Spanish for consultation. Also referred to as a divinatory "reading."

crowning or coronation: Terms commonly used to refer to the *asiento.*

derecho: Spanish for "right." Refers to a fee given to a priest for ceremony.

diloggun: Divination by specially trained Lukumi priests using cowrie shells. Each divinatory reading reveals a particular *odu.*

Elegua: A messenger Orisha who opens doorways to opportunity and allows for communication between people and the Orisha.

elekes: See *collares.*

Espiritismo: Spanish for Spiritism. A European ritual practice of communing with spirits and the dead that is commonly grafted into Cuban and Puerto Rican Lukumi practice.

estera: Spanish for mat. Treated as a clean, sacred space, separated from the profane, for ritual such as divination and for *tronos.* (One does not step on *estera* with shoes.) Because *iyawo* are made to eat (and sometimes sleep) on *estera*, it elevates these everyday routines spiritually.

godfamily: Spiritual kin consisting of one's godparents and their godchildren and sometimes the godfamily of one's godparents. A person has expectations of and responsibilities to members of one's godfamily such as godparents and godsiblings (a godparent's other godchildren).

head marking: A special divinatory consultation in which a trained diviner determines a single (tutelary) Orisha to which a person will be dedicated during the *kariocha.* Orisha are said to choose their initiates and, once "seated" on an initiate, will "rule" his or her "head." The head marking must precede the *kariocha,* and a person whose head has been marked is generally expected to undergo the *kariocha* afterward.

Ibeji (or Ibeyi): The Orisha of twins. Twins are believed to confer special blessings on a household. I was taught to treat them like children and appeal to them when in need of a miracle.

igbodu: Yoruba for grove. Refers to the space where *kariocha* occurs, a sacred space the non-initiated are not supposed to see.

ikofa: A ritual performed by *babalawos* in the Ifa religion, a tradition related to Lukumi.

ilé: See *casa de ocha.*

Inle: An Orisha who lives where the river meets the ocean; a magician associated with liminality.

itá: Diloggun consultation that occurs during the *kariocha* that provides guidance for a person's life. Unlike a regular consultation, *itá* is meant to apply for one's entire life rather than for a few months. An initiate can also receive *itá* divination outside of the *kariocha* when receiving certain Orisha singly.

iyalosha: A female *olorisha* who has one or more godchildren.

iyawo: One who has undergone the *kariocha* within the past year and is subject to the rules of the year in white.

kariocha: A seven-day Lukumi ceremony in which the initiate is dedicated to her or his tutelary Orisha. In the *kariocha* an *aleyo* becomes *abokú* and emerges as *iyawo,* commencing the year in white. Because it is seen as conferring Orisha priesthood, some describe it as "priestly initiation" or "ordination." It is also called or described as *asiento, ocha,* crowning, coronation, making santo, making *ocha,* or having one's head made.

Lukumi (or Lucumí): The language derived from Yoruba in Cuba, the ethnic group associated with the Lucumí language there. More recently, the religion is also known as Regla de Ocha and Santería (see Brown 2003 and Sandoval 2006). In this book it generally refers to the latter, though this usage dates only to the late nineteenth century and its spelling with a "k" is a late twentieth-century invention (see Palmie 2013).

madrina: Spanish for godmother.

maferefun: "Thanks be to."

Obatalá: A fatherly Orisha associated with the intellect and purity. Seen as a king and judge.

Obá: A Yoruba title meaning "ruler" or "chief." Refers to the *oriaté.*

obi: Divination accomplished with four pieces of coconut.

Ocha (or Osha): Short for Oricha/Orisha.

ocha (or osha): Short for *kariocha.* When capitalized it refers to Lukumi or Orisha religion or community, as in "house of Ocha" or "Ocha community."

Ochosi: An Orisha of the hunt and justice. One of the Warriors.

odu: One of 256 patterns of cowrie shells in *diloggun* divination. Each *odu* is associated with specific memorized verses and stories, situations, advice, rituals, and liturgies.

Ogun: An Orisha of iron, hard work, and technology. One of the Warriors.

Olodumare: The Supreme God.

Olokun: An Orisha in the depths of the ocean who is often appealed to for issues of health and wealth. Sometimes seen as masculine, sometimes feminine, S/he is also associated with the ancestors because of the many who perished in the ocean during the Middle Passage of the slave trade.

olorisha: Yoruba term meaning "owner of Orisha." An Orisha priest; one who has undergone the *kariocha* and the year in white.

oluwo: A *babalawo* who is also an *olorisha.*

oriaté: A specially trained *olorisha* who performs divination and leads ceremonies.

Orisha: Aspects of divinity in Lukumi religion. They are seen as "specialized forms of the one Supreme God" (Edwards and Mason 1985, 1). Also referred to as *santos* (saints) and Ochas.

Orula: An Orisha of divination to whom *babalawos* are specially dedicated. Also called Orunmila.

Oshun: An Orisha associated with feminine sexuality, beauty, art, and sweet waters.

otanes: Rocks that have been consecrated, generally with *ashé* of Orisha.

Oya: An Orisha of the wind associated also with cemeteries and marketplaces. A fierce wife of Chango who wields lightening.

padrino: Spanish for godfather.

pañuelos: Spanish for handkerchief. Here it refers to decorative cloth for the Orisha and sometimes to head scarves.

Santería: A term used to refer to Regla de Ocha or Lukumi religion. Originally a pejorative term.

sopera: Spanish for soup tureen. Container for the sacred *otanes* of Orisha.

Spiritism: See Espiritismo.

trono: Spanish for throne. A consecrated area in which Orisha are honored and upon which an initiate resides during the *kariocha.*

Warriors: Also called Los Guerreros, this term refers to the Orishas who are seen as professional soldiers: Elegua, Ogun, and Ochosi. As one of their initial steps in the religion, *aleyos* generally "receive" in ceremony items consecrated to these Orisha (and to the mysterious Osun), thus gaining their protection. Receiving Warriors also serves to connect an *aleyo* to a particular godparent. See Clark (2005), Mason (2002), and Murphy (1988) for more detailed descriptions of the ceremony of receiving Warriors.

yaworaje: The Lukumi year in white.

Yemaya: The maternal Orisha of salt waters.

BIBLIOGRAPHY

Abimbola, Wande, and Ivor Miller. 1997. *Ifa Will Mend Our Broken World: Thoughts on Yoruba Religion and Culture in Africa and the Diaspora*. Roxbury, MA: Aim Books.

Albrecht, Stan L., and Howard M. Bahr. 1983. "Patterns of Religious Disaffiliation: A Study of Lifelong Mormons, Mormon Converts, and Former Mormons." *Journal for the Scientific Study of Religion* 22(4): 366–379.

Ammerman, Nancy Tatom. 1997. "Golden Rule Christianity: Lived Religion in the American Mainstream." In *Lived Religion in America: Toward a History of Practice*, edited by David D. Hall, 196–216. Princeton, NJ: Princeton University Press.

———, ed. 2007. *Everyday Religion: Observing Modern Religious Lives*. New York: Oxford University Press.

Andrews, George Reid. 2004. *Afro-Latin America, 1800–2000*. New York: Oxford University Press.

Anzaldúa, Gloria. 1987. *Borderlands—La Frontera: The New Mestiza*. San Francisco: Aunt Lute Books.

Aronson, Elliot, and Judson Mills. 1959. "The Effect of Severity of Initiation on Liking for a Group." *Journal of Abnormal and Social Psychology* 59(2): 177–181.

Asad, Talal. 1993. *Genealogies of Religion: Discipline and Reasons of Power in Christianity and Islam*. Baltimore, MD: Johns Hopkins University Press.

Babbie, Earl. 2007. *The Practice of Social Research*. 11th ed. Belmont, CA: Thomson Wadsworth.

Barnes, Sandra T., ed. 1989. *Africa's Ogun: Old World and New*. Bloomington, IN: Indiana University Press.

Barro, Robert, Jason Hwang, and Rachel McCleary. 2010. "Religious Conversion in 40 Countries." *Journal for the Scientific Study of Religion* 49(1): 15–36.

Bascom, William R. (1980) 1993. *Sixteen Cowries: Yoruba Divination from Africa to the New World*. Bloomington: Indiana University Press.

———. (1972) 1990. *Shango in the New World*. Austin: African and Afro-American Research Institute, The University of Texas at Austin.

Bastide, Roger. (1960) 2007. *The African Religions of Brazil: Toward a Sociology of the Interpenetration of Civilizations*. Translated by Helen Sebba. Baltimore, MD: Johns Hopkins University Press.

Berger, Peter L. (1967) 1990. *The Sacred Canopy: Elements of a Sociological Theory of Religion*. New York: Anchor Books.

Berger, Peter L., and Thomas Luckmann. 1967. *The Social Construction of Reality: A Treatise in the Sociology of Knowledge*. New York: Anchor Books.

Bolboacă, Sorana D., Lorentz Jäntschi, Adriana F. Sestraş, Radu E. Sestraş, and Doru C. Pamfil. 2011. "Pearson-Fisher Chi-Square Statistic Revisited." *Information* 2(3): 528–545.

Bourdieu, Pierre. 1986. "The Forms of Capital." In *Handbook of Theory and Research for the Sociology of Education*, edited by John Richardson, 241–260. Westport, CT: Greenwood Press.

———. 2004. *Science of Science and Reflexivity*. Palo Alto, CA: Stanford University Press.

Brandon, George. 1997. *Santeria from Africa to the New World: The Dead Sell Memories*. Bloomington, IN: Indiana University Press.

———. 2002. "Hierarchy without a Head: Observations on Changes in the Social Organization of Some Afroamerican Religions in the United States with Special Reference to Santeria." *Archives de Sciences Sociales des Religions* 47(117): 151–174.

Bristol, Joan Cameron. 2007. *Christians, Blasphemers, and Witches: Afro-Mexican Ritual Practice in the Seventeenth Century*. Albuquerque: University of New Mexico Press.

Brown, David H. 2003. *Santería Enthroned: Art, Ritual, and Innovation in an Afro-Cuban Religion*. Chicago: University of Chicago Press.

Brown, Karen McCarthy. (1991) 2011. *Mama Lola: A Vodou Priestess in Brooklyn*. Berkeley: University of California Press.

Bruce, Steve. 2002. *God Is Dead: Secularization in the West*. Malden, MA: Blackwell Publishers.

Canizares, Raul J. 1999. *Cuban Santeria: Walking with the Night*. Rochester, VT: Destiny Books.

Carr, C. Lynn. 2010. "Conversion Hunger and Hurdles: Narratives of Cultural Newcomers to Orisha Religions in the U.S." Paper presented at the annual meeting of the American Sociological Association, Atlanta, GA, August 14–17.

———. 2011. "Negotiating Authenticity: The Case of Cultural Newcomers to Orisha Religious Traditions in the U.S." Paper presented at the annual meeting of the American Sociological Association, Las Vegas, NV, August 20–23.

Chang, Heewon. 2008. *Autoethnography as Method*. Walnut Creek, CA: Left Coast Press.

Chaves, Mark. 1998. *National Congregations Study: Data File and Codebook*. Tucson, AZ: University of Arizona, Department of Sociology.

———. 2004. *Congregations in America*. Cambridge, MA: Harvard University Press.

Christerson, Brad, Korie Edwards, and Michael Emerson. 2005. *Against All Odds: The Struggle for Racial Integration in Religious Organizations*. New York: New York University Press.

Chubin, Fae. 2014. "You May Smother My Voice, but You Will Hear My Silence: An Autoethnography on Street Sexual Harassment, the Discourse of Shame and Women's Resistance in Iran." *Sexualities* 17(1-2): 176–193.

Clark, Mary Ann. 2005. *Where Men Are Wives and Mothers Rule: Santería Ritual Practices and Their Gender Implications*. Gainesville, FL: University Press of Florida.

———. 2007. *Santería: Correcting the Myths and Uncovering the Realities of a Growing Religion*. Westport, CT: Praeger Publishers.

Conner, Randy P. 2004. *Queering Creole Spiritual Traditions: Lesbian, Gay, Bisexual, and Transgender Participation in African-Inspired Traditions in the Americas*. Binghamton, NY: Harrington Park Press.

Curry, Mary Cuthrell. 1997. *Making the Gods in New York: The Yoruba Religion in the African American Community*. New York: Routledge.

De La Torre, Miguel A. 2004. *Santería: The Beliefs and Rituals of a Growing Religion in America*. Grand Rapids, MI: Wm. B. Eerdmans Publishing Company.

Drummond, Murray. 2010. "The Natural: An Autoethnography of a Masculinized Body in Sport." *Men and Masculinities* 12(3): 374–389

Eck, Diana L. 2001. *A New Religious America*. New York: HarperCollins Publishers.

Edwards, Gary, and John Mason. 1985. *Black Gods—Orisa Studies in the New World*. Brooklyn, NY: Yoruba Theological Archministry.

Ellis, Carolyn. 2004. *The Ethnographic I: A Methodological Novel about Autoethnography*. Walnut Creek, CA: Alta Mira.

Ellis, Carolyn, Tony E. Adams, and Arthur P. Bochner. 2011. "Autoethnography: An Overview." *Forum: Qualitative Social Research Sozialforschung* 12: Article 10. http://nbn-resolving.de/urn:nbn:de:0114-fqs1101108. Accessed January 7, 2015.

Emerson, Michael O., and Karen Chai Kim. 2003. "Multiracial Congregations: A Typology and Analysis of Their Development." *Journal for the Scientific Study of Religion* 42(2): 217–227.

Ettorre, Eizabeth. 2006. "Making Sense of My Illness Journey from Thyrotoxicosis to Health: An Autoethnography." *Auto/Biography* 14(2): 153–175.

———. 2010. "Nuns, Dykes, Drugs and Gendered Bodies: An Autoethnography of a Lesbian Feminist's Journey through 'Good Time' Sociology." *Sexualities* 13(3): 295–315.

Falola, Toyin, and Ann Genova, eds. 2006. *Orisa: Yoruba Gods and Spiritual Identity in Africa and the Diaspora*. Trenton, NJ: Africa World Press.

Foucault, Michel. 1979. *Discipline and Punish: The Birth of the Prison*. Translated by Alan Sheridan. New York: Vintage Books.

Fries, Christopher J. 2009. "Bourdieu's Reflexive Sociology as a Theoretical Basis for Mixed Methods Research." *Journal of Mixed Methods Research* 3(4): 326–348.

Garfinkel, Harold. 1956. "Conditions of Successful Degradation Ceremonies." *American Journal of Sociology* 61(5): 420–424.

———. 1967. *Studies in Ethnomethodology*. Englewood Cliffs, NJ: Prentice-Hall.

Gatson, Sarah N. 2003. "On Being Amorphous: Autoethnography, Genealogy, and a Multiracial Identity." *Qualitative Inquiry* 9(1): 20–48.

Giddens, Anthony. 1991. *Modernity and Self-Identity: Self and Society in the Late Modern Age*. Stanford, CA: Stanford University Press.

Goffman, Erving. (1959) 1990. *The Presentation of Self in Everyday Life*. New York: Penguin.

———. 1961. *Asylums: Essays on the Social Situation of Mental Patients and Other Inmates*. Garden City, NY: Anchor Books.

Gordon, David F. 1974. "The Jesus People: An Identity Synthesis." *Urban Life and Culture* 3(2): 159–178.

Gregory, Steven. 1999. *Santería in New York City: A Study in Cultural Resistance*. New York: Garland Publishing.

Hadaway, C. Kirk. 1980. "Denominational Switching and Religiosity." *Review of Religious Research* 21(4): 451–461.

Hadaway, C. Kirk, and Penny Long Marler. 1993. "All in the Family: Religious Mobility in America." *Review of Religious Research* 35(2): 97–116.

Hall, David D., ed. 1997. *Lived Religion in America: Toward a History of Practice*. Princeton, NJ: Princeton University Press.

Hervieu-Leger, Daniele. (1993) 2000. *Religion as a Chain of Memory*. Translated by Simon Lee. New Brunswick, NJ: Rutgers University Press.

Hoge, Dean R., Benton Johnson, and Donald A. Luidens. 1995. "Types of Denominational Switching among Protestant Young Adults." *Journal for the Scientific Study of Religion* 34(2): 253–258.

Hucks, Tracey E. 2012. *Yoruba Traditions and African American Religious Nationalism*. Albuquerque, NM: University of New Mexico Press.

Jane, Ernesto Valdés. 2007. "Osha Ifa Rules for Santeros" http://www.reglasparasanteros
.com/eng/. Accessed 2011.

Karmakar, Sunita D., and F. Curtis Breslin. 2008. "The Role of Educational Level and Job Characteristics on the Health of Young Adults." *Social Science and Medicine* 66(9): 2011–2022.

Kleinmann, Scott Matthew. 2012. "Radicalization of Homegrown Sunni Militants in the
United States: Comparing Converts and Non-Converts." *Studies in Conflict and Terrorism*
35: 278–297.

Kumar, Krishan. 1995. *From Post-Industrial to Post-Modern Society: New Theories of the Contemporary World.* Oxford: Blackwell.

Lefever, Harry G. 2000. "Leaving the United States: The Black Nationalist Themes of Orisha—
Vodu." *Journal of Black Studies* 31(2): 174–195.

Long, Theodore E., and Jeffrey K. Hadden. 1983. "Religious Conversion and the Concept
of Socialization: Integrating the Brainwashing and Drift Models." *Journal for the Scientific
Study of Religion* 22(1): 1–14.

Lyon, David. 2000. *Jesus in Disneyland: Religion in Postmodern Times.* Malden, MA: Blackwell
Publishers.

Mason, John. 1992. *Orin Orisa: Songs for Selected Heads.* Brooklyn, NY: Yoruba Theological
Archminism.

Mason, Michael Atwood. 2002. *Living Santería: Rituals and Experiences in an Afro-Cuban Religion.* Washington, DC: Smithsonian Institution Press.

Matibag, Eugenio. 1996. *Afro-Cuban Religious Experience: Cultural Reflections in Narrative.*
Gainesville, FL: University Press of Florida.

McCormick, Donald W. 2013. "The Future of Scholarship in Management, Spirituality, and
Religion: Diversity and the Creative Nexus." In *Handbook of Faith and Spirituality in the
Workplace: Emerging Research and Practice,* edited by Judi Neal. New York: Springer.

McGuire, Meredith B. 2008. *Lived Religion: Faith and Practice in Everyday Life.* New York:
Oxford University Press.

McMahon, Jenny, and Maree Dinan Thompson. 2011. "'Body Work—Regulation of a Swimmer Body': An Autoethnography from an Australian Elite Swimmer." *Sport, Education and
Society* 16(1): 35–50.

Murphy, Joseph M. 1988. *Santería: An African Religion in America.* New York: Beacon.

———. 2015. *Botánicas: Sacred Spaces of Healing and Devotion in Urban America.* Jackson,
MS: University Press of Mississippi.

Ócha'ni Lele. 2003. *The Diloggun: The Orishas, Proverbs, Sacrifices, and Prohibitions of Cuban
Santeria.* Rochester, VT: Destiny Books.

Olmos, Margarite Fernandez, and Lizabeth Paravisini-Gebert. 2003. *Creole Religions of the
Caribbean: An Introduction from Vodou and Santería to Obeah and Espiritismo.* New York:
New York University Press.

Olupona, Jacob K., and Terry Rey, eds. 2008. *Orisa Devotion as World Religion: The Globaliza-
tion of Yoruba Religious Culture.* Madison, WI: University of Wisconsin Press.

Omo Ase. 2011. "Reflections on My Iyawo Year." *Eriwo Ya!,* December 2011. http://orisacdc
.org/reflections-on-my-iyawo-year/?utm_source=OrisaCDCandutm_campaign=
oedb362ef8-Eriwo_Ya_Nov_201111_15_2011andutm_medium=email. Accessed December 28, 2011.

Ontario Consultants on Religious Tolerance. 2005. "Santeria: A Syncretistic Caribbean Religion." http://www.religioustolerance.org/santeri.htm. Accessed January 14, 2006.

Orishanet. N.d. "Pinaldo, Receiving the Knife: The Truth and Common Misconceptions."
www.orishanet.org/knife.html. Accessed July 14, 2013.

Orsi, Robert. 1997. "Everyday Miracles: The Study of Lived Religion." In *Lived Religion in America: Toward a History of Practice*, edited by David D. Hall, 3–21. Princeton, NJ: Princeton University Press.

Palmié, Stephan. 2001. "Of Pharisees and Snark-Hunters: Afro-Cuban Religion as an Object of Knowledge." *Culture and Religion* 2(1): 3–19.

———. 2013. *The Cooking of History: How Not to Study Afro-Cuban Religion*. Chicago: University of Chicago Press.

Partridge, Christopher H. 2004. *The Re-Enchantment of the West: Alternative Spiritualities, Sacralization, Popular Culture, and Occulture*. New York: T & T Clark International.

Pearce, Lisa. D. 2012. "Mixed Methods Inquiry in Sociology." *American Behavioral Scientist* 56(6): 829–848.

Pérez, Elizabeth. 2012. "Staging Transformation: Spiritist Liturgies as Theaters of Conversion in Afro-Cuban Religious Practice." *Culture and Religion* 13(3): 361–389.

Perez y Mena, Andres Isidoro. 1991. *Speaking with the Dead: Development of Afro-Latin Religion among Puerto Ricans in the United States*. New York: AMS Press.

Petts, Richard J. 2009. "Trajectories of Religious Participation from Adolescence to Young Adulthood." *Journal for the Scientific Study of Religion* 48(3): 552–571.

Phillips, Benjamin T., and Shaul Kelner. 2006. "Reconceptualizing Religious Change: Ethnoapostasy and Change in Religion among American Jews." *Sociology of Religion* 67(4): 507–524.

Pike, Sarah M. 2001. *Earthly Bodies, Magical Selves: Contemporary Pagans and the Search for Community*. Berkeley, CA: University of California.

Pond, Allison, Gregory Smith, Neha Sahgal, and Scott F. Clement. 2010. "The Zeal of the Convert: Religious Characteristics of Americans Who Switch Religions." Pew Forum on Religion and Public Life. http://bycommonconsent.files.wordpress.com/2010/02/pond -smith-sahgal-clement-zeal-of-convert-asre09.pdf. Accessed July 10, 2014.

Prothero, Stephen. 2010. *God Is Not One: The Eight Rival Religions That Run the World—And Why Their Differences Matter*. New York: Harper Collins.

Rambo, Lewis R. 1995. *Understanding Religious Conversion*. New Haven, CT: Yale University Press.

Ramos, Miguel "Willie." 2008. "The Iyawo." http://eleda.org/blog/2008/11/11/the-iyawo -english/. Accessed July 11, 2011.

———. 2012. "Founder's Note." http://eleda.org/a-note-from-willie/. Accessed May 26, 2012.

Reilly, Rosemary C. 2013. "Me and Goldilocks . . . Searching for What Is 'Just Right' in Trauma Research: An Autoethnography." *Qualitative Report* 18(47): 1–11.

Rich, Adrienne. (1971) 2002. *The Fact of a Doorframe: Selected Poems 1950–2001*. New York: W. W. Norton and Company.

Roof, Wade Clark. 1998. "Religious Borderlands: Challenges for Future Study." *Journal for the Scientific Study of Religion* 37(1): 1–14.

———. 2001. *Spiritual Marketplace: Baby Boomers and the Remaking of American Religion*. Princeton, NJ: Princeton University Press.

Roof, Wade Clark, and William McKinney. 1987. *American Mainline Religion: Its Changing Shape and Future*. New Brunswick, NJ: Rutgers University Press.

Ruiz-Junco, Natalia, and Salvador Vidal-Ortiz. 2011. "Autoethnography: The Sociological through the Personal." In *New Directions in Sociology: Essays on Theory and Methodology in the 21st Century*, edited by Ieva Zake and Michael DeCesare. Jefferson, NC: McFarland and Company.

Sandoval, Mercedes Cros. 2006. *Worldview, the Orichas, and Santería: Africa to Cuba and Beyond.* Gainesville, FL: University Press of Florida.

Savastano, Peter. N.d. "St. Gerard, Processual Hagiography and Devotional Practices in the Lives of His Devotees." Unpublished manuscript in author's possession.

Shapiro, Judith. 1982. "'Women's Studies': A Note on the Perils of Markedness." *Signs: Journal of Women in Culture and Society* 7(3): 717–721.

Smith, Christian, Brandon Vaidyanathan, Nancy Tatom Ammerman, José Casanova, Hilary Davidson, Elaine Howard Ecklund, John H. Evans, Philip S. Gorski, Mary Ellen Konieczny, Jason A. Springs, Jenny Trinitapoli, and Meredith Whitnah. 2013. "Roundtable on the Sociology of Religion: Twenty-Three Theses on the Status of Religion in American Sociology—A Mellon Working-Group Reflection." *Journal of the American Academy of Religion* 81(4): 903–938.

Snow, David A., and Richard Machalek. 1984. "The Sociology of Conversion." *Annual Review of Sociology* 10: 167–190.

Spradley, James P. 1979. *The Ethnographic Interview.* Orlando, FL: Harcourt Brace Jovanovich.

Spry, Tami. 2001. "Performing Autoethnography: An Embodied Methodological Praxis." *Qualitative Inquiry* 7(6): 706–733.

Sremac, Srđan. 2010. "Converting into a New Reality: Social Constructions, Practical Theology and Conversion." *Nova Prisuntnost* 8(10): 7–27.

Stark, Rodney, and Lynne Roberts. 1982. "The Arithmetic of Social Movements: Theoretical Implications." *Sociological Analysis* 43(1): 53–67.

Storr, Merl. 1999. "Postmodern Bisexuality." *Sexualities* 2(3):309–325.

Strauss, Anselm L., and Juliet M. Corbin. 1990. *Basics of Qualitative Research: Grounded Theory Procedures and Techniques.* Thousand Oaks, CA: Sage Publications.

Stromberg, Peter G. 1993. *Language and Self-Transformation: A Study of the Christian Conversion Narrative.* New York: Cambridge University Press.

Thomas, William I., and Dorothy S. Thomas. (1928) 1970. *The Child in America: Behavior Problems and Programs.* New York: Knopf.

Thompson, Joyce. 2013. *How to Greet Strangers: A Mystery.* Maple Shade, NJ: Lethe Press.

Thompson, Stephen I. 1968. "Religious Conversion and Religious Zeal in an Overseas Enclave: The Case of the Japanese in Bolivia." *Anthropological Quarterly* 41(4): 201–208.

Travisano, Richard V. 1970. "Alternation and Conversion and Qualitatively Different Transformations." In *Social Psychology through Symbolic Interaction,* edited by Gregory Prentice Stone and Harvey A. Faberman, 594–606. Waltham, MA: Ginn-Blaisdell.

Van Gennep, Arnold. (1909) 1961. *The Rites of Passage.* Translated by Vizedon and Gabrielle L. Caffee. Chicago: University of Chicago Press.

Vidal-Ortiz, Salvador. 2004. "On Being a White Person of Color: Using Autoethnography to Understand Puerto Ricans' Racialization." *Qualitative Sociology* 27(2): 179–203.

———. 2005. "Sexuality and Gender in Santería: LGBT Identities at the Crossroads of Santería." In *Gay Religion,* edited by Scott Thumma and Edward R. Gray. New York: AltaMira Press.

———. 2006. "Sexuality Discussions in Santería: A Case Study of Religion and Sexuality Negotiation." *Sexuality Research and Social Policy: Journal of NSRC* 3(3): 52–66.

———. 2011. "'Maricón,' 'Pájaro,' and 'Loca': Cuban and Puerto Rican Linguistic Practices and Sexual Minority Participation in U.S. Santería." *Journal of Homosexuality* 58(6–7): 901–918.

Wagner, Brooke. 2009. "Becoming a Sexual Being: Overcoming Constraints on Female Sexuality." *Sexualities* 12(3): 289–311.

Waugh, Linda R. 1982. "Marked and Unmarked: A Choice between Unequals in Semiotic Structure." *Semiotica* 38(3–4): 299–318.

Weber, Max. 1991. "The Nature of Social Action." [1922]. In *Weber: Selections in Translation*, edited by W. G. Runciman and translated by Eric Matthews, 3–32. Cambridge: Cambridge University Press.

Wuthnow, Robert. 1998. *After Heaven: Spirituality in America since the 1950s.* Berkeley, CA: University of California Press.

———. 2002. *Loose Connections: Joining Together in America's Fragmented Communities.* Cambridge, MA: Harvard University Press.

———. 2007. *America and the Challenges of Religious Diversity.* Princeton, NJ: Princeton University Press.

Young, David E., and Jean-Guy Goulet. 1994. *Being Changed: The Anthropology of Extraordinary Experience.* Toronto: University of Toronto Press.

Yates, Daniel, David Moore, and George McCabe. 1999. *The Practice of Statistics.* 1st ed. New York: W. H. Freeman.

Zinnbauer, Brian J., and Kenneth I. Pargament. 1998. "Spiritual Conversion: A Study of Religious Change among College Students." *Journal for the Scientific Study of Religion* 37(1): 161–180.

INDEX

ABOUT THE AUTHOR

C. LYNN CARR is an associate professor of sociology at Seton Hall University. Her prior publications in journals including *Sex Roles, Gender & Society,* and *Symbolic Interaction,* emphasized the interplay between the individual and the social within sex, gender, and sexual identity construction. Her more recent work involves religious identification. Also known as Chango Dina, she is a priest in the Lukumi religious tradition.

9 780813 571195